Golden Voyages

HBJ BOOKMARK READING PROGRAM, EAGLE EDITION

Margaret Early

G. Robert Canfield

Robert Karlin

Thomas A. Schottman

Sara Krentzman Srygley

Evelyn L. Wenzel

Level 12

Golden Voyages

Harcourt Brace Jovanovich, Publishers

Orlando   New York   Chicago   San Diego   Atlanta   Dallas

ACKNOWLEDGMENTS: For permission to reprint copyrighted material, grateful acknowledgment is made to the following sources:

ALPHA IOTA CHAPTER OF PI LAMBDA THETA, CLAREMONT GRADUATE SCHOOL, CLAREMONT, CALIFORNIA: Excerpt (titled "At Home in Lagos") adapted from pages in the book *Iyabo of Nigeria* written by Rhoda Omosunlola Johnston.

AMERICAN BOOK COMPANY: Excerpt on p. 42, from Table of Contents—Unit 5 Resources, in *Patterns of Language, Level F* by Nell C. Thompson, George E. Coon, Barbara B. Cramer, H. Thompson Fillmer, and Ann Lefcourt (text and art).

ATHENEUM PUBLISHERS: "Snowy Morning" from *I Thought I Heard the City* by Lilian Moore. Text copyright © 1969 by Lilian Moore. "The Tape" and "Fantasy: For Jennie" from *The Way Things Are and Other Poems* by Myra Cohn Livingston (a Margaret K. McElderry Book). Copyright © 1974 by Myra Cohn Livingston. "P wer Lines" and "Silly Dog" from *4-Way Stop and Other Poems* by Myra Cohn Livingston (a Margaret K. McElderry Book). Copyright © 1976 by Myra Cohn Livingston.

THE BOBBS-MERRILL COMPANY, INC.: Excerpt (titled "The Miniature City") from *Europe for Young Travelers* by Elinor Porter Swiger. Copyright © 1972 by the Bobbs-Merrill Company, Inc.

CHILTON BOOK COMPANY, RADNOR, PA.: "Pompeii" from *Lost Cities and Vanished Civilizations* by Robert Silverberg. Copyright © 1962 by Robert Silverberg.

CLACK, INC.: First act from "The Phoenix and the Carpet," a radio play by Madeline Sunshine.

COLD MOUNTAIN PRESS, THE LITERARY IMPRINT OF PROVISION HOUSE, AUSTIN, TEXAS, AND JOSEPH BRUCHAC: "Birdfoot's Grampa" by Joseph Bruchac. Copyright © 1975 by Joseph Bruchac. "Camping near Trumansburg" from *Flow* by Joseph Bruchac. Copyright © 1975 by Joseph Bruchac. "Homestead" and "This Earth Is a Drum" from *This Earth Is a Drum* by Joseph Bruchac. Copyright © 1974, 1975, 1976 by Joseph Bruchac.

THOMAS Y. CROWELL, PUBLISHERS: Excerpt (titled "The Very Best") adapted from *Roberto Clemente* by Kenneth Rudeen. Copyright © 1974 by Kenneth Rudeen.

CROWN PUBLISHERS, INC.: "The Three Maidens" from *The Kaha Bird: Tales from the Steppes of Central Asia* by Mirra Ginsburg. © 1971 by Mirra Ginsburg.

DODD, MEAD & COMPANY, INC.: From "Gato and the Dragons" in *My Brother, Angel* by Hilary Beckett. Copyright © 1971 by Hilary Beckett.

DOUBLEDAY & COMPANY, INC.: Excerpt (titled "Towers All Around Us") from *Towers* by David Webster. Copyright © 1971 by David Webster.

EBONY JR! MAGAZINE: "Dreams Really Do Come True" by Karen Odom Gray from EBONY JR! *Magazine.* Copyright 1977 by Johnson Publishing Company, Inc.

RUSSELL FREEDMAN: Excerpt (titled "Toscanini Gets His Start") from "The Beardless Bambino" in *Teenagers Who Made History* by Russell Freedman.

GOLDEN GATE JUNIOR BOOK DIVISION OF CHILDRENS PRESS, CHICAGO: Excerpt (titled "A Visit to Hong Kong") adapted from *Children of Hong Kong* by Terry Shannon. Copyright © 1975 by Terry Shannon.

GROSSET & DUNLAP, INC.: "The Pedaling Man" and "Esmé on Her Brother's Bicycle" from *The Pedaling Man and Other Poems* by Russell Hoban. Copyright © 1968 by Russell Hoban.

HARCOURT BRACE JOVANOVICH, INC.: Excerpts on pp. 26 and 27, from "Studying and Resting"; on pp. 171 and 172, from "The Three S's"; on p. 69, from "How We Use Our Resources"; on pp. 368 and 369, from "Getting Tired"; on p. 508, from "What Do I Want?" in *Toward Your Future* (Brown) by Daniel A. Collins et al. Copyright © 1977 by Harcourt Brace Jovanovich, Inc. Excerpts on pp. 89 and 90, from Unit 3, "Searching for Long Life—A Problem for You and Yours"; on pp. 321–23 from "The Lively Mouse" (text & art); on p. 443, from "A New View of Change"; and on pp. 483 and 484, from "An Apprentice Investigation into a Lever" in *Concepts in Science*, Newton Edition (Brown) by Paul F. Brandwein et al. Copyright © 1975 by Harcourt Brace Jovanovich, Inc. The library floor plan on p. 48 from *Language for Daily Use*, Level Gold, used in our section titled "Using Library Resources." Excerpts on pp. 300 and 301, from "How Our Language Grows—Ups and Downs"; and on pp. 464 and 465, from "A Book to Read" in *Language for Daily Use*, Explorer Edition (Brown) by Mildred A. Dawson et al. Copyright © 1978 by Harcourt Brace Jovanovich, Inc. Abridged and adapted from *Patch* by C. H. Frick. © 1957 by Harcourt Brace Jovanovich, Inc. Abridged and adapted from *The Borrowers.* Copyright 1952, 1953 by Mary Norton.

HARPER & ROW, PUBLISHERS, INC.: Excerpt (titled "Adventure in the Desert") adapted from chapters 1 and 2 in *Lizard Tails and Cactus Spines* by Barbara Brenner. Text copyright © 1975 by Barbara Brenner. "Narcissa" (text only) from *Bronzeville Boys and Girls* by Gwendolyn Brooks. Copyright © 1956 by Gwendolyn Brooks Blakely.

HARPER & ROW, PUBLISHERS, INC., AND OXFORD UNIVERSITY PRESS: Text adaptation of Chapter 2, "Meeting in Southdale Court" from *The Nothing Place* by Eleanor Spence. Copyright © 1972, 1973 by Eleanor Spence.

HAWTHORN BOOKS, A DIVISION OF ELSEVIER-DUTTON PUBLISHING COMPANY, INC.: "Pablita Velarde: Artist of the Pueblos" from *American Indian Women* by Marion E. Gridley. Copyright © 1974 by Marion E. Gridley.

HISTORIC PRESERVATION: Excerpts on pp. 304–07, adapted from "Elephants Remembered" by Julian Cavalier in *Historic Preservation*, Vol. 29, No. 1, January–March, 1977, the quarterly magazine of the National Trust for Historic Preservation.

HOLT, RINEHART AND WINSTON, PUBLISHERS: "Steam Shovel" from *Upper Pasture* by Charles Malam. Copyright 1930, © 1958 by Charles Malam. "The Runaway" from *The Poetry of Robert Frost* edited by Edward Connery Lathem. Copyright 1923, © 1969 by Holt, Rinehart and Winston. Copyright 1951 by Robert Frost.

HOUGHTON MIFFLIN COMPANY: Excerpts on pp. 91 and 92, from "Farmers and Pharaohs—The Pyramids"; on pp. 219–21, from "A Human Being's Third Greatest Need"; on pp. 481 and 482, from "The Common Experience—Identify the Pictures"; on pp. 22–25, from "Languages Are Alike But Different" (text and art); and on p. 149, from "Putting It Together" (text and art) in *Windows on Our World: The Way People Live* by Margaret Stimman Branson. Copyright © 1976 by Houghton Mifflin Company.

ALFRED A. KNOPF, INC.: Excerpt (titled "The Great Adventures of Nicolo, Maffeo, and Marco Polo"), adapted from "Marco Polo Tells About China" in *They Put Out to Sea* by Roger Duvoisin. Copyright 1944 by Alfred A. Knopf, Inc. and renewed 1972 by Roger Devoisin.

LAIDLAW BROTHERS, A DIVISION OF DOUBLEDAY & COMPANY, INC.: Excerpts on p. 370, from "Your Emotions"; on pp. 344 and 345, from "Life Cycle of Frogs"; on pp. 201–03, from "Life Cycle of Snakes"; and on pp. 43–45, from "Comets" in *Exploring Science,* Red Book, by Milo K. Blecha et al.

J. B. LIPPINCOTT, PUBLISHERS: "Margaret Bourke-White" (titled "Woman Without Fear") adapted from *Women Who Made America Great* by Harry Gersh. Copyright © 1962 by Harry Gersh. "The Earth's Deep Freeze" adapted from *Supersuits,* Text copyright © 1975 by Vicki Cobb. "Bring 'Em Back Alive" adapted from *Skin-Diving Adventures* by John J. Floherty and Mike McGrady. Copyright © 1962 by John J. Floherty and Mike McGrady.

LITTLE, BROWN AND CO.: Excerpt on pp. 131–33, from "Your Own Mask" (titled "How to Make Your Own Mask") (text and art) from *Do a Zoom Do* edited by Bernice Chesler and including work by the Zoomdoers—Frank Durgin, Kathy Rainwater, Rebecca and Vicky Sacks, and Pauline Kim of Cambridge, Mass. Copyright © 1975 by WGBH Educational Foundation. "Why the Sea Is Salt" from *Favorite Fairy Tales Told in Norway* by Virginia Haviland. Copyright © 1961 by Virginia Haviland. This story was adapted from the 1859 translation by Sir George Dasent of Norwegian folktales gathered by Peter Christian Asbjørnsen and Jørgan E. Moe. "Limericks" from "Write Me a Verse" and "Cricket" from *Take Sky* by David McCord. Copyright © 1961, 1962 by David McCord.

LOTHROP, LEE & SHEPHARD, INC., A DIVISION OF WILLIAM MORROW AND COMPANY, INC.: "The Women's 400 Meters" from *The Sidewalk Racer* by Lillian Morrison. Copyright © 1965, 1967, 1977 by Lillian Morrison.

MACRAE SMITH COMPANY: "Lucinda Gates: Plant Breeder, Plant Hunter," an edited version of "Lucy's Love Apples" from *Green Treasures: Adventures in the Discovery of Edible Plants,* copyright 1974 by Charles Morrow Wilson.

DAVID MCKAY COMPANY, INC.: "A Dog and a Girl" (titled "The Secrets of Altamira") adapted from *The Timeless Trail* by Heinz Sponsel, translated by Hertha Pauli. Copyright © 1971 by Heinz Sponsel and Hertha Pauli.

MCINTOSH AND OTIS, INC.: "A Little About Me" by Myra Cohn Livingston. Copyright © 1979 by Myra Cohn Livingston.

LILIAN MOORE: "Go With the Poem" from *Go With the Poem* by Lilian Moore. Copyright © 1979 by Lilian Moore.

WILLIAM MORROW AND COMPANY, INC.: "Knoxville, Tennessee" from *Black Feeling, Black Talk, Black Judgment* by Nikki Giovanni. Copyright © 1968, 1970 by Nikki Giovanni.

THE NEW YORK TIMES COMPANY: "Butterfly Hunt Reveals Secret" by Boyce Rensberger from the August 1, 1976, issue of *The New York Times.* © 1976 by The New York Times Company.

RAINTREE PUBLISHERS LIMITED: Excerpts from "Terror by Fire" and "The Restless Earth" (titled "The Restless Earth") from *Volcanoes: Mountains of Fire* by Barbara B. Simons. Copyright © 1976 by Raintree Publishers Limited, 205 West Highland Avenue, Milwaukee, Wisconsin 53203.

RAND MCNALLY & COMPANY: "Insect Eaters of the Plant World" adapted from *Strange Plants and Their Ways* by Ross E. Hutchins. Copyright 1958 by Ross E. Hutchins.

RANDOM HOUSE, INC.: Adaptation of "Tragedy of the Tar Pits" from *All About Strange Beasts of the Past* by Roy Chapman Andrews. Copyright © 1956 by Roy Chapman Andrews.

THE SATURDAY EVENING POST COMPANY: "Genius With Feathers" by Josephine C. Walker adapted from *Jack and Jill* magazine. Copyright © 1977 by The Saturday Evening Post Company, Indianapolis, Indiana.

SCHOLASTIC MAGAZINES, INC.: "Treasures of a Teenage God-King" (titled "Treasures of a Teenage King") adapted from *Senior Scholastic* Magazine. Copyright © 1977 by Scholastic Magazines, Inc.

SCOTT, FORESMAN AND COMPANY: Excerpts on pp. 302 and 303, from "Interpreting Remainders" (text and art); and on pp. 506 and 507, from "Using Decimals: The 1972 Summer Olympics" in *Mathematics Around Us,* Book 6, by L. Carey Bolster et al. Copyright © 1978, 1975 by Scott, Foresman and Company.

CHARLES SCRIBNER'S SONS: Excerpt from *The Wind in the Willows* by Kenneth Grahame. Text copyright 1908 by Charles Scribner's Sons.

SILVER BURDETT COMPANY: Excerpts on pp. 67 and 68, from "Ties to the Past—Answers from the Past"; on pp. 441 and 442, from "Australia: A Case Study"; on pp. 346 and 347, from "The Ability to Make Things"; on pp. 199 and 200, from "Tame Animals Work for People"; on pp. 320 and 321, from "Technology Helps Pests Too" (text and art); and on pp. 462 and 463, from "Stories of Early Government" in *Silver Burdett Social Science: People and Change.* © 1976 by Silver Burdett Company. Excerpts on pp. 173 and 174, from "Life in Single Cells—What Do You Call Them?"; and on pp. 147 and 148, from "Investigation 25—How Can You Show That Air Has Weight?" (text and art) in *Science: Understanding Your Environment* (Level 6). © 1975 by General Learning Corporation.

WILLIAM JAY SMITH: "Seal" from *Boy Blue's Book of Beasts* published by Atlantic–Little, Brown, 1957. Copyright © 1956, 1957 by William Jay Smith.

SPORTS ILLUSTRATED: "Young Olympic Star" adapted from "Nadia Awed Ya" by Frank Deford, *Sports Illustrated,* August 2, 1976. © 1976 by Time Inc.

VIKING PENGUIN, INC.: Excerpt from "The Story of Theseus" (titled "Theseus: A Hero of Ancient Greece") in *Lord of the Sky: Zeus* by Doris Gates. Copyright © 1972 by Doris Gates.

WALKER AND COMPANY: Adapted from *The Heavenly Hosts* (titled "Danger or Not?") by Isaac Asimov. Copyright © 1975 by Isaac Asimov.

FREDERICK WARNE & CO., INC.: "The Legend of the Royal Palm" from *Once in Puerto Rico* by Pura Belpré. Copyright © 1973 by Pura Belpré.

FRANKLIN WATTS, INC.: Excerpts (titled "The Viking Age") from *The First Book of the Vikings* by Louise Dickinson Rich, copyright © 1962 by the author. Excerpts (titled "Builders in the Sky") from *The Incas* by Barbara L. Beck, copyright 1966 by Franklin Watts, Inc.

WESLEYAN UNIVERSITY PRESS: "The Base Stealer" from *The Orb Weaver* by Robert Francis. Copyright © 1948 by Robert Francis.

THE H. W. WILSON COMPANY: Entries on p. 51, from *Reader's Guide to Periodical Literature.* Copyright © 1975, 1976 by The H. W. Wilson Company.

Contents

APPRECIATING LITERATURE

Part **2** On Your Own   95

READING TO LEARN

Part **3** The World Around Us

APPRECIATING LITERATURE

Part **4** **Flights of Fantasy**

APPRECIATING LITERATURE

Part **6** The Storyteller's Answer: Myths 373

READING TO LEARN
Part 7 Nature's Ways   417

APPRECIATING LITERATURE

Part 8 Poets and Their Poetry: Impressions

To the Reader

Golden Voyages are waiting for you. In this book, you will take journeys that may be remembered for a lifetime. You will travel through time and space. You will learn about the past and about other lands. You will learn about people and their hopes, goals, and achievements. You will even meet some fantastic characters and visit other worlds. You will read myths and poems. You will read interesting selections about the Earth and the secrets of nature.

Your book, *Golden Voyages,* is divided into eight parts. In Parts 1, 3, 5, and 7, you will learn to improve your reading skills through Skills Lessons, Vocabulary Studies, and Textbook Studies. The reading selections are yours to enjoy as you explore new information. In Parts 2, 4, 6, and 8, you will discover ways to understand and appreciate literature. The selections and poems are yours to enjoy as you travel with the characters and writers.

The voyages you take in a book are special because they are yours forever. They are journeys that you will learn from, share with others, and remember. Are you ready to go? *Golden Voyages* is filled with exciting journeys just for you.

Part 1

Other Times, Other Places

Developing Good Study Habits

Osgood studies with his friends.

Ed studies one hour every night.

Teresa studies in the library.

Elena studies only on weekends.

What do you notice about the study habits of the four people shown above? They're all different from one another. Who, then, has good study habits? They all do, because each person has developed a method that works. Now read about the three people below.

- Roger can't seem to find more than ten minutes at a time to study.
- Doris watches TV a lot and glances at her textbook during the commercials.
- Patricia always finds other things to do when she has to study.

Roger, Doris, and Patricia may have good intentions. But good intentions alone aren't enough. Until you actually begin reading the book and begin thinking about what you're reading, you haven't begun to study. In other words, you have to carry through your good intentions. You should set aside a certain amount of time for the material you have to study. Then you should stick to your schedule.

Setting the Scene

If you haven't found a successful study method, here are some tips to help you develop good habits.

Find a quiet place. This may not always be easy. Some people, in fact, have difficulty concentrating when there is no noise at all. However, you should not let the background sounds—no matter what they are—distract you.

Make sure you have enough light. Any eye doctor will tell you about the importance of proper lighting. If you're having trouble seeing the words on the page, you can't concentrate on what the words are saying. Adjust the lighting so that you can read comfortably. Many people like to study outdoors. As long as you're not bothered by shadows or bright sunlight, studying outdoors can be very pleasant.

Have writing material handy. If you take notes while you study, keep pencils and paper within easy reach. If you have to jump up to look around for a pencil, there's a chance you'll forget what the pencil is for!

Work out a schedule. When you think about it, you'll discover that every activity in your life fits into a time slot. Some things—such as school, club meetings, and sports practice—have fixed time periods. They can't be changed. But you probably have several hours a week that are free. Some of this time can be blocked out for studying.

3

How much time is enough? The amount of time you spend each week studying depends on a number of things.

If social studies seems easy to you but math is a problem, you'll need to spend more time on math. If you have a test coming up, you may want to "borrow" a few hours from another subject to prepare for the test. Whatever your time slot for studying is, be sure you stick to it. If you've planned to study science on Tuesday between 7:00 and 8:30, don't give in to the urge to either watch TV or visit a friend instead.

How to Begin Studying

Starting to study can be easy. Here are a few suggestions.

Preview the material. If you have to read a chapter, look at the headings, subheadings, and graphic aids. Read the questions and/or summary at the end of the chapter. This will help you focus on the most important information.

Read the chapter carefully. Look for key words and ideas. Notice words and phrases that are in italics or boldface. Make sure you understand graphs, charts, and tables. Ask yourself whether these graphic aids are illustrating information in the text or adding new information.

When you come to a paragraph you don't understand, stop and reread it. Ask yourself, "What is the author saying?" Then try to explain the information in your own words.

Review the material. Make sure you understand what you've read. You may want to do this with a friend. Discuss anything you have questions about.

These are just a few suggestions. Perhaps they will work for you. Perhaps you've developed your own method. Remember, the heart of studying is reading. Once you start reading your textbook, you're halfway there.

Try This

Look at the pictures below. Who has good study habits? Whose habits need improvement? What improvements can you suggest? Tell some other good study habits.

Leonard

Barbara

Jenny

Paul

Compound Words

The general cleared his throat and looked around the table. "It says here," he began, " 'To whom it may concern: please send us one **stonecutter**, two **shipbuilders**, and a **shoemaker**. We'd like some samples of your craftspeople to bring back to our planet. Thanks.' "

The general folded the note. "Well," he said. "There you have it. It seems that we have been invaded by beings from outer space. They are demanding a person who cuts stone, two people who build ships, and someone who makes shoes. The question is: do we give up these people to the aliens?"

"Absolutely!" cried the stonecutter.

"Most definitely!" shouted the shipbuilders.

"Hooray!" screamed the usually quiet shoemaker.

The general could hardly believe his ears. "Hold on," he sputtered. "You mean you *want* to go?"

"Sure," said the stonecutter. "If the aliens' planet is rocky, I can cut some fantastic designs in it."

"And just imagine building a real starship!" breathed one of the shipbuilders.

"And I can make my first pair of antigravity shoes," said the shoemaker. "Come on, general, please let us go."

"Well, I suppose it *is* the chance of a lifetime, but don't forget to send me a postcard when you get there."

"Right," said the stonecutter. "As soon as we touch down. Gee, I wonder what the aliens look like."

"I believe they have two arms and two legs," said the general.

"No tentacles?" cried the shoemaker.

"Sorry. No tentacles," said the general, stretching his twelve tentacles. "Yes, my friends. Things will be very different once you get to Earth."

Word Play

1. Compound words are made of two or more words. There are five more compound words besides the three in boldface in the story. Find them and use them in sentences.
2. Try to combine other words in the story to make compound words. Use the new words in sentences.

Before you read this selection, preview it. Use the subheadings, illustrations, and captions to get an idea of what the selection is about.

How do we know about the kinds of animals that lived a million years ago? We have learned about some of them through . . .

THE TRAGEDY OF THE TAR PITS

by Roy Chapman Andrews

Imagine time turned back almost a million years. That was the beginning of the Ice Age in North America. Great fields of ice covered much of the northern part of the continent.

The countryside near what is now the city of Los Angeles, California, looked much as it does today. In the wide valley at what is now called Rancho La Brea, clumps of trees and bushes were sprinkled through tall grass.

To the east, the silver thread of a river could just be seen. In the foreground lay several strange-looking pools. Each was surrounded by a bare black patch of ground on which nothing could grow. The pools were half-liquid asphalt, resembling tar. In fact, these pools of asphalt are usually known today as "tar pits." At certain times, bubbles of oil and terrible-smelling gas broke through them. After a rain, the surface was probably covered with a few inches of water. It was not good water, but it was drinkable. During dry weather, a film of wind-blown dust made the tar look like solid ground.

The Time of the "Tiger"

A saber-toothed "tiger" had just awakened from sleep. It was a powerful beast, the most dreaded killer of the country. It had a short tail and huge front legs. From either side of its upper jaw, nine-inch teeth grew downward. They were curved like sabers, sharp and pointed. It wasn't really a tiger, but it looked so much like a tiger that this is what it is usually called.

All of the country belonged to the saber-toothed tiger by right of its strength, ferocity, and terrible teeth. Its teeth were like knives or daggers. Those teeth could cut through skin, flesh, even bone.

The saber-tooth was hungry. The sun beat down with a blazing heat, making the tiger lazy. Food in plenty roamed nearby. The tiger had only to choose. But the day was hot, and the tiger didn't want to move.

In the valley below, the tiger's eye caught something moving. Two huge, shaggy, golden-brown animals were pushing through the brush near a dry creek bed.

Instantly the tiger's body grew stiff. Its yellow eyes blazed. Here was a favorite prey—the big, slow-moving ground sloths. They were distant cousins of the small sloths living today in South America.

The sloths waddled about, sure that they were safe. They were safe enough from wolves and even lions, but not from the saber-tooth. The tiger's dagger-like teeth could cut through their tough skin.

The beasts were working their way toward the black pools. They were thirsty, and water from the last night's rain shone in the sun. They crossed the bare, black rim around the largest pool and splashed in to drink. For a few moments nothing happened. Then slowly the bottom began to give way. Their feet sank into tar. Struggling in fright, they tried desperately to pull themselves out. But their back legs only went deeper and deeper into the black ooze. Escape was impossible.

The saber-toothed tiger had left the hill. It crept quietly through the brush. Belly down, chin almost touching the grass, its body seemed to flow smoothly across the ground like a snake. With eyes blazing, the tiger watched the great beasts struggling in the pool. The time had come. In one leap, the tiger jumped on the back of the nearest sloth. With a desperate move, the animal threw the tiger off. The tiger rolled over in the tar. Snarling, the saber-tooth turned to strike at the sloth's golden-brown neck. But the tiger couldn't raise its feet. The sticky tar held them in a clutch of death. Forgetting the sloths, the tiger tried to drag itself out. It was too late. The tiger was sucked down slowly into the black depths of the pool.

Half a dozen great black vultures watched what was happening below them. These were huge birds with naked red heads, giant beaks, and ten-foot wings. These vultures were close relatives of the California condors that live today. Like all vultures, they fed on dead or dying animals.

While the animals were still fighting for their lives, the vultures circled over them. One dropped down upon the surface of the pool, then another and another. As each bird tried to move, the tar grabbed its feet. Like insects on a sheet of flypaper, their wings and feathers were caught and held. Soon all the animals were only black balls of tar. Long before the sun dropped behind the mountains, all traces of birds and beasts had disappeared. The pools shone like silver. The traps were ready for new victims.

CALIFORNIA

Los
Angeles

•La Brea
Tar Pits

PACIFIC
OCEAN

A Million Years Later

The story you have just read is true. It is imaginative only in details. We know it is true because of the fossil bones buried in the tar. We also know because we can see the same tar traps working today, although the pits are not as large as they were a million years ago.

One morning I stood on the edge of one of the La Brea pools. A rabbit and a bird were struggling in the black tar. A hawk circled overhead, coming lower and lower. I watched it dive for the rabbit. It sank its claws in the animal's body and tried to lift it out. In two minutes, the bird itself was caught. Such has been the fate of many animals and birds through the years. Today the pits are closed off so that wandering animals cannot be trapped by the deadly tar.

The pools were first formed by oil that oozed up from the earth in springs. Around the springs the tar remains soft. Elsewhere it hardens into a solid mass mixed with earth and dust. In the Ice Age, the oil springs were more active than now.

When asphalt was taken out of the La Brea pits to make roads, thousands of bones buried in the tar were discovered. For a time, little was done about it. Then scientists at the University of California began to study the strange bones. Thousands of skulls and tens of thousands of other bones have been dug out. The bones are filled with the tar, but they have changed very little. Of course, nothing is left of the flesh, skin, horns, and hoofs. The bones are mixed up in a crowded mass so that no animal's skeleton is together.

The La Brea tar pits are famous as the richest fossil deposit ever discovered. Nowhere else are the remains of so many different kinds of extinct animals found in one place. Nowhere else are the bones so well preserved. Nowhere else are they so easy to dig out and study.

As scientists have examined the La Brea fossils, they have identified more than fifty different kinds of birds and mammals. Many of these creatures have been extinct for thousands and thousands of years.

Most of the bones are those of flesh-eating mammals, birds of prey, and wading birds. The story of the saber-toothed tiger and the sloths and vultures gives the reason. The larger animals caught in the tar were bait for the trap. They lured flesh-eating birds into the tar. Day after day this went on for a million years.

The La Brea tar pits show which mammals lived in southern California since the Ice Age. It is a whole chapter in the past life on this Earth, written in black asphalt tar.

Understanding What You've Read

1. What was the "tragedy" of the La Brea tar pits?
2. How do scientists know that almost a million years ago animals were trapped in the pits?
3. Why was the saber-toothed "tiger" the most dreaded beast that lived almost a million years ago?
4. Why were most of the fossils found in the tar pits mainly flesh-eating animals and birds?
5. Why have the La Brea tar pits become famous?

Applying the Skills Lesson

Why are the following study habits good to use in reading this selection?

1. previewing the selection
2. turning to the glossary or a dictionary
3. using the map on page 12 to locate the tar pits
4. writing down any important ideas

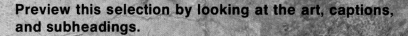

Preview this selection by looking at the art, captions, and subheadings.

It was by luck that a dog found an ancient cave in northern Spain. It was luck, too, that led a five-year-old child to . . .

THE SECRETS OF
ALTAMIRA

by Heinz Sponsel
and translated by Hertha Pauli

Dawn broke in the small village of Santillana [sän·tē′yä′nä] del Mar, in northern Spain. José, steward to Don Marcelino, left with hunters and dogs to catch the foxes that had been raiding Don Marcelino's chicken coops.

The hunt lasted well into the afternoon. Suddenly, José noticed that one of the dogs was missing. He called and whistled in all directions, but it was no use. The dog had disappeared.

Finally, one of the other dogs seemed to find a scent. The hunters followed. A short time later, they stood in the middle of a meadow facing a deep crack in the earth. They stared at it in surprise. They had never noticed it before. José bent forward and listened. He heard a whimper from deep in the earth. The dogs jumped around, scratching and scraping. The men joined the dogs and dug. Soon, they saw that the crack was an entrance to a cave underneath the earth. A cave? Could there really be a cave? When they had made an opening large enough for a person to squeeze into it, the lost dog suddenly shot up from underground.

When José reached the castle, he told Don Marcelino about the dog and the cave. Don Marcelino found the story hard to believe. He had heard of caves in the mountains, but never of one in a field. So he rode to the spot with José to check the story. Sure enough, there was a deep crack leading down into the earth!

Step by step, holding a torch, the two men entered. They saw the narrow opening widen into a rocky cave. There were low hollows in the walls, but nothing in them. The men looked around and then left the cave to return to the castle. There, Don Marcelino ordered José to write in the castle chronicle: "A cave has been discovered under a meadow near Altamira."

José made the one-sentence entry in the book with the year 1869 stamped in gold letters on the cover.

Nobody gave the cave any further thought. Children started to use the cave as a playground. But one day Don Marcelino told José: "Close the cave with a door and an iron lock. It's too dangerous to serve as a playground."

The Secrets of the Cave

Nine years went by. Don Marcelino returned to his castle in northern Spain from a trip to the World's Fair in Paris. There he had seen an exhibit of stone tools made by people who lived about twenty thousand years ago. It was then that he got the idea that primitive people might have once lived in the cave of Altamira.

Upon his return to Spain, Don Marcelino immediately called for his steward, José. Together they rode across the fields of Altamira. Once more they stood in front of the cave. The lock was so rusty that José could barely open it. After a long struggle, they entered the cave, holding a blazing torch.

The two men explored the cave but found nothing. They locked the door again with great care.

During the next year, Don Marcelino explored the cave thoroughly but found nothing.

Then, on a gray November day, Don Marcelino was digging when, all at once, he felt his shovel strike against something. He dropped the shovel to one side and began to dig with his bare hands. His fingers trembled. Then he stopped. He had touched something! He clutched it firmly. After months and months, now he was holding a wedge tool in his hands. There it was—proof that people had lived in this very cave—ten or perhaps twenty thousand years ago.

He continued to dig swiftly. He found weapons that early people had used to kill animals now long extinct: bison, mammoths, and cave bears.

More digs gave more finds: a stone knife, stone blades, and other arrowheads. Soon a trunk in Don Marcelino's home was filled with these objects.

Advice from an Expert

After a long train journey, Don Marcelino and José arrived in Madrid, the capital of Spain. It was December. They went to the home of Professor Vilanova.

When they arrived, the professor greeted them. "So, you have discovered a cave, Don Marcelino?" Professor Vilanova began.

"Well, to be correct," replied Don Marcelino, "the real discoverer was the dog that fell into a crack in the field. That was almost ten years ago. Please take a look at what I found there!"

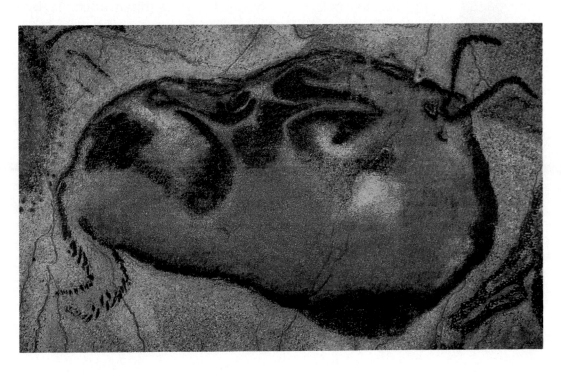

Professor Vilanova carefully examined the stones, one after the other. After a long time, he said, "There's no doubt that these are weapons and tools of early people. Go on with your digging. Perhaps you will discover even more secrets in your cave."

More Secrets

Upon his return from Madrid, Don Marcelino spent all his time digging in the cave.

Each time Don Marcelino left the castle for the cave, his five-year-old daughter Maria pleaded, "Please, Papa, take me along."

Finally, Maria won her case. One day, her father lifted her onto his saddle and set out for Altamira. When he reached the cave he took her hand.

"Always stay close to me," he told her. "There's very little light in the cave except where my torch burns."

Don Marcelino was so interested in his digging that he did not notice his daughter's disappearance. It was only when he heard her scream that he dropped the spade and went in the direction of the sound of her voice. Where was Maria? Crawling on the ground, he suddenly saw the child in one of the hollows. "Papa!" she shouted happily. "Look! There are animals in the stone!"

Don Marcelino first took Maria into his arms. Then he held his torch close to the stone. He could hardly believe his eyes! Ancient bison, wild boars, and other animals had been drawn in color on the walls of the hollows. He just stood there and stared.

Little Maria broke the silence. "Papa, don't you like my *toros*?" She thought the bison were bulls.

Don Marcelino, still unable to speak, just kissed her.

"You must come right away," he wrote Professor Vilanova that night. "My five-year-old daughter Maria has discovered drawings of animals in the cave."

When Professor Vilanova arrived, Don Marcelino rode with him to the cave. They stayed there for hours. Over and over, the professor scrutinized the colors and drawings that Maria had discovered.

After many days he still wondered if they were really drawn by early people.

"Can you swear, Don Marcelino, that nobody but you and your daughter has ever entered the cave?" he asked.

"My fox hunters were in the cave. And a few village children before I closed it. That's all I can say."

"Is it possible that one of the hunters made the drawings on the walls?"

"You don't believe that!" Don Marcelino burst out. "This kind of bison has been extinct for thousands and thousands of years."

"I am convinced that people from the Ice Age made these drawings on the walls," said Professor Vilanova. "I believe that they are more than fifteen thousand years old. But how can we prove it?"

"Professor Vilanova, if *you* will make such a statement, everybody will have to believe it."

The News Spreads

The news of the finds in the cave of Altamira soon spread from Spain all over Europe. The tiny village became famous overnight. Newspapers carried the picture of little Maria. Visitors from many lands arrived to see the wonderful drawings in the cave.

Many archaeologists, however, did not agree that Don Marcelino and Professor Vilanova were right about the drawings. There was talk that an artist, once a guest of Don Marcelino, had made the drawings on the wall.

The artist was found and made a statement that he had never been in the cave at Altamira. The statement was sent to the newspapers and to scientists all over the world. But nobody cared. The road to Altamira lay deserted again, and the cave was closed.

Twenty-three years passed. Don Marcelino had died before he could prove the truth of the discovery. One day, a famous archaeologist arrived at the castle of Santillana and told Maria, "The drawings on the cave walls *are* authentic. They *are* fifteen to twenty thousand years old. Caves with similar drawings have just been discovered in southern France. There is no longer any doubt."

Soon after, the door to the wonders of Altamira was reopened.

20

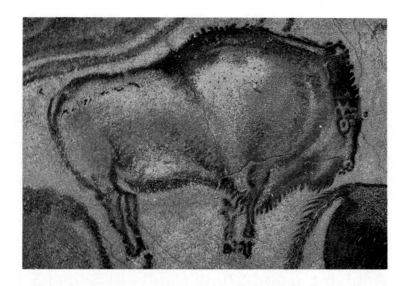

Understanding What You've Read

1. How was the cave at Altamira first discovered?
2. Why did Don Marcelino and his steward, José, begin to explore the cave nine years after its discovery?
3. What did Don Marcelino first discover in the cave?
4. What greater secrets were found in the cave?
5. There was talk that an artist, a guest of Don Marcelino, made the cave drawings. Why was the cave closed after this talk?
6. What happened later that helped to prove that the drawings in the cave were authentic?

Applying the Skills Lesson

Which things below did you learn by *previewing* the selection? Which did you learn by *reading* the selection?

1. The selection would deal with tools found in a cave.
2. The selection would deal with cave paintings.
3. Altamira is in northern Spain.
4. Paintings were found in a cave in southern France.

Applying Good Study Habits to Reading

During most of your school years, you'll need to apply your good study habits to reading textbooks. Throughout this book you'll find several Textbook Studies. Each of them has selections taken from different textbooks. As you read the selections, use the sidenotes. They will give you hints about the best way to apply your reading skills and good study habits to textbooks.

Applying Good Study Habits in Social Studies

On the next few pages are several headings, paragraphs, and illustrations from a social studies textbook. If you were *previewing* a chapter on languages from this textbook, you would examine the parts shown on these pages.

Here are several headings and subheadings from the chapter. Notice the different sizes of the headings. Which is a general topic that includes all the other topics?

Just by looking at the subheadings you can answer this question: In what three ways are all languages alike?

LANGUAGES ARE ALIKE BUT DIFFERENT

HOW ARE ALL LANGUAGES ALIKE?

Spoken Sounds

Words

Grammar

Words are not enough. To communicate through language, people must agree about more than just what certain words mean. They also need certain agreements about how to use those words.

For example, how do you change a word to show when you are talking about one cat (*singular*) and when you're talking about several cats (*plural*)? It's useful, too, to have rules for changing action words, or verbs, to show whether something happened in the past or will happen in the future. How is that done in English? Most languages also have rules about the order in which words are used in sentences. All of these kinds of rules are what is meant by **grammar.** Every language has its own grammar.

When you preview, you do not read whole paragraphs. However, words in italics or in boldface type may catch your attention. Such words are often defined. Quickly find out what is meant by *grammar.*

Sometimes interesting information is put in a box. You'll see tables, maps, or explanations of key ideas presented in this way.

Swahili Plurals

Different languages use different ways of making a singular word (*cat*) into a plural (*cats*). Below you see how some plural words are formed in Swahili, an African language. After studying the first two examples, can you infer what the plural of *kiti* (*KEE'tee*) would be?

Singular	**Plural**
kitu (*thing*)	vitu (*things*)
kisu (*knife*)	visu (*knives*)
kiti (*chair*)	? (*chairs*)

The Indo-European family tree. Branches labeled: Spanish, Italian, French, Romanian, Slovene, Bulgarian, Serbo-Croatian, Polish, Czech, Slovak, Portuguese, Latvian, Lithuanian, Russian, Ukrainian, German, Dutch, Flemish, Romance, Balto-Slavic, Hindi, Bengali, Urdu, Bihari, English, Romany, Norwegian, Germanic, Indo-Iranian, Persian, Afghan, Icelandic, Danish, Swedish, Irish Gaelic, Scottish Gaelic, Celtic, Welsh, Albanian, Greek, Armenian. Trunk: THE INDO-EUROPEAN FAMILY TREE.

You can learn from a quick look at art as you preview a chapter.

Each of these headings is part of the general topic *Languages Are Alike but Different.*

LANGUAGES ARE RELATED

THE INDO-EUROPEAN LANGUAGE FAMILY

THE EVIDENCE OF RELATIONSHIP

Another important language family is the one called Sino-Tibetan. Chinese, the most important member of this family, has many dialects that differ in words and sounds. All the dialects, however, use the same writing system. Notice how Chinese writing is done with an upright brush (below). Chinese writing often appears in old paintings (left).

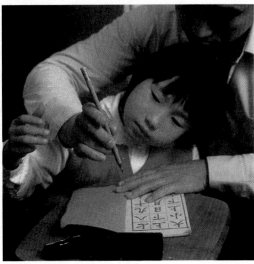

—*The Way People Live*
Houghton Mifflin

25

Building Skills

Just by previewing parts of this chapter, you have learned several things. Which of the following things have you learned by previewing?

1. Languages are related.
2. Languages have spoken sounds, words, and rules of grammar.
3. English is derived from the Indo-European family of languages.
4. The word *three* is similar in many different Indo-European languages.
5. The word for *three* in Hungarian is *harom*.
6. Chinese writing is done with an upright brush.

Applying Good Study Habits in Health

Studying and Resting

Notice that this paragraph mentions some of the things you read about in the Skills Lesson on study habits.

Study habits are formed just like other habits. You have to set goals for yourself. Then you have to plan. Find a good place and set aside a regular time. If you stick to your plan, you will soon form study habits that will help you reach your goal.

George does his homework when he can't think of anything else to do. He usually works on the living room floor. He watches TV while he studies. After a half-hour, he gets tired and stops.

What study habits has George formed? What would you change if you were George? Why?

Celia does some of her homework after school. She works at the library because it's quiet. At home, she studies for a while after dinner. Before school the next day, she looks again at what she has studied the night before.

What study habits has Celia formed? How are her habits different from George's?

— *Toward Your Future:* Brown
Harcourt Brace Jovanovich

> **When you come to questions within a paragraph, stop and think. Try to answer the questions before you continue to read.**

 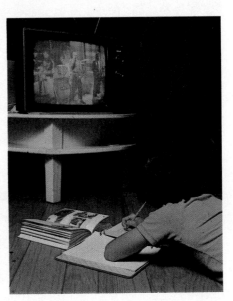

Building Skills

1. Why are George's study habits poor?
2. Why are Celia's study habits good?

Adjusting Your Reading Speed
to Your Purpose

In the cartoon above, the hare is reading very quickly. The tortoise is reading slowly. Who do you think is the better reader? The best answer to this question is, "You can't tell. You'd have to know what purpose each animal has for reading and what it is reading."

Suppose both animals are reading an exciting story. If that is the case, *both* animals are good readers. The tortoise wants to read every detail carefully because that's the way it likes to read. Good for the tortoise! The hare can hardly wait to see what's going to happen next, so it's reading very fast. Good for the hare, too!

Now suppose that both animals are just trying to find out what the book is about in general. The tortoise might be wasting a lot of time by reading every word.

Finally, suppose that each animal is studying a math book. By reading very quickly, the hare might be missing some important details.

Your reading speed may be affected by the material you're reading and by your reason for reading it. However, when you read, *you* are the only one who can judge whether you're going fast enough or slow enough to get the most out of your reading.

Skimming

Suppose you were in a library or a bookstore and you found a book with the title *Gadgets You Can Make Yourself.* How could you find out whether this book would be useful to you? You might **skim** through the book.

When you skim a book, an article, or a chapter, your purpose is to get a general idea of what it's about. You have most likely used skimming many times in the past, though you might not have known it was called skimming.

How would you skim the book *Gadgets You Can Make Yourself?* You might start with the table of contents. You'd glance at the chapter titles first. Do any of the chapters deal with clocks?

Table of Contents

Would you take the book because one or more of the chapter titles seemed interesting? Maybe you would. But maybe you'd want to skim through the book rapidly to find out more about it. If you were interested in Chapter 2, "Glass Wind Chimes," you might want to *preview* that chapter. (*Previewing* is one kind of skimming.) You'd look at the illustrations, or pictures, to see whether the finished gadgets were something you'd like to make. You might read all the headings or a few sentences to make sure you can follow the directions. Why might you also look for a list of the materials and tools you'd need?

Scanning

Skimming is a kind of rapid reading you do to get a general idea about a book, chapter, or article. **Scanning** is another kind of rapid reading. You scan when you want to find a *specific* piece of information quickly.

Suppose you want to know when Dolley Madison was born. You might first scan the index at the back of a book to see whether *Madison, Dolley,* is listed. You would move your eyes rapidly along the *M* listings. If you found *Madison, Dolley,* you'd turn to the pages that the index lists. Then you'd scan those pages for information about Dolley Madison.

When you scan a printed page, names of people or places, dates and other numbers, and words printed in italics or boldface seem to stand out. Perhaps you'd find this date first: 1809. You'd read the whole sentence:

In 1809 James Madison became the fourth President.

This is not the information you want. So you'd continue to scan, looking for dates earlier than 1809. Maybe you'd see this date: 1768. Read the whole sentence. Does it give the information you're looking for?

His wife, Dolley Payne Madison, was born in 1768.

When you scan, you don't read every word. You keep certain key words in your mind and look for them as you let your eyes move over the page.

Try This

1. Skim through the selection called "The Viking Age," which begins on page 61. What do the subheads and illustrations tell you about the Vikings?
2. Scan the selection called "The Secrets of Altamira," which begins on page 14. Find the year that the cave was discovered. What clue did you look for?
3. Scan this book's table of contents. On what page do you find an author study of Joseph Bruchac? Skim this author study. Give a summary in a few sentences.

VOCABULARY STUDY

Getting Meaning from Context Clues

Mrs. Sparks led me into the living room. The first thing I saw was the huge object on the sofa. A robot!

"His name's Futuro," she said.

Futuro's faceplate **glinted** in the lamplight. His **ebony** eyes **resembled** two black coat buttons. I moved closer to get a better look at Futuro. But the more I **scrutinized**, the less amazed I became. His eyes really were coat buttons. His nose was a funnel. His body was made of dozens of pie plates nailed together. What a **shabby** sight he was!

"Don't let his ragged **appearance** fool you," said Mrs. Sparks. "He's really very intelligent."

Naturally, I didn't believe her. "Prove it," I challenged.

Mrs. Sparks commanded Futuro to stand up, but just as I expected, nothing happened. "Perhaps he's tired," said Mrs. Sparks. "The novel he's writing keeps him very busy."

Novel? Well, this was too much!

"Really! Mrs. Sparks!" I cried. "This is the silliest thing I ever heard." Mrs. Sparks had fallen silent and was sitting with a glassy look in her eyes.

"Mrs. Sparks! MRS. SPARKS!"

Just then Futuro leaped to his feet and grabbed Mrs. Sparks's wrist to take her pulse. Futuro shook his head. "Please forgive Mrs. Sparks," he said. "I'll have her back to normal in a jiffy."

"What's wrong with her?" I asked.

"Nothing serious," said Futuro. "She just needs a new battery."

Word Play

Context clues are words or phrases that give a hint to the meaning of a word. Use the context clues in the story to help you match each word in the column on the left with its meaning in the column on the right. Then use each word in a sentence.

glinted	black
ebony	studied
resembled	shone
scrutinized	ragged
shabby	looked like
appearance	sight

Before you read this selection, skim through it to get a general idea of what it is about. Remember, *previewing* is one kind of skimming.

What was hidden away over three thousand years ago and became a great discovery? Find out about the . . .

TREASURES
OF A
TEENAGE KING

by the editors of *Senior Scholastic* magazine

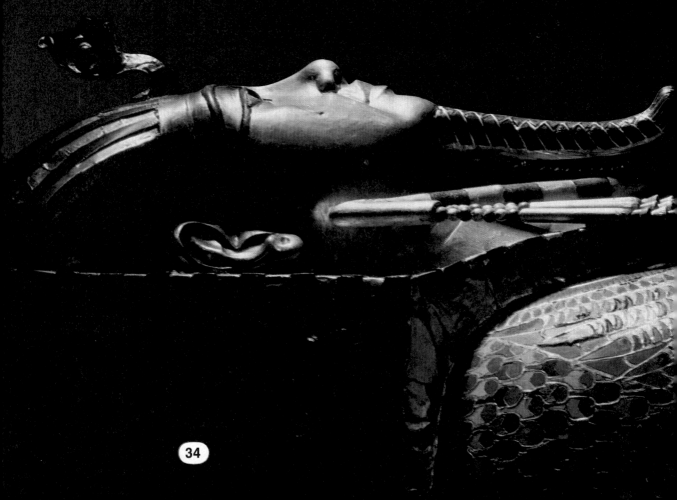

"At first I could see nothing. The hot air escaping from the chamber caused the candle flame to flicker. As my eyes grew accustomed to the light, details of the room emerged slowly from the mist. I saw strange animals, statues, and gold — everywhere the glint of gold."

These were the words archaeologist Howard Carter used to describe what happened in 1922 as he first looked into the tomb of King Tutankhamun. King Tut had been a boy-pharaoh of ancient Egypt. This king belonged to a civilization which had developed three thousand years before. It still fascinates many people in the world today.

The discovery of the tomb was the beginning of a dream-come-true for Carter and his partner, Lord Carnarvon. They had been searching for it for more than ten years in a desert area nearly 400 miles upriver from Cairo, Egypt. They were in the *Valley of Kings,*

Gold casket of King Tut.

Right:
Miniature sarcophagus (front).

Below: *Howard Carter and staff examine Tutankhamun's body (1922).*

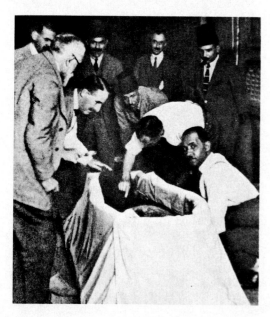

the burial ground of the pharaohs. Many tombs had already been found there, but none for King Tut.

Unlike the great pyramids — tombs of earlier pharaohs — these tombs were underground. But like the pyramids, these tombs were built with secret passages and fake doorways in the hopes of discouraging robbers. However, none of these things had stopped robbers from entering and looting the tombs.

Howard Carter believed that he could find King Tut's tomb. He remembered the glazed cup, the painted vases, and the shawls with King Tutankhamun's seal. These had all been found earlier in the Valley of Kings. They were clues that perhaps the tomb was somewhere nearby.

One day, Howard Carter was searching with a team of workers. The team dug some ancient mud huts out of the sand. The presence of the huts made it seem an unlikely place for the tomb. But the spot, Carter felt, was his last hope.

Under one of the huts, a worker's shovel struck something hard. A few shovelfuls of sand revealed a stone step. More digging uncovered fifteen more steps. Then Carter saw it—a plaster door, stamped with two seals. Writing on the seals said that the mummy of a teenage pharaoh named Tutankhamun lay inside.

Carefully Hidden Away

Carter carefully poked a small peephole through the door and inserted a flashlight. He saw a passageway filled from floor to ceiling with stones. He knew it was a blockade. He was sure that, in more than three thousand years, no one had opened the door!

With Carnarvon and Carter leading the way, the stone blockade was removed. This opened up a passageway that sloped down another thirty feet to a second

Left:
Miniature sarcophagus (back).

Below: *The Valley of Kings, the Tomb of King Tut.*

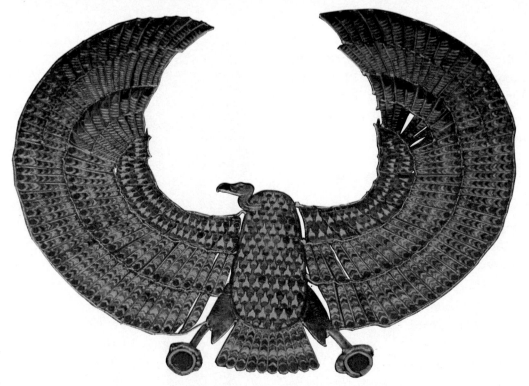

A golden vulture. The vulture was the symbol of upper Egypt.

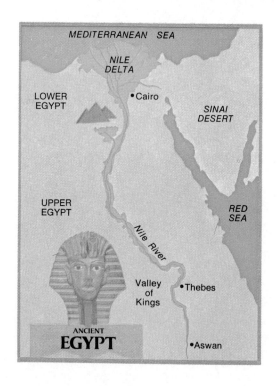

MEDITERRANEAN SEA

NILE DELTA

LOWER EGYPT

•Cairo

SINAI DESERT

UPPER EGYPT

RED SEA

Nile River

Valley of Kings

•Thebes

ANCIENT EGYPT

•Aswan

sealed doorway. Carter punched a peephole through this door.

Behind the door was a room so filled with treasures there was little space to walk. When Carter and Carnarvon broke down the door, they stepped into another world.

As they recovered from their amazement, they realized something else: there was no coffin in the room. Then they took a better look at two life-sized statues of King Tutankhamun which faced one another along one wall. The statues guarded a sealed door. Apparently, there were more

Detail of colored glass decoration worn on Egyptian clothing.

rooms in the tomb. It turned out there were four rooms. Each one was jammed with treasures. The king was buried in the second burial room.

Evidence showed that robbers had broken into the tomb soon after the king's burial. But they seemed to have taken little. They may have been caught in the act. It was probably shortly after this that huts were built above the tomb.

What the Treasures Revealed

Egyptians believed that death was the end of life in Egypt and the beginning of another life in the next world. So they felt that the dead person's possessions should be put into the tomb for use in that next life. When people died, things such as fine clothes, jewels, furniture, and mounds of food and drink were buried with them.

King Tut's people provided him with gold chairs and animal-shaped couches, chariots, clothes, perfumed jars, and roast ducks. All these were jammed into the first room of the tomb.

This room also held the pharaoh's symbols of power. His

Gold jewelry with inlaid glass.

wand, a blue-and-gold-striped rod, showed his high office. His throne was made of ebony and ivory which came from central Africa. A perfumed jar was shaped like a lion to show his power.

Carter and his crew spent two years clearing the first room before entering the burial room itself. When he finally peeked through the doorway between the statues of the two kings, Carter saw a solid wall of gold. It blocked the entrance to the room.

The gold wall turned out to be a shrine—wood, covered with gold. Inside it was another shrine—and then another and another and another. Pictures on each shrine described the pharaoh's life. His coronation, wedding feast, and funeral feast were shown.

Inside the innermost shrine, Carter found the king's *sarcophagus* [sär·kof′ə·gəs], or coffin. Inside this coffin lay a coffin within a coffin. Three coffins protected the dead pharaoh! Each was topped with a gold, jeweled statue of King Tut.

The work team found the coffins unusually heavy. When they made their way to the third coffin, through a maze of linen wrappings, charms, and other small treasures, they learned why. The coffin weighed 2,448 pounds. It was made of solid gold.

The Royal King

Inside lay King Tutankhamun, as he had for three thousand years. On his face and head was a mask made of pure gold. The blue stripes which covered the mask were colored glass. The Egyptians felt this colored glass was more valuable than precious stones. The cobra, symbol of lower Egypt, and the vulture of upper Egypt were both part of the headpiece. They symbolized the nation's unity under one ruler.

Little is known of King Tut's reign. He was born in 1343 B.C. As a child, he was married to the daughter of the then-reigning pharaoh. He became king when he was nine, but died of unknown causes in 1325 B.C., when he was eighteen or nineteen years old. He was quickly buried and forgotten, supposedly for all time.

With the discovery and opening of the tomb, a glimpse of King Tutankhamun's ancient land was revealed to the whole world three thousand years later.

Understanding What You've Read

1. Who was King Tutankhamun?
2. How was King Tut's tomb discovered?
3. What treasures did King Tut's tomb reveal?
4. Why was the discovery and opening of the tomb such a great event?
5. Why were possessions placed in the pharaohs' tombs?

Applying the Skills Lesson

1. When you previewed the selection, which of the following things did you look at to help you find out what the selection was about?
   a. subheads
   b. every word in the selection
   c. map, photographs, and captions
   d. a few sentences
   e. words in italics

2. Scan the selection to find the answers to the following questions:
   a. When was King Tutankhamun born and when did he die?
   b. When was King Tutankhamun's tomb discovered?

Adjusting Reading Speed to Purpose

As you read textbooks, you'll find you can adjust your reading speed to your purpose. When you want to find specific information, you'll find yourself scanning. When you want to get a general idea about something, you'll skim. The sidenotes will help you think about how to use these skills.

Adjusting Reading Speed to Purpose in Language Arts

The tables of contents at the front of your textbooks can help you quickly find information. On which page would you find information about how to use the card catalogue?

Sometimes titles or headings do not clearly tell you what information appears on the page. Can you guess what is meant by *human resources* in this table of contents?

—*Patterns of Language:* Level Six
American Book Company

Building Skills

Scan the table of contents on the preceding page to answer the following questions.

1. On which pages would you find information about the library?
2. On which page would you find information about magazines? (Hint: Another name for magazines is *periodicals*.)

Adjusting Reading Speed to Purpose in Science

Do not read this selection now. Just preview it by looking at the illustrations and the headings. Then go directly to *Building Skills*.

Heads or tails! When most comets travel near the sun, they form what is called a tail. The tail extends from the head. It is the tail which makes comets different from each other. Some people believe that no two comets are alike.

The tails of most comets appear as smokelike streamers. Tails may be curved or straight. They may be short or long. Some of the longest tails may be 161 million kilometers (100 million miles) long. However, some comets have no tails at all. And some comets have two tails.

The tail of a comet always faces away from the sun. As the comet travels toward the sun, the tail is behind its head. After the comet goes around the sun and travels back in its orbit, the tail is in front of its head!

Comets lose some of their mass on each orbit. The sun causes some of the frozen particles to melt and break off. Each orbit causes a comet to become smaller and smaller. At some time a comet will lose practically all its mass.

You read captions as part of previewing.

How are the tails of these two comets different?

A famous comet. Probably the most famous comet is Halley's comet. This comet is named for the British astronomer Edmund Halley. In 1682, Halley carefully watched the path of this large comet. By doing this, he was able to figure out the exact size and shape of its orbit. Halley also read many old books about comets. He was able to show that this same comet had probably appeared in 1066, 1456, 1531, and 1607.

—*Exploring Science:* Red Book
Laidlaw Brothers

Building Skills

1. Scan the selection above in order to answer the following questions.
   a. How long may a comet's tail be?
   b. What is the name of a famous comet?
   c. When did Halley first sight the comet?

2. Now go back and read the selection about comets. Then answer *true* or *false* to the following statements.
   a. Tails of comets may be curved or straight.
   b. All comets have tails.
   c. Comets travel in orbits around the sun.
   d. Comets stay the same size no matter how many times they travel around the sun.

Using Library Resources

Suppose your favorite sport is ice skating. Once you arrived at the library, how would you begin your search for information?

A good place to start your search is the **card catalogue.**
This is a set of drawers holding cards that list all the books in
the library. Most likely, you wouldn't have an author or the
title of a book on ice skating in mind. So you would look for
subject cards. Here are three cards you might find if you
looked under *Sports, Ice Skating,* and *Skating.*

YA   SPORTS
796.4
         Durant, John.
            Highlights of the Olympics: from ancient
         times to the present. Hastings House (1973)

         160 p. illus.
         Includes Index.

J   ICE SKATING
796.9
         Sullivan, George.
            Better Ice Skating for Boys and Girls.
         Dodd, Mead & Co. (1976)

         64 p. illus.
         Includes Glossary

J   SKATING
796.9
         Lindsay, Sally.
            Figure Skating. Chicago, Rand McNally
         (1963).
         96 p. illus. (A Rand McNally fact book)
         Bibliography

Which of the three books are about skating in particular?
Which of the books is about sports in general?

Now how would you find these books in the library? Notice the number listed on the top left corner of each card. This is a **call number.** Nonfiction books are shelved in the library according to their call numbers. Each of the three books on sports has a call number that begins with 796. To find them, you'd look for the section of the library that has books with call numbers in the 700's. In that section you'd find books that have the call number 796 on their spines. The diagram below is a sample of a library floor plan. How is it similar to your local or school library? How is it different?

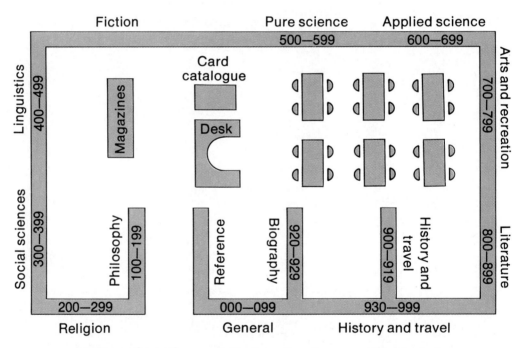

Notice that the nonfiction books are divided into ten classes. The ten classes of books, numbered from 000 to 999, make up the **Dewey Decimal System.** A call number is also called a **Dewey Decimal number.** Where in the library pictured above would you find *Figure Skating*? Its call number is 796.9. It would be on the shelves marked 700–799.

Where would you find each of the following books listed?

Book	Call number
Better Ice Skating for Boys and Girls, by George Sullivan	J 796.9

The letter **J** in the call number means that this book can be found in the *juvenile,* or children's, section of the library.

The Concise Encyclopedia of Sports, by Keith Jennison	R 796.03

The letter **R** in the call number means that this book is part of the library's *reference* collection. You may look at reference books in the library. But most likely you may not take such books home with you.

Highlights of the Olympics, by John Durant	YA 796.4

In some libraries, **YA** before a call number means that the book is part of the *young adult collection.* These books are easier than adult books but harder than children's books. Right now you're able to read young adult books.

Skate to a Mountain Song, by Alberta Eiseman	no call number

This book has no call number. It is a fiction book and can be found on the fiction shelves in alphabetical order by the author's last name.

Peggy Fleming, by Charles Morse	B 920 F

The letter **B** before the call number means that the book is a *biography.* Most libraries have a special section for biographies. Individual biographies are arranged alphabetically by the last name of the person whom the book is about.

Of course, most libraries have more than books. You can usually find records and tapes, and films and picture files as well. In some libraries—sometimes called "media centers"—you can use listening machines or machines that store information on tapes.

Reference Materials

Nonfiction books like those listed on the catalogue cards on page 47 are not the only source you could use for a report on ice skating. When you want information on a topic, a good place to look is in a **general encyclopedia.** This is a book or a set of books (called *volumes*) that contain articles on almost every topic you can think of. The articles are listed in alphabetical order by topic. Most encyclopedias also have an **index.** The index is sometimes a volume by itself. It lists, in alphabetical order, all the topics in the encyclopedia.

Specialized encyclopedias can also be helpful reference tools. There are specialized encyclopedias on many different subjects—airplanes, coins, furniture, and even cartoons.

Another useful reference tool is a **specialized dictionary.** Such dictionaries include foreign language dictionaries, biographical dictionaries, and dictionaries of synonyms and antonyms.

Atlases are also useful references. Atlases are books containing many different kinds of maps.

Keeping Current

Sometimes you need the latest information on a subject. **Almanacs** may give you information that is less than a year old. Other reference books usually contain information that is a year old or older. Recent magazines and newspapers can be the best sources for up-to-date information.

Most libraries have many magazines. They are often kept in binders in the reference section of the library. How can you quickly locate which magazines have articles on a subject you are interested in? You can use a reference book called the *Readers' Guide to Periodical Literature*. ("Periodical literature" means magazines.) This guide offers a list of the articles found in many different magazines. The articles are listed alphabetically by topic and by author.

If you wanted to find some magazine articles on skating, you would look for the topic—*skating*. To save space, the *Readers' Guide* uses abbreviations. The sidenotes will help you to read the following sample from the *Readers' Guide*.

SKATING

Old sport cuts a new figure: figure skating. K. D. Tulenko. il Parks & Rec 10:16-18 + N '75

This is the title of the article. The author's name follows the title.

Competitions

All packed and waiting: speed skating

North American indoor championships. D. Levin. Sports Illus 42:70 Mr 31 '75

This is a subheading of the topic *skating*. It lets you know what the article focuses on.

SKATING, rinks

Footloose: Rockefeller Center's skating rink. J. Bruce. Sports Illus 43:14 D 8 '75

Iceless skating. R. Field. il Sci Digest 78:79 S '75

This means *Sports Illustrated*, volume 43, page 14, December 8, 1975 issue.

—Readers' Guide to Periodical Literature

Try This

1. Use the three cards on page 47 to answer the questions below.

    a. Who is the author of each book?
    b. Which book would appear to be the best source for facts about figure skating?
    c. Which book would appear to be the best source for finding out what some of the ice skating terms mean?
    d. Which book was published most recently?
    e. In what order would these cards be in a card catalogue if they were filed by subject? By title? By author?

2. To which library source would you turn if you wanted to find a recent magazine article on ice skating?

3. In which library source would you probably find the answers to the following questions?

    a. What is the highest mountain in the world?
    b. What products does Japan export?
    c. What do the French words *très bien* mean?
    d. What kinds of rare coins do people collect?

VOCABULARY STUDY

Homophones

We leave the following awards to our classmates . . .

. . . For Maria Fizzlehammer, who always got the most **loot** at birthday parties, we leave a sixty-kilogram **lute**. . . .

. . . For Herbert "Big Blast" Wilson, the class chemist, we leave twelve **cents**, to remind him of the twelve horrible **scents** he produced in chem lab this year. . . .

. . . For Donald Igg and Eleanor Snorch, the **reigning** king and queen of the prom, we leave an umbrella, to help them out when it's **raining**. . . .

. . . And because of our passing grades, for Mrs. Davis, our principal, we leave the school. . . .

Word Play

1. Homophones are words that are pronounced alike but have different meanings. Tell which homophone fits each of the following definitions.

   a. ruling, governing with royal power (*reigning; raining*)
   b. a slang term for money (*lute; loot*)
   c. odors, smells (*scents; cents*)

2. Look up *principal* in the glossary. Then look up *principle*. Note their different meanings. Use each word in a sentence.

As you read this selection, you may find you want to learn more about something that is mentioned. What reference books will help you?

We've found out a lot about the life of the ancient Romans through the discovery of . . .

POMPEII

by Robert Silverberg

Not very far from Naples, a strange city sleeps under the hot Italian sun. It is the city of Pompeii, and there is no other city quite like it in all the world. Only bugs and lizards live in Pompeii. Yet every year, thousands of people come from distant countries to visit.

No one has lived in Pompeii for nearly two thousand years— not since the summer of the year A.D. 79, to be exact. Until that year, Pompeii was a wealthy city of 25,000 people. Nearby was the Bay of Naples, an arm of the blue

55

View of Pompeii with Mt. Vesuvius in the distance.

Mediterranean. Rich people came down from Rome, 125 miles to the north, to build fine seaside homes. Good farmlands surrounded Pompeii. Rising sharply behind the city was the 4,000-foot Mount Vesuvius, a grass-covered slope where the shepherds of Pompeii took their goats to graze. Pompeii was a busy city and a happy one.

It died suddenly, in a terrible rain of fire and ashes.

The tragedy struck on a hot summer afternoon, August 24, A.D. 79. Mount Vesuvius, which had slept quietly for centuries, exploded with savage violence. Tons of hot ashes fell on Pompeii,

burning it, hiding it from sight. When the eruption ended, Pompeii was buried. A busy city had been destroyed in a single day.

Centuries passed; Pompeii was forgotten. Then, almost 1,700 years later, in 1748, it was discovered again. Beneath the protecting cover of ashes, the city lay intact. Everything was as it had been the day Vesuvius erupted. There were still loaves of bread in the ovens of the bakeries. In the wine shops, the wine jars were in place. On one counter could be seen a stain where someone had thrown down a glass and fled.

Modern archaeology began with the discovery of buried Pompeii. Almost fourth-fifths of the city has been uncovered.

A Visit to the City

Going to Pompeii today is like taking a trip backward in a time machine. The old city comes to life all around you. You can almost hear the sound of horses' hoofs on the narrow streets, the cries of children, and loud laughter of the shopkeepers. You can almost smell meat sizzling over a fire. The sky is blue, with the summer sun almost directly overhead. Sunlight shines on the water of the bay a thousand yards from the city walls. Ships from

every nation are in port, and strange languages can be heard in the streets.

Such was Pompeii on its last day. And so it is today, now that the ashes have been cleared away.

Arriving at Pompeii today, you leave your car outside and enter through an age-old gate. First you see a museum that has been built to house many of the smaller things found in the ruins. There are small statues and toys, saucepans and loaves of bread. There are glass cups, coins, burned beans and peas. The little things of everyday life in Pompeii have all been preserved for your startled eyes.

Then you enter the city itself. The streets are narrow and deeply marked with the tracks of chariot wheels. Only special, narrow chariots could travel inside the town. Travelers from outside had to change vehicles when they reached the walls of the city. This allowed for a good business for the Pompeiian cab drivers of twenty centuries ago!

The city is roughly oval in shape. Streets stretch straight ahead of you. They are very carefully laid out, crossing each other at right angles everywhere except in a few parts of the city.

The houses and shops are made of stone. The upper wooden stories either were

burned away or simply crumbled with the passing of time. The biggest of the shops are along the Street of Abundance. Silversmiths, shoemakers, and manufacturers of cloth all had their shops here.

The Houses of Pompeii

Many ancient buildings have survived in other places. What makes Pompeii so important is the wealth of knowledge that it gives us about the *private* lives of its people. Nowhere else do we have such complete information about the houses, customs, and living habits of the ancients.

The houses in Pompeii show the changes in styles over a period of several centuries. Many of the houses were built to a simple plan. There is a main court, known as the *atrium*. Around it are a living room, bedrooms, and a garden. This was the Roman style. Some of the later and more costly houses follow the Greek way of life. The Greek-style homes have baths, sitting rooms, huge gardens, and sometimes a second court. Their walls are decorated with paintings and *mosaics*—pictures made from bits of colored glass or stone.

The houses of Pompeii are known by name, and a good deal is known of their owners. One of the most famous is the "House

of the Vetti Brothers." It is rich with paintings, mosaics, and sculptures.

The writings on many houses are often amusing today. On the walls of one house is *WELCOME PROFITS!* Another has the words *PROFITS MEAN JOY!* At the so-called "House of the Tragic Poet," a mosaic shows a barking dog, with the Latin words *cave canem*—"Beware of the dog."

One of the most interesting things about Pompeii is the large number of scribbled street signs. Messages were painted directly on the stone. At the theater where plays were given, a message to an actor reads, "Actius,

beloved of the people, come back soon. Fare thee well!"

There are messages everywhere. "Romula loves Staphyclus" is on one wall. Some Pompeiians wrote sayings, such as, "A little evil grows great if disregarded." A person with a very good sense of humor left another message: "Everyone writes on the walls — except me."

To enter Pompeii is to step into the ancient world of the Romans. A whole city, forever frozen in the last moment of its life, awaits the visitor. Thanks to the careful work of Italian archaeologists, we can know what life was like two thousand years ago in a Roman city.

Understanding What You've Read

1. What happened to the city of Pompeii in A.D. 79?
2. When the ashes were cleared away, what was found?
3. What makes Pompeii so important to us?

Applying the Skills Lesson

1. Which two reference sources might you use to find out more about the location of Pompeii?

   a general encyclopedia   an atlas
   Readers' Guide to Periodical Literature

2. Under which two topics in a general encyclopedia would you look for each of the following items?

   a. information about Mount Vesuvius
      Vesuvius   Volcanoes   Greece

   b. information about the Roman road system
      Roads   Rome, Ancient   Transportation

3. Where in the card catalogue would you look for each of the following items?

   a. books by Robert Silverberg
   b. a book about the art of the ancient Romans
   c. a book called *The Riddle of the Past*

As you read, look for topics that you'd like to know more about. What reference books would give you information about the Vikings?

You may already know that the Vikings came to America before Columbus did. But you may not know about . . .

The Viking Age

by Louise Dickinson Rich

What do many people think of when they hear the word *Vikings*? They think at once of tall people sailing the North Atlantic in their dragonlike ships a long, long time ago. They remember that the Vikings visited the lands that are now Newfoundland, Nova Scotia, and New England almost five hundred years before Columbus discovered America.

How do we know about the Vikings? The information comes from several sources. First there are the writings and pictures made at that time by people other than the Vikings themselves.

Then there are the Vikings' own writings and their works of art. These works help us to see the Vikings as they saw themselves. And last, we have thousands of objects made and used by these people in their everyday lives. These objects have been dug up and studied in recent times by trained archaeologists who have used very new ways to explain their discoveries.

All sources seem to agree on some things. The Vikings were *very* brave, fearing almost nothing. They had a high sense of justice and fair play. They were extremely loyal to their own people. If they made a promise, they kept it.

When we say that the Viking Age began around A.D. 800, we do not mean that suddenly, out of nowhere, a new people came into being. Actually, they had been living in southern Scandinavia for many centuries, although they were not yet called Vikings. That name came later.

Builders of Fine Boats

People who live on a coast must learn to get along well with the sea. This was certainly true of the Vikings. Their shores and seas were among the roughest and most dangerous anywhere in the world. Long sea arms called *fiords* [fyôrdz] reached far inland. They made it much easier to get from one place to another by water than by land.

These Northern people learned early to build boats—first, little rowboats, then larger boats called *skuta* [sko͞o′tə]. They finally learned to build big ships called *langskips* [lang′ships], or "long ships," and *knorrs* [kə·nôrz′], a shorter, heavier type. Since the Scandinavian currents were strong and tricky, the boats had to be seaworthy. They also had to be handled skillfully. So, from necessity, the Vikings became the best shipbuilders and sailors in the world of their time.

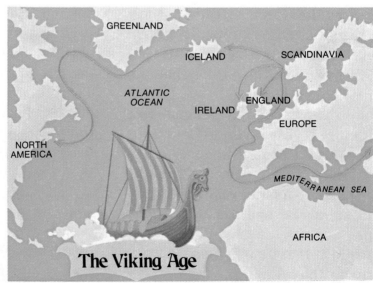

The Viking Age

The Vikings at Sea

As their ships became bigger and better, the Vikings sailed further and further along the coasts and up the rivers of Europe. They went far into Russia and France, and around Spain into the Mediterranean. They visited Italy and Greece and went across the North Sea to the British Isles, and finally across the Atlantic to Iceland. At this time the name "Vikings" was given them. There is some dispute over its exact meaning. Some say it comes from the Anglo-Saxon word *wic*, meaning "camp," and that the Vikings were therefore "campfolk." Most authorities agree that the name "Vikings" means people who come from the *viks*, or fiords.

At first, long before the year 800, the Vikings' journeys were largely peaceful trading voyages. They loaded their ships with fish, furs, whale oil, and ivory. They had plenty of these and other things. They traded for silk, dyes, honey, silver and gold, and other items from the countries they visited.

More valuable, however, than the things brought home in their ships were the things they brought home in their minds. They saw how other people did things, and they adopted some of their ways of making life more comfortable and pleasant. The most important thing they learned was the expression of ideas by means of marks on paper, wood, or stone—that is, writing and reading. Quite early they developed an alphabet of their own, called the "runes" or the "runic alphabet." It is probably based on a Greek alphabet.

During the period from 800 to 900, many European countries were too weak to defend themselves against attacks. The Vikings were quick to see this, and they took advantage of it. It was much cheaper to take things they wanted than to trade for them, and much more exciting.

Viking artifacts.

63

There were no aids to navigation at all during any of the Vikings' trips. There were no compasses to tell direction and position. The Vikings did not have log books to tell the speed and distance covered. On the open sea, the captain followed the sun, moon, and stars. The sailors arrived at the goals exactly as planned.

The Vikings' voyages were successful, and their ships were very happy ships. No one was there who did not want to be. Once a Viking was asked a question by a foreigner: "Which of you is the leader?" Surprised, the Viking said, "We have no leader. As sailors, we are all equal."

That was their secret. On the ocean, the Vikings were all equal in rank, courage, skill, strength, and ability. They were equal in training and understanding. They were friends — sailing fine ships of which they were proud, and sailing on adventures of their own choosing.

Many later voyages had a purpose other than robbing or trading. After the year 900, many Vikings left their northern homes and settled in new lands.

The Vikings Ashore

We are likely to think of the Vikings as mainly seafaring people. Actually, they spent as much time doing other things. They farmed, hunted, and fished. Their lives, though lived on a grander scale, were very much like the

lives of the early settlers along the coast of North America.

The Vikings lived their lives based on the seasons and the Earth. They didn't sail until the spring plowing and planting were done. They returned from their voyages at harvest time. After the crops were under cover, the trading journeys could begin again.

The Viking women had much freedom and authority in their community. They made decisions, held property, and voted at some public meetings. These rights were unknown to women in other parts of the world at that time.

The authority and rights of the Viking women had developed naturally, as a result of the ordered life of the people. After planting the crops, many of the men were often absent for weeks or even months on end. The women did not share in these trips. They were in charge of the life on shore.

The Vikings did not have formal schools, but they did spend a great deal of time teaching their children. The children learned reading, writing, singing, and other arts. Courage, endurance, and athletic ability were valued very highly. Both boys and girls were strictly trained in order to develop these qualities.

The striking thing about the life of the Vikings is not that it differed so much from ours, but that in some ways it differed so little. The general ideas behind most things were much like our own

ideas: that people should be treated equally and fairly by the law; that children should be aided and encouraged to make the most of their abilities.

The Vikings were a people who worked hard and played hard. They were very much at home in their world, whether on the sea or ashore.

Understanding What You've Read

1. From what sources have we learned about the Viking people?
2. What things do most sources agree on about the Viking people?
3. Why had the Vikings become the best shipbuilders and sailors in the world of their time?
4. How were the Vikings' lives affected by the seasons?
5. In what ways were the Vikings' ideas very similar to some of our ideas today?

Applying the Skills Lesson

1. How would you find the following books in your library?

   a. a book about Viking ships
   b. a book by Louise Dickinson Rich
   c. a book called *Leif Ericson*

2. Under what topics in a general encyclopedia would you look to find the following information?

   a. information about the names Vikings gave their children
   b. information about the ships the Vikings sailed
   c. information about the runic alphabet

Using Library Resources

You may often want or need to find more information about certain topics related to your textbook reading. The library has many resources that you can use. As you read the following selections, think about what resources you can turn to for more information. The sidenotes contain comments and questions to help you think about these resources.

Using Library Resources in Social Studies

Answers from the Past

Singapore is a country that looks forward. It must in order to live.

Yet people who study or visit Singapore today cannot help but think about the city's history. They think about the past when they try to answer such questions as these: Why is this Chinese city found outside of China? Why are there four languages? Why is English used by people who are so proud of not being English? Why is this small island an independent country? To answer these questions, they must learn about the past.

The library has books and reference sources that answer each of these questions.

Singapore lies at one of the world's meeting places. For hundreds of years, people have been coming here to trade and settle. Some of the groups that live together today in Singapore have been doing business with one another for a long time.

What subject card or cards would you look for in the card catalogue for books on trading in Singapore long ago?

Early trade. Traders met here long ago partly because of the way the winds blow. From October to March, winds blow from the northeast. They blow away from Asia. From May to August, they blow in the other direction, toward Asia. These winds, called monsoons, were very useful in the days of sailing ships.

—*People and Change*
Silver Burdett

A monsoon is a seasonal wind. If you wanted to find a recent article on monsoons, where would you look?

Building Skills

1. Use the library floor plan on page 48 to answer this question: In which section would you find a book about the history of Singapore?
2. What reference source or sources would help you find the answer to each of the following questions?

   a. Where is Singapore?

   almanac   atlas   dictionary

   b. How large is Singapore?

   atlas   general encyclopedia
   Readers' Guide to Periodical Literature

   c. When did the British begin to trade in Singapore?

   atlas   general encyclopedia
   Readers' Guide to Periodical Literature

   d. What was the population of Singapore last year?

   atlas   dictionary   almanac

Using Library Resources in Health

There are no sidenotes for this selection. Read it and then answer the questions that follow.

When Jonas Salk was a boy, a disease called polio changed many people's lives. Jonas always wanted to help people in some way. He studied in college and medical school. He spent 4 years working with his teacher on flu viruses. Finally he began to research for a vaccine to stop polio.

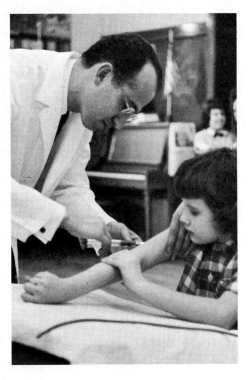

The work was slow. Dr. Salk had to study more than 100 different viruses that cause polio. He had to test the same viruses again and again. He spent 3 years at this work.

For the next 2 years, he tried one vaccine after another on the viruses. In 1954, one of the vaccines Dr. Salk had tested was given to children. For the first time, children were safe from polio.

—Toward Your Future: Brown
Harcourt Brace Jovanovich

Building Skills

1. Suppose you wanted to find a biography about Dr. Salk. Use the library floor plan on page 48. Where would you find such a book?
2. The oral vaccine you get for polio was later invented by another person, Albert Sabin. What reference book might tell you this fact?

Gathering Information/Taking Notes

How do *you* remember to do something? Many people write notes to themselves—and it works! They remember what they had planned to do.

How do you remember information from your reading? Perhaps you already know the best trick for remembering something—write it down immediately. There are two good reasons for noting new information: First, just the *act* of writing something reinforces it in your mind. Second, if you later want to remember the information, you just have to look at your notes. The second point, however, is true only if you've taken good notes.

What are *good* notes? Good notes are the kind of notes that work best for you. They should include the most important information: answers to the *W-H* questions—*Who? What?*

When? Where? Why? How? Generally, notes should not include so much information that the important facts are lost among too many details. Read the following article. As you read, think about how *you* would take notes on the topic of the article. Look for the facts that tell *who, what, when, where, why,* and *how.*

Around 300 B.C., the Chinese realized they needed protection from the Mongols. The Mongol people, who lived north of China, often attacked Chinese towns and villages. So the Emperor decided to have a wall built. Work on the Great Wall would go on for nearly 2,000 years. At first the Wall was only in sections, built near the villages.

At one time there was a law that one out of every three men in China had to work on the Wall. Of these millions of workers, hundreds of thousands died. The work went on in the worst weather. Often there was no food for the workers.

By 1646, when the present Wall was finished, it was 2,400 kilometers long—half the distance across the United States. The Wall, at that time, had 40,000 watchtowers. Most of these later wore away or were torn down.

More than *350 million* cubic meters of material had been used. This was enough material to build a two-meter-high wall around the equator. It was 120 times as much material as was used in Egyptian King Khufu's great pyramid. The Wall is the largest structure ever built. Nevertheless, it didn't serve its purpose. It never really provided security.

Today it stands from six to twelve meters high. It is four meters wide. Its only real value is as a tourist attraction.

Now look at the two sets of notes below. Which is the better set? Why?

Heather's Notes:

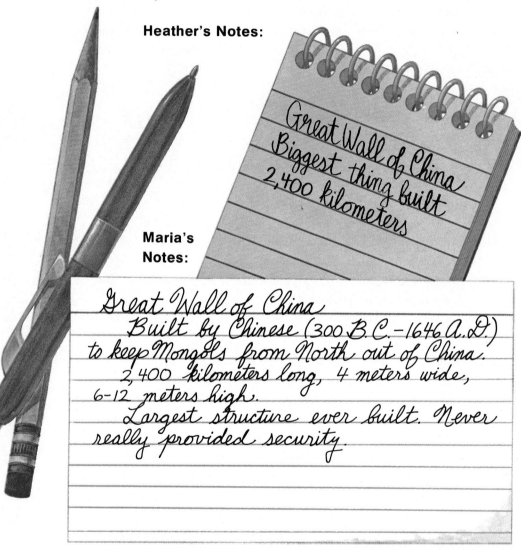

Great Wall of China
Biggest thing built
2,400 kilometers

Maria's Notes:

Great Wall of China
Built by Chinese (300 B.C. – 1646 A.D.)
to keep Mongols from North out of China.
2,400 kilometers long, 4 meters wide,
6–12 meters high.
Largest structure ever built. Never
really provided security.

What's wrong with Heather's notes? Notice that she gives only two facts about the Great Wall. She doesn't tell when or why the Wall was built. She doesn't give a very important fact that Maria gives: "Never really provided security."

Maria is a good note-taker. She has found that the best way *for her* to take notes is to do these things:

1. Note the topic at the top of a set of notes.
2. Write only the main ideas and *important* details about the topic. (Look for facts that answer the W-H questions.)
3. Use only key words and phrases.

Try This

As you read the following article, take notes about it. Look for facts that tell *who, what, when, where, why,* and *how.* Remember to use only key words and phrases.

The Roots of Written Language

The first known writing was done by the ancient Egyptians about five thousand years ago. The Egyptian *hieroglyphics,* meaning "sacred writing," were really just pictures. The pictures stood for things, people, or ideas.

After many, many years (it is not known exactly how many), symbols for sounds entered into Egyptian writing. Sound-symbols were better than pictures in most ways. Pictures could cause confusion.

The Phoenician people used both sound-symbols and pictures in their writing. Later the Greeks borrowed their system of nineteen sound-symbols and added five vowels. The Romans, in turn, borrowed from the Greeks and made a few more changes. The Roman alphabet had twenty-three letters. The Romans used *i* for both *i* and *j* sounds. They used *v* to show *v, u,* and *w* sounds. The Romans, of course, introduced their alphabet to the rest of Europe.

73

Multiple Meanings

"... and the villain said, 'Aha! Now you're in my **clutches**....'"

"**Clutches**? You mean 'nests of eggs'? What kind of a villain is he anyway? An animal lover?"

"No. **Clutches**, 'tightly held hands.' The villain's a bad guy."

"Never mind the villain. What about the hero?"

"He wasn't thinking too straight. He'd been wounded in the **temple**."

"What was he doing in a 'house of worship'? I thought he was in the villain's clutches."

"Not that **temple**! The 'flat space on each side of his forehead.' The **temple**! Anyway, the hero was in big trouble."

"Sounds that way. I hope the heroine had a plan."

"Oh, yes. She jumped out from behind a rock with a long **blade** in her hand."

"Her plan was to fight that villain with a piece of grass? I don't believe it! She'll lose!"

"The villain thought so, too, until he saw the sword."

"What sword?"

"The **blade**. A sword can be called a **blade**."

"Never mind the blade. What about the hero?"

"The hero was in the villain's clutches."

"Hey, Mom! Let's get a couple of heroes in *our* clutches. I'll get the bread if you get the salami."

Word Play

1. What is the meaning of each word in boldface as it is used in the sentence below?

   a. Lila visited the ancient **temple** in Greece.
   b. The thief let the money slip from his **clutches**.
   c. The ancient **blade** was rusty but still beautiful.

2. The words below are in the *Vocabulary Study* you just read. Use each word in two sentences; use a different meaning of the word in each sentence.

   a. mind   b. saw   c. kind   d. mean   e. rock

As you read, think about how you would take notes on the selection. Look for the facts that tell *who, what, when, where, why,* and *how.*

For hundreds of years, historians and poets have retold the story of . . .

The Great Adventures of Nicolo, Maffeo, and Marco Polo

by Roger Duvoisin

In the year 1260, two brothers from Venice, Italy, named Maffeo and Nicolo Polo, sailed east from the city of Constantinople, in Turkey. (This city is now called Istanbul.) The brothers set out to trade in the land of the Tartars. The Tartars were Turkish and Mongol peoples who had settled in several parts of Eastern Europe and Asia.

Nicolo and Maffeo traveled far

beyond the Black Sea. They finally came to the great city of Bokhara [bō·kä′rä] in the southern part of what is now Asian Russia. The brothers remained in Bokhara for three years. Bandits had made further travel too dangerous.

One day, there came into Bokhara a very important-looking gentleman. One hundred horsemen rode behind him. This stranger was an ambassador from Persia (now called Iran) on his way to China, which the Europeans called Cathay. Nicolo and Maffeo could not help noticing the man. Before long they became good friends. The Persian ambassador invited Nicolo and Maffeo to come with him to Cathay.

So it came about that Nicolo and Maffeo, instead of going home, went in quite the opposite direction.

The Polo Brothers Reach Cathay

After many months of traveling, the Polo brothers arrived in Cathay. They went to the palace of Kublai Khan—the khan, or emperor, of the Tartars.

The khan was truly glad to see these merchants from Venice. Europe was as mysterious to Kublai Khan as Cathay was to Nicolo and Maffeo. The khan asked the brothers to tell all they could about their homeland.

"How great is it?" he asked. "As great as Cathay? How many kings are there in Europe? Are they fair to their people?" Nicolo and Maffeo answered so well that the khan, judging them to be very clever, asked them to go back to Europe as his ambassadors. So Nicolo and Maffeo, who had come to Cathay as traders, now left as ambassadors in 1266.

It took three years for the brothers to return home. When Nicolo arrived in Venice in 1269, he learned that his wife had died. His sorrow was made less by the sight of his son, Marco, now fifteen years old.

Marco Polo Journeys to the East

Two years passed before Nicolo and Maffeo were ready to return to China. It is at this point that Marco Polo's great adventure began. At the age of seventeen, in 1271, he set out with his father and his uncle, bringing gifts for the khan.

After four years of travel over dangerous mountains and deserts, Marco, Nicolo, and Maffeo

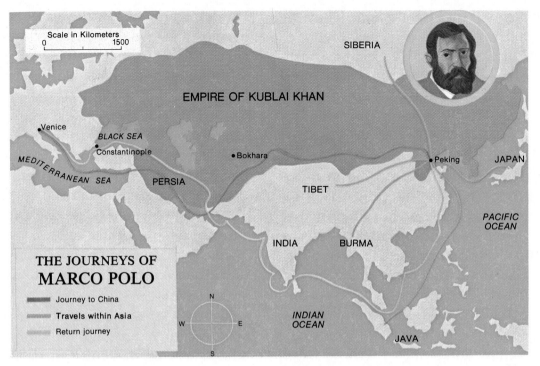

Scale in Kilometers
0   1500

SIBERIA

EMPIRE OF KUBLAI KHAN

Venice
BLACK SEA
Constantinople
MEDITERRANEAN SEA
PERSIA
Bokhara
Peking
JAPAN
TIBET
PACIFIC OCEAN
INDIA
BURMA
THE JOURNEYS OF
MARCO POLO
Journey to China
Travels within Asia
Return journey
N
W   E
S
INDIAN OCEAN
JAVA

finally arrived at the khan's palace in Peking in 1275.

"Tell me about your travels," said Kublai Khan.

Nicolo told of their adventures and gave Kublai Khan the gifts. Then Kublai Khan ordered a great feast and there was much rejoicing in honor of Nicolo, Maffeo, and Marco.

The Polos stayed in the palace for some time. Marco quickly learned the Tartar language, as well as four other languages that were spoken in Cathay. The khan was impressed by Marco's intelligence and interest in Cathay. He decided to send Marco on spe-

cial missions to many places throughout his empire. Later, Marco was also sent on missions to foreign countries. On these trips Marco learned about many of the unknown countries of Asia. These countries had never been drawn on any map.

Before Marco had left Venice, he had believed that Europe was the richest, most learned part of the world. He was surprised to find that this was not so. Civilization in Europe was new, but in China it was very old.

The Chinese knew how to dig coal and burn it to keep warm. Marco had never even seen coal.

He was astonished that black "stones" could burn like wood.

In Europe, when a book was written, it was copied by hand. But long before that time, the Chinese had already learned to print their books. Millions of Chinese people could read. The Chinese also printed paper money, which was easier to carry than heavy gold and silver coins.

The Chinese system of delivering messages seemed wonderful to Marco. Along the roads, fast messengers ran from post-house to post-house with letters and packages. There were larger stations, too, in which four hundred horses were kept to carry travelers along the post roads.

Marco recorded all these wonders in his notebook.

During all the years he spent in Asia, traveling for the khan, Marco never forgot to write about the marvelous things he saw or heard. He wrote about crocodiles which he had thought were snakes with four legs. He wrote about the gold and silver towers he saw in Burma. On top of each tower were bells that made music when the wind blew. Marco wrote about the dog sleds and the big white bears of Siberia and the people of the North who rode upon reindeer instead of horses. And, of course, Marco wrote about Kublai Khan's palace and many, many other wonders.

Returning to Europe

While Marco traveled, Nicolo and Maffeo continued to trade in Cathay. They had become very rich, but their black beards had turned white. They now began to think of their homeland more and more often.

At first, Kublai Khan told them he did not want them to go back to Venice. If they left, who would tell him the wonderful stories about foreign countries? But then, in 1292, the khan finally said the Polos could go home if they would escort a young Tartar princess named Kogatin to Persia. Kogatin was to be married to the king of Persia.

At that time, some Tartar princes started a war among themselves. They made the country unsafe for traveling. But Marco Polo had just returned from a long voyage to the island of Java and knew a safe way to travel to Persia by sea.

After bidding good-by to Kublai Khan, Nicolo, Maffeo, and Marco at last set sail from Cathay.

It was three more years before Marco, his father, and his uncle finally arrived in Venice. It was the year 1295. Twenty-four years after they had left it, they easily found their old home. However, the servant who answered their knock at the door did not recognize them. They were wearing foreign clothes, their faces were sunburned and tired, and they had bushy hair and beards. But finally they were allowed in.

Portrait of Marco Polo, from the first printed edition of his book.

A great feast was held at Nicolo's house to reunite old friends and relatives. At this feast, Nicolo, Maffeo, and Marco decided to astonish their friends. They came in wearing long Tartar robes of red satin. Then the three travelers went into another room and soon reappeared in robes of red velvet.

After the meal, they brought in the old, torn clothes which they had worn home. When they ripped them apart, streams of diamonds, pearls, and other jewels poured out onto the table.

No one doubted now. They were Nicolo, Maffeo, and Marco, and they must indeed have had wonderful adventures!

In 1298, Marco wrote a book about all the things he had seen. People who read it or heard about it did not believe he told the truth.

"What a tale-teller Marco Polo is!" they said. And they called him "Marco of the Millions" because he said that there was so much of everything in China.

But in truth, no traveler before him had ever seen so many new birds and animals, people and cities. And no one had added, all at once, so many countries to the map.

Understanding What You've Read

1. Who were Nicolo and Maffeo Polo?
2. Why was Kublai Khan so glad to see the merchants from Venice?
3. Why was Marco Polo sent on missions by the khan?
4. What were some of the things Marco wrote about when he went on these missions?
5. Why were Marco's notes so important?

Applying the Skills Lesson

Listed below is a set of notes about the selection you just read. Most ideas listed are important to remember from the selection. Tell which idea listed could be omitted from the set of notes.

The Great Adventures of
Nicolo, Maffeo, and Marco Polo

Time period—middle to late 1200's.

Venice merchants, Nicolo and Maffeo, went to China and left as ambassadors for Kublai Khan.

Marco accompanied father and uncle when they returned to China—1275.

Marco sent on missions throughout China and to many unknown countries in Asia. Took notes about all he saw.

Marco saw crocodiles that he thought were snakes with four legs.

Returned home in 1295—24 years after leaving.

Wrote book of his travels and his adventures.

Marco known as "Marco of the Millions" because of his tales of so much of everything in China.

First source of information about China.

Added many new countries to the map.

To find the important ideas in this selection, look for the answers to the W-H questions. You would list the answers to these questions if you were to take notes on the selection.

From records that the Spanish explorers kept and from the remains of their roads, bridges, and cities, we have learned about the Incas, . . .

BUILDERS IN THE SKY

by Barbara L. Beck

In Quechua [kesh'wa], a native Peruvian language, the word *Inca* means "lord." In their day, these people of the Andes were not called Incas. This is a name that has been given to them by historians.

About eight hundred years ago, around A.D. 1200, the first Inca people entered Cuzco [kōo'skō] in what is now Peru. In time, this city, high in the Andes Mountains of South America, became the center of a great empire.

We know very little about what happened in Cuzco between the years 1200 and 1438. But we do know that from 1438 to 1532 — a period of less than one hundred years — the Incas forged a great empire. It stretched two thousand miles up and down South America and included some six million people. In 1532, this mighty empire was conquered by a very small force of Spanish soldiers. It became a Spanish possession.

◀ *Machu Picchu.*

83

Inca pottery.

Finding out about the Inca people and those who lived before them has been difficult. None of these peoples had a system of writing. But because the Incas were conquered by the Spanish, who could write, there are some early records.

History is one source of our knowledge. Archaeology is another. Many Inca ruins have been found by archaeologists. They have studied how the Incas buried their dead, painted their pottery, wove their clothing, and made their roads and buildings. Through these studies, the archaeologists have learned a great deal about the Incas' mighty civilization.

The Incas' strong system of government was probably their greatest achievement. Next to this came the famous Inca roads and buildings. At the height of the empire, the roads covered nearly 10,000 miles. A coastal highway stretched for 2,520 miles from the north almost to present-day Chile in the south. High in the Andes was another highway that ran for 3,250 miles along the spiny back of South America. Other roads crisscrossed back and forth between these two great highways.

The Incas did not understand the principle of the wheel. So roads were made for pack-carrying llamas and foot travelers.

The Incas' rope bridges were generally built of five great cables. The cables were

An Inca rope bridge.

made of braided or twisted fibers taken mostly from a plant, the *maguey* [mä·gā']. The cables, often as thick as a person's body, were stretched across ravines. The ends were attached to beams that had been sunk into great piles of stones and earth. Although these suspension bridges swayed dangerously, both people and llamas passed over them safely.

One such 250-foot-long bridge, the Bridge of San Luis Rey [sän lwēs' rā'], spanned the Apurímac [a'pōō·rē'mäk] River. It was kept in good repair for over 500 years—from 1350 to 1890.

Runners, called *chasquis* [chäs'kēs], ran swiftly over the roads and bridges. They carried messages and small packages from town to town, and to the Lord Inca in Cuzco. These couriers often carried *quipus* [kē'pōōz], dangling, knotted strings used for counting and for keeping records.

The Incas' network of roads joined together hundreds of villages and cities. The cities had nearby *pucaras* [pōō'ka·ras'], or hilltop fortresses. The *pucaras* were often tiny cities in

Inca vase.

themselves. Each had a sun temple, houses, and reservoirs for water. They also had living quarters for troops. When an enemy threatened, the city people fled to the safety of their *pucaras.*

Perhaps the most amazing piece of architecture in all the Americas is a huge *pucara*

Quipus.

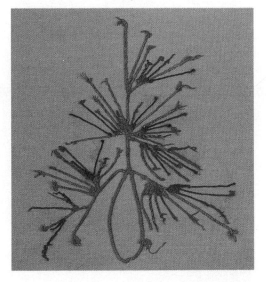

with the name *Sacsahuaman* [säk′sä·wä·män′]. This great fort stands on the edge of a high hill above Cuzco. Thirty thousand workers took seventy years to build it.

Farther north is the Urubamba [o͝or′ə·bäm′bə] River. High above the river, clinging to the steep sides of the mountains, are several fortresses. They are joined by a stone-paved road. These forts lead to Machu Picchu [mä′cho͞o pēk′cho͞o]. This well-known stone citadel was never found by the Spaniards.

Discovered in 1911, Machu Picchu stands hidden between two mountain peaks. It had terraces for farming, houses, living quarters for soldiers, temples, plazas, and royal homes. The town's water supply came by means of a stone aqueduct from springs about a mile away. Just inside the city wall, the water was made to fall over steps into a series of sixteen stone basins, one lower than the other. People filled their water jars at these stone basins. This water system is called "the Stairway of the Fountains."

This city of stone buildings is being restored by archaeologists and South American Indian workers. Today, Machu Picchu looks very much as it did over four hundred years ago when it was full of life.

Fortress of Sacsahuaman.

The finest Inca buildings were built of carefully cut and polished stone. No cement was used to hold the stones together. It is amazing that the Incas could build as they did, since most of their tools were also made of stone.

Building stones were quarried and placed on rollers to which ropes were attached. The stones were then pulled to the building site. Here, each stone was shaped and polished by skilled stonecutters. They chipped at the rough surface of

Narrow stairway of stones at Machu Picchu.

the rock with stone tools and rubbed it smooth with sand. Each stone was then hoisted with ropes up an earth ramp and fitted exactly to the stone next to it, maybe by rubbing the two stones together. The fitting was so exact that even today a knife blade cannot be inserted between them!

Many Inca buildings have all but disappeared because their stones were removed by later peoples to make new structures. Others have disappeared because trees, vines, and grass have grown up through them and caused them to topple over.

There is much more to be discovered in Peru. Hidden on the sides of the great gorges in the shining, snow-capped Andes, or on some high plateau, more Inca ruins are waiting to tell their secrets.

Understanding What You've Read

1. How have archaeologists learned about the Incas' civilization?
2. Why are the Incas' system of roads and their buildings considered great achievements?
3. In what ways were *pucaras* often tiny cities in themselves?
4. Why have some Inca buildings disappeared?

Applying the Skills Lesson

Using key words and phrases, tell the answers to the following questions.

1. *Who* were the Incas?
2. *Where* was the center of their empire?
3. *When* was their great empire?
4. *What* were their greatest achievements?
5. *Why* did the empire end in 1532?
6. *How* have we found out about the Inca empire?

Taking Notes

Very often, as you study your textbooks, you'll find it useful to take notes on what you read. Remember to note only the main ideas and important details. Don't use whole sentences if you can clearly note information using only key words and phrases. Refer to the sidenotes to help you understand the important information.

Taking Notes in Science

A Problem—for You and Yours

You drink water every day. You are not worried about getting diseases from bacteria in the water. Yet, there was a time when this was a problem. Two diseases carried by water killed many people. These diseases were cholera and typhoid.

These sentences give important details. Your notes, using key words and phrases, might read: *Cholera and typhoid—carried by water; killed many people.*

You take safe drinking water for granted. How do most cities make water safe to drink?

Your glass of water starts in the clouds. It falls as rain. Some rain soaks

into the ground. Some rainwater runs along the ground, down slopes and mountains into lakes and streams. Some rain falls directly into lakes and streams. The water collected in lakes and streams is used to fill **reservoirs.** Reservoirs are large lakes used for storing water. Water used by most large cities is collected in reservoirs. This reservoir holds water for a big city—Newark, New Jersey.■

New words in boldface type should usually be noted. What is a reservoir used for?

The main idea is stated in the middle of this paragraph. Find it. Remember, a good set of notes is a record of main ideas.

A reservoir should be located in clean surroundings, away from the city. There the water is kept free from garbage, sewage, wastes from factories. In other words, the water in a reservoir should not be polluted. This polluted water (page 89) is near the city.● Do you see factories or homes around the reservoir in the picture? ■ Why not? The reservoir is in northwest New Jersey, about 50 kilometers (30 miles) away from the city of Newark.

—*Concepts in Science:* Brown
Harcourt Brace Jovanovich

90

Building Skills

Below are two sets of notes. Which is the better set? What is wrong with the other set of notes?

1. Water
   Drinking water generally safe today. In past cholera and typhoid carried by water; killed many people. Water from lakes and streams fills reservoirs, used for storing water for cities. Reservoir water should not be polluted.
2. Water — A Problem for You and Yours
   We drink water every day. We are not worried about getting diseases. Cholera and typhoid are diseases that used to kill many people. Water starts in the clouds, runs along the ground, down slopes and mountains, into lakes and streams. The water in the lakes and streams fills *reservoirs*. These are large lakes used for storing water. Water used by most large cities comes from them. They should be clean, free of garbage, sewage, and wastes. A reservoir in New Jersey is clean.

Taking Notes in Social Studies

Read the following selection and take notes on the important ideas and details. Use key words and phrases. There are no sidenotes.

The Pyramids

Along the banks of the Nile stand the world's oldest stone buildings. Once those Egyptian **pyramids** shone gleaming white. Today they are more than 5,000 years old. No wonder they look a bit run-down! But the pyramids remain one of the wonders of the world. And they are lasting evidence of the Egyptians' belief in a life after death.

The pyramids were built

as tombs for the Pharaohs. The Egyptians believed that when they had finished life on Earth, they would begin another life. Helping their Pharaoh get ready for the next world was an important matter for the Egyptians. They believed the Pharaohs held the key to their own happiness after death. If they had served him or her well, the Pharaoh would put in a good word for them when that ruler joined the gods.

So the dead bodies of the Pharaohs were preserved as mummies. Mummies were made by wrapping the bodies in linen bandages that had been soaked in special liquids. Starting long before a Pharaoh's death, thousands of workers labored for years to build the pyramid-tomb that would house his or her body.

To build each pyramid, workers mined millions of tons of limestone and granite under the hot desert sun. They moved these stones to the Nile River and loaded them onto boats. Sailors rowed the heavy loads down the river. Meanwhile, on the construction site other workers laid the layers of huge limestone blocks. Inside the pyramids they built secret rooms, airshafts, hallways, and even bathrooms.

When a Pharaoh died, the mummified body was placed inside the pyramid. Along with it went everything the Pharaoh might need in the next world. Such things as food, wine, silver and gold, tools, boats, carvings, paintings, and even the bodies of favorite pets were buried with the Pharaoh.

Over the ages robbers found their way into the pyramids and stole most of the gold and silver. But they left some things of greater value. Today in many museums we can see the mummies of the Pharaohs and many of the things entombed with them. These remains tell us much about life in ancient Egypt.

—The Way People Live
Houghton Mifflin

A close-up view shows the huge stone blocks that make up the pyramids' walls. Teams of workers had to drag the heavy blocks up sloping ramps to get them into place.

Building Skills

Compare your set of notes to the main ideas and important details below. How many of these ideas and details are in your notes?

Pyramids

World's oldest buildings—5,000 years old
On Nile River in Egypt
Built as tombs for Pharaohs
Workers believed Pharaohs held the key to their own happiness after death
Bodies of Pharaohs preserved as mummies
Mummy and everything the Pharaoh might need in next world put in pyramid
Robbers stole most of gold and silver

Books About Other Times, Other Places

A Glorious Age in Africa: The Story of Three Great African Empires by Daniel Chu and Elliott Skinner. Doubleday, 1965. The authors tell of Ghana, Mali, and Songhay — nations that were rich and powerful over 1,000 years ago.

Golden Days of Greece by Olivia Coolidge. T. Y. Crowell, 1968. The original Olympic games, great people, and customs of ancient Greece are all told about in this book.

How the Plains Indians Lived by George S. Fichter. Illustrated by Alexander Farquharson. David McKay, 1980. This book describes the clothing, customs, dwellings, tools, and weapons of twenty American Indian tribes who lived on the Great Plains.

The Art of Egypt Under the Pharaohs by Shirley Glubok. Macmillan, 1980. This book is about Egyptian art and life from Menes, the first pharaoh, to Cleopatra VII.

Kingdom of the Sun: The Inca, Empire Builders of the Americas by Ruth Karen. Four Winds, Schol. Bk. Serv., 1975. This book describes the world of the Incas and the great cities they built so long ago.

Pyramid by David Macaulay. Houghton Mifflin, 1975. Detailed drawings help trace the building of a pyramid from its beginnings to when a pharaoh was buried inside it.

The First Artists by Dorothy Samachson and Joseph Samachson. Doubleday, 1970. The author tells about the early people who were the first "artists." She explains how and why they made paintings and engravings on cave walls.

Part **2**

On Your Own

UNDERSTANDING AND APPRECIATING LITERATURE

Point of View

My hands were steady as I sent the ball straight toward the basket.

Her hands were steady as she sent the ball straight toward the basket.

The two pictures above show the same scene. How are they different? Which picture shows the scene through the eyes of a character who is in the picture? Picture 1 shows the scene as the basketball player shooting the ball sees it. Picture 2 shows the same scene as someone who is not part of the action might see it. Each picture shows the scene from a different **point of view.**

Understanding Point of View

Authors write stories from different points of view. Some-times an author pretends to be a character in a story. This author writes the story as if a character were telling it. Such a story is written from a **first-person point of view.** *First person* means that a character tells the story.

Picture 1 on page 96 shows what one character, the basket-ball player, sees. Read the sentence under picture 1. This sentence is written from the first-person point of view. The sentence contains two pronoun clues to who is speaking. What are they? The two pronouns are *my* and *I.* These two pronouns, along with *me, we, us,* and *our,* are often called first-person pronouns. They appear frequently in stories written from the first-person point of view. They are clues to who is telling the story, or to the point of view.

Read the following sentence. As you read it, look for the first-person pronouns used by the author.

> As I walked to the plate, I was very nervous: my mouth was dry, my hands and my knees were shaky; it felt to me as though I had never held a bat in my hands before.

What pronouns tell you this sentence is from the first-person point of view? The pronouns *I, my,* and *me* tell you. The narrator uses *I, my,* and *me* to tell the story. How do you know the narrator feels nervous about coming up to bat? The narrator says, "I was very nervous: my mouth was dry, my hands and my knees were shaky; it felt to me as though I had never held a bat in my hands before." The narrator uses the pronouns *I, my,* and *me* to refer to the batter. You see the in-cident through the eyes of one character. You see it from the first-person point of view.

Often an author tells a story from the point of view of an invisible observer, not as a character participating in the story. Such a story is told from the **third-person point of view.**

Look back at picture 2 on page 96. It is drawn from the third-person point of view. It shows that what the artist saw from the sidelines. The sentence under picture 2 contains two pronoun clues to the point of view. What are they? They are *her* and *she*. These two pronouns, along with *he, him, his, they, them,* and *their,* are often called third-person pronouns. They appear frequently in stories written from the third-person point of view.

Look for clues to the point of view in the next paragraph.

As Mark stepped up to the plate, the pressure on him was visible: his face was pale, his knees seemed to shake. But there was determination in his eyes. As the ball came toward him, he took a mighty swing. Crack! The ball flew far over the left-field fence. He had done it!

From what point of view is this story written? It is written from the third-person point of view. What are the pronoun clues to the point of view? The author uses the pronouns *him, his,* and *he.* How do you know the story is told from the third person? The author is an observer, not a character in the story.

How is the first story different from the second? The narrator of the first story is *in* the story. The narrator of the second one is not in the story. The first story is told from the first-person point of view. The second is told from the third-person point of view.

The point of view of a story tells you who is narrating, or telling, the story. A narrator who tells a story from the first-person point of view is a character in the story and uses the pronouns *I, me,* and *my.* A narrator who tells a story from the third-person point of view is an observer and uses the pronouns *she, he, her, him, his, they, them,* and *their.* As you read, notice the point of view that an author has chosen. Authors use different points of view to tell stories in different ways.

Try This

Read the following sentences. Then answer the questions.

a. As Jerry neared his home, it was clear to him that the flames were coming from his house; they were destroying everything he owned.

b. As I turned the corner of my street, the darkness seemed to lighten, a faint smell of smoke reached me, and a strange crackling sound filled the air.

1. Which sentence is written from a first-person point of view? Which is written from a third-person point of view?
2. What are the pronoun clues to point of view in each sentence?

Writing

1. Read the sentences below. If the sentence tells about an event or incident from the first-person point of view, rewrite the sentence from the third-person point of view. If the sentence tells about an event or incident from the third-person point of view, rewrite it from the first-person point of view.

   a. Yelling "Fire!" as he ran from his burning house, Jamie looked toward his neighbors for help.
   b. I went to the beach to sun myself and swim with my friends.

2. Use one of the sentences in *Try This* as the first sentence in a paragraph. Add details to write a complete paragraph. Keep the point of view of the original sentence.

As you read "On Your Own," look for the point of view of each story: Who is the narrator—who tells the story?

Patch

by C. H. FRICK

The loudspeaker squawked once, vibrated, and uttered a tinny announcement. "First call for the mile run! Milers assemble at the south goal post."

Dirk Ingersoll, the student manager, studied the neat score sheet on his clipboard with a pleasant feeling of importance. He ran a finger down a column of figures and turned to a grizzled bear of a man who stood at his elbow.

"So far, Coach, the juniors and seniors are tied."

Coach Anderson grunted absently, his eyes focused on the far end of the field, where the milers were trotting up.

Dirk followed his glance. "There's Grover Godwin. He ought to win this."

Coach Anderson, strolling away, said nothing. Dirk was rechecking the score sheet when a hand touched his elbow. He turned to see a slight, sandy-haired boy.

"Can anyone enter this race?"

100

"Anyone that wants to run a mile." Dirk looked him over. "Where's your track suit?"

"Track suit? You mean — can't I run like this?"

Dirk shrugged. "Mr. Anderson!" he called, and the coach turned around. "Fellow here wants to know can he race in jeans?"

"No law against it," the coach said, coming over. "But why didn't you dress?"

"Dress? Golly, I thought I did. I thought this was just another assembly — you know, speeches — till everybody headed out here into the stadium."

"Just another assembly?" the coach roared like a wounded lion. "After all the publicity we gave it last month? Announcements in gym classes, articles in the school paper, posters in the halls. . . ." He shook his head. "Two weeks ago I called an organizational meeting and explained the setup. All students interested in track signed up for their events at that meeting. This assembly is the interclass track meet and varsity tryouts combined. Everyone has been practicing for two weeks. Where were you?"

"Millville."

Mr. Anderson looked a bit dazed. "How did Millville get into this?"

"You asked about it, sir. That's where I was. We moved here three days ago."

"Oh!"

The boy glanced toward the south goal post, where seven or eight boys were jogging about, warming up for the mile.

The loudspeaker squawked again. "Last call for the mile run!"

The coach grinned. "Get moving. Report to Tom Martin. He's the letterman in charge of this race. Tell him *I* said it's all right."

"Gee, thanks, but—"

"But what now?"

"But I don't know your name."

The coach chortled. "Anderson."

"*Coach* Anderson," Dirk put in.

"Yes, sir!" The boy was off, charging across the field.

Coach Anderson smiled after him. "He won't run a four-minute mile in those two-ton army boots."

"Here they come up to the starting line," Dirk said a moment later. "He made it."

When Tom Martin had lined up the milers across the track in front of the grandstand, Mr. Anderson moved to the starting line. "Four times around the track," he reminded them for the benefit of the stranger in jeans. "Now on your marks."

The milers hunched forward nervously.

"Get set."

The gun cracked. Eight runners leaped ahead with a spatter of cinders. The ninth, in jeans, jerked up his head, looked startled, and catapulted away.

In the lead was Grover Godwin, already moving smoothly along the pole. A pack of white-suited figures followed, bare legs pumping as they jockeyed for position. The boy in jeans moved up, pounding hard, and passed the pack on the outside. When they headed into the first curve, he lay off Grover's right shoulder.

The crowd watched in near-silence: too early to cheer.

Moving easily, the runners rounded the U-curve at the south end of the track. On the backstretch the pack began to pull slowly apart. The slight figure in jeans was floating along in the lead, followed a few yards back by Grover and then by the others in a lengthening chain.

They rounded the opposite curve and were on the straightaway passing the grandstand. The boy in jeans was romping along a good twenty yards in the lead.

"That kid can *really* run!" Dirk said.

"Poor devil doesn't know how long a mile can be," Mr. Anderson muttered, but Dirk detected a note of hope. "Grover is pacing himself pretty well," the coach continued. "He's not trying to keep up with the kid."

The runners passed the stands at the end of the first lap and moved away.

"Hey!" somebody shouted, pointing. "Look at the patch!"

Dirk saw it too—a glaring blue patch on the right hip of the faded jeans.

"Look at the patch," another shouted.

"Hooray for Patch!"

"Keep going, Patch!"

The runners glided around the south curve and nosed again into the backstretch. The boy in jeans still headed the ever-lengthening chain. But Dirk, watching closely, saw that his strides were shorter now, and the gap between him and Grover was narrowing inch by inch. Grover's knees rose and fell with machine-like precision in the seemingly effortless gait of the picture athlete.

As they entered the straight stretch in front of the stands, the gap was a scant four yards. Grover was closing in without altering his pace.

"Come on, Patch!"

"Get movin', Patch!"

The student body rose and shouted.

At the fifty-yard line Grover put on a burst of speed. The boy in jeans must have heard him coming, for he glanced back over his right shoulder. His head followed Grover's progress as the tall blond swept past him into the lead. Suddenly the boy in jeans slowed and, as Dirk watched appalled, stepped off the track and dropped to one knee on the infield grass.

A groan went up from the crowd. "Gah," Coach Anderson snorted. "Front runner. Only two laps. And how I could have used a good miler!"

Dirk trotted along the edge of the track and leaned over the boy as he knelt on the grass. "What happened? You had a lot left."

"Still have." The boy was fumbling with a shoelace. "Anchors," he panted. He jerked off one heavy boot, flung it aside, and started yanking at the lace of the second boot. Dirk was watching the other runners glide past when he heard the boy talking.

"Who's this Patch everybody's yelling for?"

Dirk looked down and grinned. *"You!"*

A look of amazement spread across the boy's face, followed by one of sheer joy. He stared at Dirk a second, tore off the other boot, and leaped back onto the track in his socks.

Dirk winced. The last trailing runner had just passed, and Patch took off after him, his stockinged feet pounding the sharp cinders. He passed the last man and drew abreast of the man just ahead. Dirk saw Patch flinch and break stride. He hobbled a few yards farther, glanced back, limped diagonally across the track to the outside, and stepped off onto the grass.

This time Dirk groaned.

"On-again, off-again," somebody shouted.

"One down!" came a gleeful cry.

But Patch was off and running on the narrow rim of grass along the outer edge of the track. Now he was last again, and Grover was far ahead, already on the backstretch.

Around the south end of the oval swept the other runners, Patch on the outside like a shadow. Dirk watched him across the field as the milers moved along onto the backstretch. Patch was running easily now, with a smooth, rhythmical stride that contrasted sharply with the disjointed movements of the tiring tailenders. Two stragglers were running in jerky slow-motion, like an old phonograph running down. But Patch was already well beyond them, pulling abreast of the middle group. As he entered the north curve, Grover was coming off it onto the straightaway, running smoothly, tirelessly, as if he could hold the pace forever.

Grover passed the starting line and began the last lap with a lead that looked insurmountable.

"Love to watch that guy run," said Dirk.

"Gah," said Anderson.

"What's wrong?"

"Those knees that are flashing so high and so pretty. If he'd keep them a little lower, he wouldn't run out of steam toward the end. Those long, reaching strides. If he'd keep them a few inches shorter, he'd have more push—and less pulling to do."

Dirk sighed. "Looks beautiful to me."

"That's the trouble. Everyone tells him so, and what's the coach's opinion against the school's?"

"Well," Dirk said slowly, "he *did* win first in the city last year in the mile."

"Last year's crop of milers was mediocre. Actually, Grover's best distance is the half-mile, even though he didn't win it. . . . Look, he's tiring."

Dirk studied the runners as they struggled along the backstretch in the final lap. "Yeah. That little sophomore—fellow who ran all week with a stopwatch in his hand—he's moving up."

"It's just that Grover's coming back to him. That's Benny Díaz. He made up ten yards, but he still has

forty left to make up." The coach shook his head. "Nice economy of form. Too tense though."

As they watched, Patch in his outside "lane" moved closer to Benny and swept on past him. The runners were rounding the last curve.

"I wonder how many extra yards that fellow's run, taking the outside," mused Dirk.

"This track isn't wide, and he had the pole for two laps. Still, if you run a mile in the second lane, they say you go eighteen yards farther than the man on the in-side—"

"Hey, look at the kid cut loose!"

Unleashing a sudden burst of speed as he hit the head of the homestretch, the boy in jeans came driving for the tape. The gap that had been shrinking by inches began to close a foot at a stride. The fans were shouting his name as Patch came roaring toward them along the grassy edge of the track.

Grover, hearing the tumult, glanced behind him. He saw Benny Díaz inching closer on the crunching cinders.

But Benny was still a safe twenty yards behind. Grover did not seem to notice Patch, gliding silently along on the grass.

Coach Anderson smelled trouble. He jerked into action. "Move the tape!" he shouted. "Move over. Move the tape!" But the two students who were holding the tape across the track stood at the finish line as immobile as posts. Anderson shouted louder. "Move! Get over onto the grass!" But again his words were drowned by the din.

Patch, on the grass, zipped past to the right of the tape. It was still taut and untouched a split second later when Grover Godwin snapped it with his chest. It fluttered to the track.

The student nearest to Coach Anderson stood holding one end of the broken string. He looked from Patch to Grover to the tape and then turned blankly to the coach. "Who won?"

As if in answer to the question, a spontaneous cheer rose for Patch. His name filled the air.

Dirk glued his eyes to the score sheet and jotted down the results as Coach Anderson called them off. "Díaz, third . . . Warner, fourth . . . Bauer, fifth," the coach snapped as the runners crossed the line. ". . . and Tompkins, sixth. That's all. The others dropped out."

A hand grabbed Dirk's arm. Grover Godwin, rasping for breath, asked hoarsely, "Got me—for first?"

"Second," Dirk said.

"I—" Grover protested, gulping in air, "broke the tape."

Coach Anderson turned to Dirk. "Do you know the name of the kid who won?"

Dirk shook his head.

"Bring him over here."

The boy was nearby, panting and grinning as the other runners gathered about, puffing congratulations.

"Hey, Patch," Dirk called.

"My name's—not really Patch," he panted. "It's Sherrill."

"From now on," said Dirk, "I'll bet it's Patch."

"But why?"

Dirk pointed to the bright-blue rectangle on the jeans. Patch twisted around. "Oh, that? Naw. My little brother got the patch. This is where it came from."

One of the boys leaned over to verify. "That's right. No patch. The pocket's gone."

"Well, now that that's settled," said Dirk, "the coach wants to see you."

Grover's voice reached them even before they joined the group. "He sneaked past me out on the grass. I couldn't hear him coming or I could've speeded up."

"The guy didn't run on the track," protested Sax Warner, who finished fourth. "I thought you had to run on the track."

"Well, he sure didn't cut any corners," Coach Anderson rumbled. "He took the long way around." He caught a glimpse of Patch and thrust out a huge hand. "Congratulations. You ran a good race, though somewhat—uh—individualistic. What's your name?"

"Sherrill Jones," said Patch.

"I still say," insisted Grover, "that I broke the tape. If that doesn't make me the winner, why have a tape?"

Patch looked at him curiously, then glanced around at the circle of tense faces. His own was frankly puzzled. "What does it matter?"

"Huh?"

"Who cares who won?" Patch asked. "I sure don't. I was just running for fun—and I had it." His eyes crinkled with laughter.

A circle of stares looked back at him.

"Well, I guess I better put my shoes on," Patch murmured. He turned and walked away in his stockinged feet.

Understanding What You've Read

1. Is the narrator of "Patch" a character in the story or someone outside who is watching it happen? How do you know? What pronouns in the second paragraph on page 100 tell you this?
2. What details does the author use to describe Patch?
3. What details tell you what kind of person Coach Anderson is?
4. Do you think the narrator of the story approved of Patch's method of running? How do you know? Find details in the story to support your answer.

Writing

1. Who was the real winner of the race, Patch or Grover? Write a sentence in which you defend your choice.
2. The author of "Patch" tells the story from the point of view of someone outside the story—from the third-person point of view. Rewrite the story from Patch's point of view. Begin with the sixth paragraph from the end of the story: "I still say," insisted Grover, "that I broke the tape."

Gato and the Dragons

by HILARY BECKETT

At first, I didn't pay much attention to my brother, Angel. He yells a lot, and I wasn't at all sure he was yelling at me.

But when the room began to get cold (it was late October) and Angel's screams got louder, I looked up from my math homework to see what he was up to. He hung half in and half out of the garden door, screaming.

"He's been eaten up! The dragons have got Gato, Carlos! Gato! Gaa-to!" He sounded scared to death.

"Hey, Angel, shut the door! I'm freezing! Can't you tell me what the trouble is without all that yelling?"

He was shivering. I couldn't tell whether it was from the cold or from being afraid. He had to be slightly freezing from wearing nothing but his thin pajamas. I'd made him put them on when Mom had gone out to shop, because it was so near his bedtime.

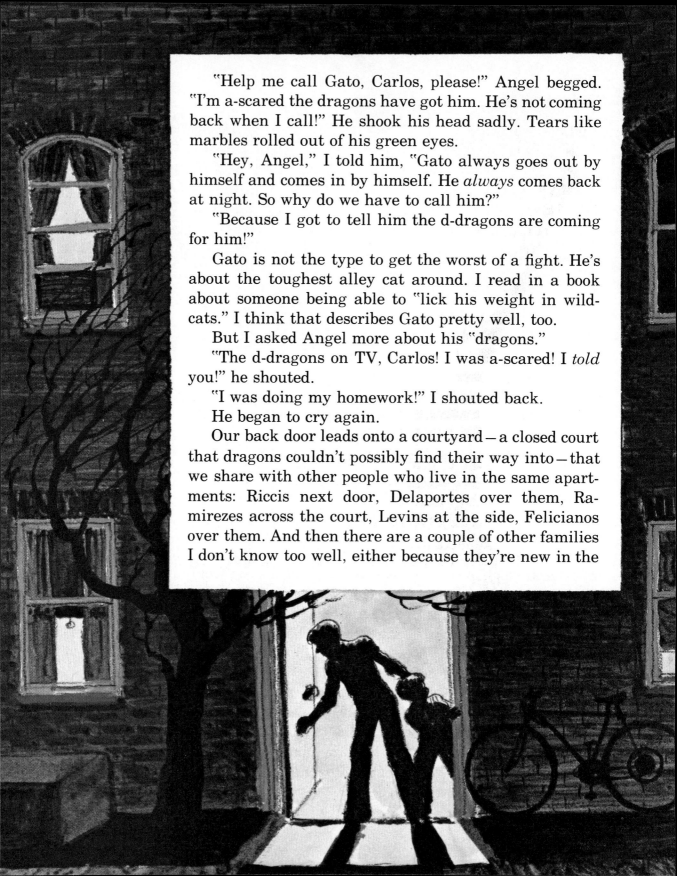

"Help me call Gato, Carlos, please!" Angel begged. "I'm a-scared the dragons have got him. He's not coming back when I call!" He shook his head sadly. Tears like marbles rolled out of his green eyes.

"Hey, Angel," I told him, "Gato always goes out by himself and comes in by himself. He *always* comes back at night. So why do we have to call him?"

"Because I got to tell him the d-dragons are coming for him!"

Gato is not the type to get the worst of a fight. He's about the toughest alley cat around. I read in a book about someone being able to "lick his weight in wild-cats." I think that describes Gato pretty well, too.

But I asked Angel more about his "dragons."

"The d-dragons on TV, Carlos! I was a-scared! I *told* you!" he shouted.

"I was doing my homework!" I shouted back.

He began to cry again.

Our back door leads onto a courtyard—a closed court that dragons couldn't possibly find their way into—that we share with other people who live in the same apartments: Riccis next door, Delaportes over them, Ramirezes across the court, Levins at the side, Felicianos over them. And then there are a couple of other families I don't know too well, either because they're new in the apartments or because they haven't got any kids my age. We all have back doors opening on the courtyard—or at least the garden-level apartments do. There are four other courts like ours side by side on our street.

Our apartments are arranged in the shape of a square, the courtyard inside. We stack our bikes out there in the garden, and we cook out on summer nights. There are a couple of swing sets there for the little kids, and a sandbox.

Like a cold, Angel's fear was catching. I figured the door might just as well be locked. By this time, there was practically frost on the furniture. I went over to shut it.

"Hey, Carlos, no! Help me call, please!"

We called together for Gato.

No answering miaow. Just a couple of barks from the Riccis' dogs next door.

"They've got Gato!" Angel insisted. "I know they d-do! He's n-never coming back no more, Carlos! I know he isn't! Gato! GATO!"

Just as I reached to shut the door, a big gust of wind rattled this tree by our house. The tree bent and scraped against the wall. For a moment, it looked as if someone or something were crouching behind it—someone or something too big to be Gato.

Angel didn't need to be any more scared than he already was, so I didn't say anything about the tree to him. I also didn't say anything about the hundred ways Gato could get out of our court and not hear us, no matter how loud we yelled. A cat is able to climb under or over or through practically anything.

I asked Angel more about the dragons. You certainly never know what on TV is going to scare a kid.

I remember when I was five—Angel's age—I believed something really crazy I'd seen on TV.

I believed a people-eating GLOB was coming to eat me up. I thought this GLOB knew exactly where to zero in on me — Carlos Ríos — in this little town in Texas, where we used to live.

This extremely bright idea came from watching the people-eating GLOB devour the entire city of Los Angeles on a late-late night horror movie my parents didn't know I was watching on TV.

About that time I stopped watching so much TV and started to read more.

It seems Angel's "dragons" were lizards — fantastically big lizards, if you can believe him — that lived out on this island somewhere in the Pacific Ocean. On TV they'd shown a scientist living with the giant lizards, measuring them, trying to check out their eating habits — nothing that sounded very scary to me. But Angel had this idea in his head that the lizards were somehow going to leave their island home and swim all the way to our city to get Gato.

He climbed me like I was a tree and he was Gato — he does it very well when he's scared — and hung onto my neck for dear life. "They went *Ss-ss, Ss-ss!* Like that, Carlos," he sniffed.

"Hey, Angel," I said. "We'll shut the door. And I'll read to you or we'll sing before you go to sleep. OK?"

He gulped once or twice, but he stopped crying.

He let me shut the door.

He only pulled back one last time to press his nose against the window to look out into the dark courtyard for Gato.

Angel got up on my shoulders near the ceiling and I gave him a piggyback ride into the bedroom. I detoured to the sofa to get my guitar. At his bed, he slid over my head and onto his quilt.

We share a bedroom — Angel and I — not my idea of the greatest thing in the world. But then, our apartment has only two bedrooms.

My mother says I can sleep in the living room if I want to have privacy. Don't think I haven't considered it.

There was this time, for instance, when Angel got into the stamps Kevin Feliciano and I were getting ready for our albums and stuck them all over the bedroom walls. And there was that other time he gave all his vitamin pills to my guppies.

But whenever I think of the privacy I could have out in the living room, and yes, the extra space—because then I wouldn't have to share a chest of drawers with Angel—I also think of the quietness and the aloneness and how I would miss Angel and Gato at night. Sometimes I have nightmares. When I do, I'm glad to have company.

In the bedroom Angel and I have beds lined up next to each other, and over on his side, near the window, we share this chest. We tried dividing the room exactly down the middle once—one side Angel's, the other side mine. But then he couldn't leave the room! The doorway was on my side. So now, his junk litters one side of the room, mine covers the other. When I think I've outgrown a book, I stick it in Angel's bookcase, but I'm really glad the book is still in the same room with me in case I ever feel like picking it up to read over again sometime.

"Hey, Angel, watch out for my glasses!" He'd grabbed them out of my pocket.

"Can I try them on?"

"Sure, if you're careful."

"Wow! Hey, Carlos, look at me!" Angel jumped up and down on his quilt like the bed was a trampoline, to get a look at himself in the mirror. "Hey, can I have glasses when I'm thirteen and grown up like you, Carlos?"

"I guess so."

"Carlos, did you have glasses when you were as little as me?"

"Yep."

"Wow! Hey, Carlos, was that last week?"

Angel's idea of time is very strange. He thinks almost everything happened "last week" — Halloween, Thanksgiving, the Fourth of July — except for those things he figures might happen "*next* week."

I guess he'll grow out of it. Have you ever met a grown-up that didn't have time mostly straightened out?

"Hey, Carlos, where's Mommy?"

"She went to the store."

"Will she get my ice cream? And more milk for lunch? That I can put in my thermos all by myself?"

"Sure! Now, into bed, Angel."

"You said you'd sing!"

"OK. Hang on, I've forgotten my pick. I'll be right back."

I'm not too great at the guitar yet, but Debby, my next-door neighbor, is teaching me. I've been able to pick out a couple of *ranchero* songs my grandfather used to sing me, ones with *gritos* in them — Mexican cowboy yells. And Debby has taught me stuff like "500 Miles" and "This Land Is Your Land, This Land Is My Land."

I sang Angel these, then I played "Mañanitas," which he knows is a song they sing in Mexico on your birthday.

"When's my birthday, Carlos? Is it next week?"

"Not for a couple of months, Angel." I also sang him some verses of "As I Walked Out on the Streets of Laredo," and that made me think of Texas.

Angel shut his eyes.

I tried to sneak out.

One eye opened — the eye I could just see above the quilt. "Hey, Carlos!"

"Yeah?" I didn't go back. I stood at the door.

"Leave the light on. For Gato, I mean. In case he needs it to find his way in. I think he might."

"OK. Good night, Angel!"

"Good night, Carlos!"

Understanding What You've Read

1. Who is the narrator of "Gato and the Dragons"? From what point of view is the story told?
2. What does the narrator of "Gato and the Dragons" say on page 113 that tells you the kind of person he is? Is the narrator in the story or an observer? What pronouns tell you this?
3. How does the author of "Gato and the Dragons" show you that Carlos takes good care of Angel?
4. Narrators describe characters from their own point of view to tell you how they feel about the characters. Find words and phrases in the story that tell you what kind of person Carlos thinks Angel is.
5. Do you think the story "Gato and the Dragons" would be a good story if it were told from the third-person point of view? Why or why not?

Writing

1. Write one or more sentences describing someone you know. Consider the following questions before you begin writing. What does the person look like? What is the person interested in? What does the person like to do? From what point of view will you write your sentences?
2. Reread the beginning of "Gato and the Dragons," pages 111–112. Rewrite four paragraphs from Angel's point of view. Begin with the sentence "He was shivering" (on page 111) and end with "Because I've got to tell him the d-dragons are coming for him!" (on page 112).

Meeting at Southdale Court

by ELEANOR SPENCE

Lyndall crossed the parking lot and entered South-dale Court Shopping Center. She knew all the shops well by now, but many failed to interest her. Lyndall climbed the stairway to the upper level. Here were clothing stores, a pet shop, a pharmacy, and a bookshop. It was not the kind of bookshop that Lyndall would have liked. In reality, it was only a newsstand that also sold books. But it was the only one in the court, so it had to suffice. Lyndall passed by the racks of magazines and paperback fiction. She seldom read for pleasure alone, but for information and hard facts. Science journals and books about biology and zoology were her particular delight. Medicine or veterinary science were her choices of future careers. She knew that to study

either she would have to win scholarships, so even at thirteen she could not afford to waste too much time.

Long ago she had discovered that a certain display rack was tall enough to hide her as she browsed through the "Technical" section at the back of the shop. True, she had already looked through the few books that interested her, but there was always the hope that new stock might have arrived. This morning she was in luck: Among the well-known titles was a new volume, *Marine Life*. This book had many pictures and was full of promising small print.

She settled herself for half an hour of private study, ignored or unseen by the busy salespeople. She did not hear the constant shuffle of feet, the clatter of the cash register, or the requests of customers. It was only when one of the salesclerks raised her voice in unmistakable exasperation that Lyndall frowned. She lost her place in the text, just as she was beginning on the life cycle of the octopus.

"I said, 'Where do you live?' " the clerk was repeating. "Don't you speak English?"

How rude! thought Lyndall. She peered around the rack. To her surprise, she saw only a boy of about her own age. He was a slender, fair-haired boy with blue eyes, dressed in quite normal shorts, T-shirt, and sandals. He was staring in obvious bewilderment at the clerk behind the counter. The presence of several interested bystanders was causing his face to flush with embarrassment.

Lyndall looked back once at her book. Then she sighed and replaced it on the shelf. She felt obliged somehow to go to the boy's rescue, if only to show the salesclerk that children were not to be bullied. And had not Lyndall's last school report stated, "shows definite leadership qualities"?

"Can I help?" asked Lyndall politely.

"Dunno, I'm sure. You his sister?" asked the clerk.

"No," replied Lyndall, glancing sideways at the startled boy. He had transferred his perplexed gaze to her face. "Why? What's he done?"

"Look," said the clerk, with exaggerated patience. "All I want to know is his name and address, see, because he says he wants the papers delivered. We have to know where to send them, don't we?"

"Did you understand that?" Lyndall asked the boy kindly.

His reaction was unexpected. He grew redder than ever. He glowered at Lyndall with even more anger than the salesclerk had exhibited.

"Of course I did! I'm not stupid!"

He took the salesclerk's pad and pen. Then he printed

a name and address in large, firm capitals. Lyndall read it over his shoulder.

" 'Calder, 12 Kennedy Place.' You must be the boy Shane Halliday was talking about."

"Who's Shane Halliday?" the boy asked, adding rudely, "I've never heard of him."

Lyndall followed the Calder boy out of the shop.

"What's your first name? I'm Lyndall Hunter."

"Why don't you mind your own business?" demanded the boy, turning to look at her. He was still flushed, and something in his expression reminded Lyndall of a trapped creature unable to fight back — like a bird in its cage, perhaps.

"I only asked your name," she pointed out.

"My name's Glen."

He set off along the gallery at a brisk pace. Clearly, he hoped that the conversation was at an end. Lyndall, however, was not easily put off, especially when her scientific curiosity was aroused. When he reached the Health Foods Store, Glen immediately pretended to take a great interest in racks of dried fruits and jars of golden honey.

"Shane is the boy you're supposed to be playing cricket with after school," Lyndall said, right in his ear. "But he'll probably be kept in today, because he was late."

"You do know everything, don't you?" remarked Glen scornfully.

He resumed his study of the crystallized pineapple. However, Lyndall's next words, clearly and precisely spoken, brought his head up in a sudden jerk.

"Not everything. But I know you're deaf."

Glen backed into the alcove. He looked about to see if anyone else was listening. This end of the gallery, however, was unusually quiet in contrast to the central court, from which arose a steady drone of sound.

"If that's a joke, it's not very funny. Why don't you go home?"

"You're shouting," said Lyndall in surprise. She leaned on the railing and gazed unseeingly at the fountain. She didn't want to look at Glen anymore. He was now so pale that she was afraid he might be ill, and it was her fault. Scientific curiosity was all very well. But the boy beside her was a human being. She felt as if she had pinned a butterfly on a board, only to find it was alive and struggling frantically to be free.

"I wasn't," said Glen, without conviction.

Lyndall felt in her pocket for her money. This was a crisis of a kind. She had to give Glen the chance for a dignified escape. Not looking at him, she went into the shop and bought the first item she could think of, which was crystallized pineapple.

Glen was still in the alcove. His elbows were on the rail and he supported his head on clenched fists. Lyndall thrust the little white bag under his nose.

"Go on—have some. It's fabulous."

He hesitated, then gave in.

Lyndall tried to remember what she was supposed to buy for the weekend, but for once her orderly memory had let her down.

"Did that boy—Shane—tell you?" asked Glen suddenly.

"Tell me what? That you were deaf? No, he wouldn't notice."

"Notice?" repeated Glen. "You mean, no one told you? You just knew?"

"Well, yes, but you see, I'm going to be a doctor. And I had an aunt who was deaf. She used to look at people's faces all the time they talked."

"If you knew, other people might, too," said Glen despairingly.

"Probably not," answered Lyndall. She considered

the question carefully. "Lots of people talk so much they never notice if anyone's listening. And anyway, you can hear some of the time, can't you?"

Glen nodded. "Depends who's speaking. Sometimes it just sounds—well—mixed up. Sort of blurred, like the television picture is when the set's not working properly."

Lyndall tried to imagine what it would be like, but it was beyond her.

"Let's go downstairs," she suggested. "I have to do some shopping. Are you in a hurry?"

Glen shook his head. "There's nothing to do at home. Graham—he's my brother—is helping sort out all the furniture and stuff. I kept getting in the way."

Lyndall nodded sympathetically. "Getting in the way" was an experience quite familiar to her. She was tall for her age, and clumsy, which secretly alarmed her—who ever heard of a clumsy doctor?

She bought as many items as she could remember. Then she rejoined Glen at the fountain.

"Come on!" she called.

But Glen was not looking at her. The noise of the splashing water, the many footsteps on the tiled floor, and the chatter of other voices all combined to drown her own. Finally she had to stand in front of him. She was not able to nudge him because her arms were full of bundles. He started when he saw her. Then he glanced quickly around to find out if any strangers were watching. Lyndall felt a sudden, keen compassion. She positively glared at a woman who seemed to be looking at Glen with curiosity.

They went home by a back route, chosen by Lyndall because of its quietness. In the distance the flat roofs of the high-school buildings gleamed in the autumn sun. She pointed them out to Glen. After a brief period of trial and error, Lyndall found that if she spoke clearly and not too fast, and from slightly in front of him, he could understand everything she said. It was not necessary, as he pointed out himself, for her to shout or make exaggerated mouth movements.

"I don't go to that school," Lyndall explained. "But Shane does, and his big sister, and Gina and Polo Dalmati, who live next door to us. Their father and mother are from Malta. Did you know people spoke English in Malta?"

"Well, it belonged to England, didn't it?" Glen asked. "Just the same as we did."

"I didn't know that," said Lyndall, genuinely respectful. "Do you read a lot?"

"Most of the time, when I'm not at school. I watch TV sometimes, but it gets boring. I'm not supposed to play around much outside."

Instinctively, Lyndall stopped herself from asking the obvious "Why?" She felt now that Glen had begun to talk, he would probably continue without any prompting.

"Last year I was sick for weeks. I missed an awful lot of school, only that was in Melbourne, not here. And when I got better I was deaf."

125

"Just like that?" asked Lyndall in surprise.

"Oh, everyone said it would get better. I've got things to take, and the doctor in Melbourne told Mum to take me to another specialist in Sydney. There hasn't been time yet."

"I'm certain there must be lots of good ear doctors in Sydney," said Lyndall, in defense of her chosen profession. Since meeting Glen she had given up once and for all the idea of veterinary science. Humans were more interesting than animals, after all.

"Oh, sure!" said Glen bitterly. "But how would you feel if you were thinking all the time that you might never hear properly again?"

Lyndall could not think of a good answer, so they walked on in silence. At last Glen said, "It's the Captain Cook Bicentenary thing. That's why they were putting up those flags at the shopping center."

"I didn't notice," said Lyndall. "I don't think I care very much about Captain Cook. We learned about his discovering Australia in third grade."

"But think how lonely he must have been," Glen went on dreamily. "All those years at sea. He was all by himself, in command. If you're captain, you can't go around chatting to the crew."

"I never thought of that," admitted Lyndall.

"Lots of great people must have been lonely people," said Glen.

Baffled, Lyndall stopped at the corner of Kennedy Place. She watched him go toward his own gate. He walked quickly, as if he were suddenly ashamed of talking so freely to someone he had met only an hour ago. But at the gate he paused and waved to her.

"See you!" Lyndall called.

She had no way of knowing, however, whether Glen heard her or not.

Understanding What You've Read

1. Does the narrator of "Meeting at Southdale Court" tell the story from the point of view of an observer outside the story or through one of the characters? How do you know?
2. Sometimes the narrator of a story tells you how a character thinks and feels. Find a paragraph on page 121 that tells you how Glen feels. Find a sentence on page 120 that tells you what Lyndall is thinking. Find a sentence on the same page that tells how Lyndall feels.
3. Why do you think Glen got angry when Lyndall asked whether he understood the clerk at the newsstand? Why did Glen try to walk away from Lyndall after she told him she knew he was deaf?
4. In what ways are Glen and Lyndall believable characters? What details does Eleanor Spence include to make them seem real? Find three sentences in the story that contain details that make Glen seem real.

Writing

1. Imagine a meeting between Glen and Lyndall several days after they met at Southdale Court. Write a sentence telling what Glen might say to Lyndall. Write another sentence telling what Lyndall might say to Glen.
2. Reread the first paragraph on page 119 of "Meeting at Southdale Court." Rewrite the paragraph in the first person from the point of view of Lyndall.

More Stories About People

A Gathering of Days: A New England Girl's Journal, 1830–32 by Joan W. Blos. Scribner, 1979. A novel about life in New England in the early 1800's as seen through the eyes of a thirteen-year-old farm girl.

Ramona and Her Family by Beverly Cleary. Morrow, 1979. A continuation of the Ramona series, which follows a young girl through stages and events in her life.

Philip Hall Likes Me. I Reckon. Maybe. by Bette Greene. Dial, 1974. The friendship between Beth Lambert and Philip Hall grows as they share experiences, some funny, some scary.

A Ring of Endless Light by Madeleine L'Engle. Farrar, Straus & Giroux, 1980. The author describes the struggles of a young girl to cope with her grandfather's fatal illness.

A Book for Jodan by Marcia Newfield. Atheneum, 1975. After her parents' divorce, Jodan's father makes her a special book to keep alive the memories and love they share.

Zia by Scott O'Dell. Houghton Mifflin, 1976. Karana, rescued after many years alone on the Island of the Blue Dolphins, goes to live with her niece Zia.

Hang Tough, Paul Mather by Alfred Slote. Lippincott, 1973. Paul has an incurable disease. But he's determined to make the most out of the time he has left to play baseball.

Part 3
The World Around Us

Following Directions

Maybe we should have read the directions.

Almost every day you give or follow directions. Many of them are written directions. Following directions is an important reading skill that you use:

- when you make or build something
- when you take a test
- when you want to get from one place to another
- when you fill out a form

When else might you read directions?

Numbered Directions

Before you start to follow a set of directions, you should carefully read all the steps. By reading all the directions before you start working, you do these things:

- You learn what the necessary materials are.
- You get an idea of how easy or difficult the task is.
- You get an idea of how much time it will take to complete the task.
- You learn about **options** you may want to take. (An option is a choice between two or more things. An option can also be something you do only if you want to. It is not a necessary step.)
- You get an idea of the things that may go wrong and how to prevent or fix them.

Read the following directions. Look for steps that contain options. Look for steps that tell you what problems may arise and how to solve them.

How to Make Your Own Mask

To make your own mask you will need:
    a hard flat surface
    potter's clay (about 5 pounds)
    1 bag of plaster of Paris (You won't
        need to use the whole bag.)
    gauze strips (It's easy to find surgi-
        cal gauze in drugstores.)
    sandpaper
    chisel or scissors
    string
    decorations (paint, feathers, beads,
        buttons, etc.)

Here's what you do:

1. Mold the clay on the board into the shape you want the mask to be. Try to make it just a little bigger than the size of your face.

   You can make the nose any size and shape you want.

   You can make pointy ears or a funny chin—and cheeks.

   Remember that the mask will take on the shape of the clay.

2. Let the clay dry 8 to 10 hours or until it is dry when you touch it.

3. Mix the plaster of Paris with water. The instructions are on the box. The solution should be liquid, but thick enough to coat the gauze.

4. Soak the gauze strips in the wet plaster, and cover the clay form with them.

   Plaster dries quickly. If your supply begins to harden, you can add some water or mix up another batch.

   The clay should be completely covered by the gauze, with no cracks showing. Let the gauze strips dry for about 15 to 30 minutes, or until it feels dry all over when you touch it. (Before it dries completely, you can put some feathers or beads in it. But don't paint the mask yet!)

5. The plaster mask should separate from the clay as it dries. If it doesn't, carefully pry it off the form around the edges.

6. Smooth the front and edges of the mask with sandpaper and/or a chisel. You can also cut out eyes, a nose, and a mouth with the chisel or scissors.

7. Cut one hole on each side where you put strings to hold the mask on your head.

8. Decorate the mask with paint, beads, or whatever else you want to use.

9. Tie strings through the side holes and wear your mask!

— Do a ZOOMdo
Little, Brown and Company

There are several options in the set of directions you just read. The following options appear in the list of materials above the numbered steps.

- chisel or scissors
- decorations (paint, feathers, beads, buttons, etc.)

The word *or* in "chisel or scissors" signals an option. You are also given options in the materials you can use to decorate the mask. The abbreviation *etc.* (for *et cetera,* meaning "and so on") shows that the decoration is up to you.

What might go wrong when you work with the plaster? Step 4 warns you that "Plaster dries quickly." What does step 4 say to do if the plaster begins to harden?

Unnumbered Directions

Sentence order and time words help you to follow directions that are not numbered. In the set of directions below, look for time words such as *first, next, then, before.* Such words help you in the same way that numbered steps do.

In some sets of directions, pictures or diagrams are keyed to one or more steps in the directions. As you come to parentheses and an abbreviation like *illus., fig.,* or *diag.,* followed by a number, look at the illustration. (The abbreviation *illus.* stands for *illustration; fig.* stands for *figure; diag.* stands for *diagram.*)

String Sculpture

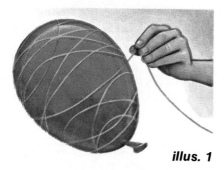

illus. 1

illus. 2

Would you like to make string sculptures? To make one, all you need is a balloon, about one meter of colored string or yarn, and some liquid laundry starch or white glue.

First blow the balloon up. Next, soak the string or yarn in the starch or cover it with glue. Then wrap the string around the balloon (*illus. 1*). Now let the string dry completely. (Drying may take a day or two.) Before you hang the sculpture, pop the balloon (*illus. 2*). Carefully remove the pieces of the broken balloon. Finally, tie a string to your sculpture and hang it from a ceiling.

Which should you do first—hang the sculpture or pop the balloon? The sentence order and the time clues *before* and *finally* show you the order of steps to follow.

Everyday Directions

Tests

A common mistake when taking tests is not following the directions carefully. Look at the test paper below. What is wrong with it?

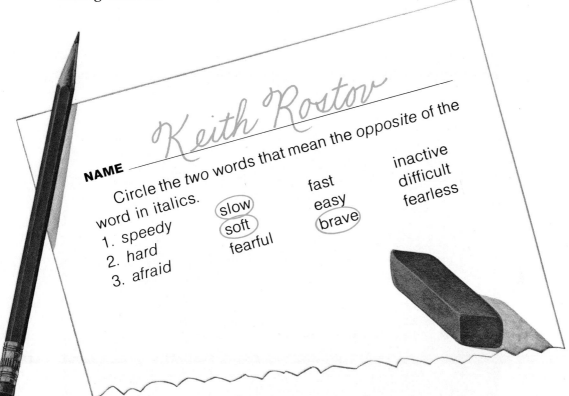

As you can see, only one answer is circled in each row. The directions said to circle two.

When you take a test, read all the directions carefully before you begin. Pay attention to key words such as *underline, cross out, choose only the best answer.* Then answer the first question. Check the directions again to make sure you followed them correctly.

135

Forms

Forms that ask for information about you have written directions. You should treat these directions like any other ones. *Read all the directions first before you begin to write.*

Below is a form that Sharon filled out. She didn't read the directions first. Look for the mistakes she made by not reading the directions at the top and under each blank.

Please *print* the information in the spaces provided. Use only the pencil that is given to you. These forms are checked by a machine that cannot read ink or ordinary pencil.

Sharon Graves 21/3/70
_____
Last name   **First name**   **Date of Birth**
                                              Month/Day/Year

2816 Batchelder Street El Paso 3A
_____
Street address Number   **Street**   **Apt.**

El Paso   Texas
_____
City or Town   **State**   **Zip Code**

Sharon Graves
_____
Signature

136

Try This

1. Read the directions for the following example. Then tell what is wrong with it. Were the directions followed?

   Use a red pencil. Place an X on the line next to each word that names a part of your body.

   arm ___✕___   hat _____   leg ___✕___   head _____
   ring _____   ear ___✕___   shoe ___✕___   toe ___✕___

2. Refer to the directions for making a string sculpture on page 134. Then answer the following questions.

   a. What options are given in the first paragraph for the kinds of materials you can use?
   b. Suppose you didn't let the string dry completely and you popped the balloon about an hour after you covered it with string. What do you think would happen?
   c. What do you do *after* you pop the balloon?

3. Study the map below. Then give directions for the shortest route from Ann's house to the art museum. Give two sets of directions from Jackson High School to Bulldog Stadium.

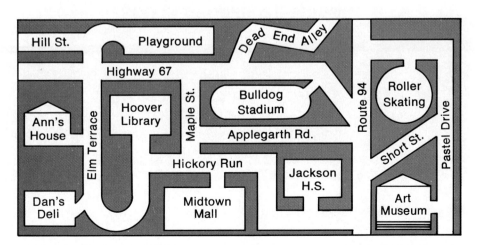

VOCABULARY STUDY

Synonyms

Museum of Unnatural History

GUIDE TO FIRST FLOOR

On this floor you will find stuffed animals that are quite rare. For **instance**, here is an example of the world's only stuffed capsnaffler. This dangerous animal lives entirely on a diet of baseball caps. This particular specimen drowned when it tried to drink a ten-gallon hat. Live capsnafflers are extremely rare. In recent years, a few have been spotted prowling around Little League baseball games.

GUIDE TO SECOND FLOOR

Visit our **invaluable** collection of shoes worn by famous people. Among these priceless exhibits, you will see a pair of galoshes worn by the Abominable Snowman. And don't miss the only ballet shoes with wheels on them. These were worn by the great dancer Isadora Graham Kracker, who was known around the world for her high-speed turns.

GUIDE TO THIRD FLOOR

Here you can view our fine assortment of unusual **decorations**. Among the ornaments you will see is a diamond comb worn by the world's richest rooster. We also have a complete set of centerpieces from the Invisible Girl's eleventh birthday party. However, no one is sure just *where* we have them.

GUIDE TO MUSEUM GIFT SHOP

Our gift shop has many fine goods for sale. It offers such **wares** as the Make-a-Mammoth Kit. With only this simple kit and a few thousand tubes of glue, you can put together your own skeleton of a giant elephant. Tusks are sold separately.

Word Play

Match each word in boldface with its synonym, or word that has a similar meaning. Then make a sentence using each word in boldface.

1. **instance**   a. ornaments
2. **invaluable**   b. goods
3. **decorations**   c. priceless
4. **wares**   d. example

When you come to the directions on making towers with clay and straws, you will see that the author does not use numbered steps. Look at the drawings as a guide. Also note the options and tips that are given.

The Earth is covered with tall, vertical structures of all kinds. Trees, buildings, and statues are a few of the . . .

TOWERS
ALL AROUND US

by David Webster

Towers, those tall vertical structures, are found everywhere in the world. There are both natural towers and towers made by people.

Different kinds of towers serve different purposes. Many natural towers are homes for animals and insects. These towers are also things of beauty in themselves. Towers made by people support bridges, hold things, send radio waves, warn of danger, and so on. The uses of towers are almost endless.

If someone asked you to quickly think of a natural tower, you might say the giant redwood trees in California—and you would be right! Some of these trees "tower" above every other plant on Earth—to a height of 368 feet.

Another natural tower you might not have thought of, however (and an unusual one), is the *saguaro* [sə·wä′rō] cactus.

Some saguaro cacti grow to fifty feet tall and have fifty arms. These cacti are often called the "apartment houses of the desert" because they provide living space for so many bird species.

The saguaro cactus sometimes lives as long as two centuries. It takes seventy-five years to develop its first branches, and years more before it reaches its full weight—from six to ten tons. It thrives in the desert in the southwestern United States and supplies food as well as homes to many animals. Some people use its fruit for cakes and syrup.

Towers Built by People

People have been making towers out of every available material since around 3000 B.C. In ancient Egypt, obelisks were built as decorations. An obelisk is a square column of stone that gets thinner as it gets higher. The top of an obelisk is shaped like a pyramid.

The *Leaning Tower of Pisa* is a marble tower that is one of the world's most famous architectural wonders. After the first three stories had been built, the ground under the tower began to sink, causing the tower to tip. It has tipped one foot during the last hundred years and is now

Saguaro cacti.

The Leaning Tower of Pisa.

more than sixteen feet out of line. Cement has been forced into the soil beneath the 179-foot tower to help prevent it from leaning further.

The *Statue of Liberty* is the largest statue ever made. It stands proudly at the entrance to New York Harbor. The torch towers 305 feet above the base of the pedestal. The statue itself is a little more than 151 feet high.

The *Empire State Building* in New York City was the world's tallest structure for almost forty years. This building reaches a height of 1,250 feet — almost a quarter of a mile. This height is now surpassed by buildings such as the *World Trade Center* towers in New York (1,353 feet), and by the *Sears Building* in Chicago (1,454 feet).

Making Towers with Clay

You have probably built towers before. When you were younger, you might have made towers with wooden blocks or sand castles at the beach. Perhaps you have even built a real lookout tower to use for climbing or for secret club meetings.

You can build a model tower with clay. Get one pound of the

kind of modeling clay that will stay soft. Using just one pound of clay, you will be able to make a tower up to eighteen inches high. Start your tower with a wide base and make it narrow as you go up. (See illustration 1.) Be careful, however, not to stretch the clay too far. When it is stretched out too far, it begins to sag and bend.

One way to stiffen clay is to cool it in the refrigerator. Try forming a skinny tower with warm clay and then chilling it for an hour in your freezer.

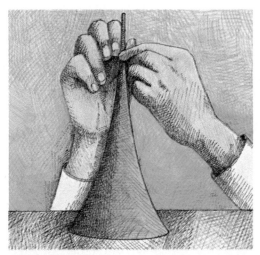

illustration 1

You may not know this, but a solid tower is not the most efficient kind to build. Much of the clay on the inside does very little to support the tower. A hollow clay structure can be made much higher than a solid one.

To build a hollow tower, first flatten out your clay in thin sheets. Then use the thin sheets to shape a hollow, conical tower. (See illustration 2.) The clay walls should be thickest at the bottom. A very thin piece of rolled clay can be placed on top. Can you make a hollow clay tower that stands more than twenty-four inches high? Try it.

To make even better use of your clay, cut out and remove

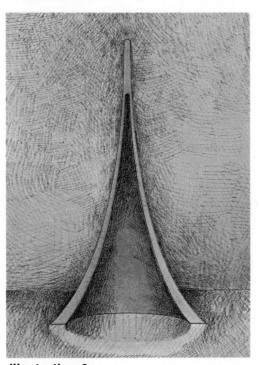

illustration 2

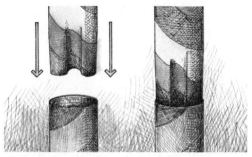

illustration 3

illustration 4

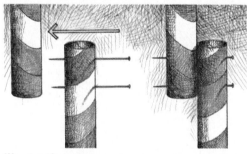

illustration 5

illustration 6

flat circles from the tower wall. With this extra clay you should be able to build a little higher. The author was able to build a one-pound clay tower twenty-eight inches high. See if you can possibly beat this record.

Making Towers with Straws

A paper or plastic straw is a tower in and of itself. However, you can make a higher tower by connecting straws.

Two straws can be joined together by squeezing in the end of one straw and forcing it into the end of another. (See illustration 3.) Anchor the two straws to the floor in a small lump of clay. Then extend the height of the tower by adding more straws. (See illustration 4.) Can you build your thin tower as high as the ceiling? What happens when the tower gets too tall?

Another method of connecting straws is with pins. Lap over two straws about one inch and push pins through both of them at the joints. (See illustration 5.) You can build a tower by connecting more straws with pins. (See illustration 6.) Which tower is stronger—the one connected with pins or the one without pins? Why?

A much sturdier straw tower can be built by pinning together several thin towers. More straws are needed near the bottom to make a wider base. (See illustration 7.)

illustration 7

A different kind of straw tower can be made with an open structure. A most important element in such a structure is the diagonal. Four straws pinned together in a square are free to move. When a fifth straw is added as a diagonal, however, the structure becomes rigid. Diagonals are used to divide a structure into a number of immovable triangles.

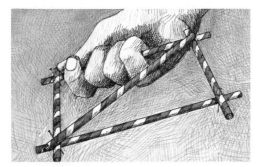

illustration 8

You can build a tower with an open structure. First pin four straws together. Then add a fifth straw as a diagonal. (See illustration 8.) Continue to add straws to increase the height. Always add a straw as a diagonal. Anchor the bottom straws in lumps of clay. (See illustration 9.)

A model tower can be made with clay and straws. Real towers, however, must be strong enough to withstand the force of strong winds and hold up their own weight as well. Concrete and steel are the basic materials from which the strongest towers are made.

illustration 9

Many different towers have been built, from the obelisks of ancient Egypt to the modern structures of today. And each day more and more towers appear, to be used and appreciated by all of us.

Understanding What You've Read

1. What are towers?
2. Why is the saguaro cactus an unusual natural tower?
3. Why is a hollow clay tower more efficient than a solid tower?
4. What must real towers be able to do?

Applying the Skills Lesson

1. Refer to the directions for making a model clay tower on pages 142–143 to answer these questions.

   a. What tips are you given about working with the clay?
   b. How do you begin to make a hollow, conical tower? (Hint: The word *first* is a time clue.)

2. Refer to the directions for making a straw tower on pages 144–145 to answer the following questions.

   a. What options are given for joining the straws to make a thin tower?
   b. Which illustration shows a tower that you can make by using squares divided by diagonals? How do you anchor this kind of tower?

3. What is the most important element in the directions for making the open structure tower on page 145?

TEXTBOOK STUDY

Following Directions

In most of your textbooks you come across directions. Some form part of a practice, a review, or a test on something you have learned. Other directions explain how to do something. Whenever you are given directions, read each step before you begin to follow them. Check yourself to make sure you have followed the directions correctly. The sidenotes for the following selection will help you to understand the directions.

Following Directions in Science

Investigation 25

How can you show that air has weight?

This sentence tells you the reason for the directions.

Materials
Spring scale
Basketball "without" air in it
Strip of cloth
Pump and needle

A. Tie the strip of cloth into a sling-shaped loop. Place the basketball in the loop. Hang the loop from the hook of the spring scale. Record the weight of the ball and strip of cloth.

Notice that letters are used instead of numbered steps. The letters are keyed to the illustrations on the following page.

B. Remove the ball from the loop. Put the needle into the needle valve of the ball. Attach the pump to the needle. By pumping, completely fill up the basketball.

C. Place the ball in the sling and weigh it again. Record the weight of the cloth and the basketball once again. Compare the two weights.

—Understanding Your Environment
Silver Burdett

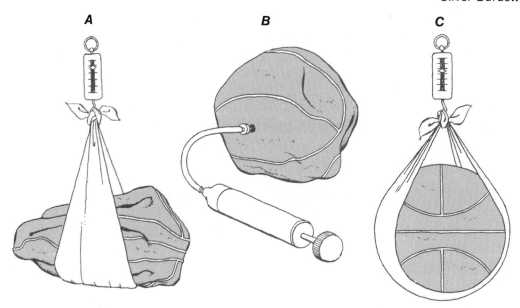

A   B   C

Building Skills

1. What materials do you need to perform the investigation you just read about?
2. How many steps are there in part A of the investigation? How many steps are there in part B?

Following Directions in Social Studies

The following selection is part of a review from a textbook chapter. There are no sidenotes. Read the selection and study the directions. Then answer the questions that follow it. *You do not have to do the exercises in the selection.*

Putting It Together

What Do You Remember?

On separate paper, draw and label a time line like the one shown at the foot of this page. Then read over the items numbered 1 to 5. Each of these items describes a stage in the language development of every human being. Above each mark on your time line, write the number of one of the stages of language development. Put them in the correct time order.

1. Speaks one language expertly
2. Cannot speak
3. Has spoken a billion words
4. Knows 1,500 words
5. Uses two-word sentences

Each group numbered 6 to 10 includes English words that come from a language spoken in one of the regions listed below. On separate paper write the number of each group. Then write the name of the correct region.

Germany   Africa   Spain

Italy   North America

6. cola, banana, jazz
7. ranch, cafeteria, rodeo
8. canoe, moose, pecan
9. piano, studio, ballot
10. noodle, pretzel, kindergarten

—*The Way People Live*
Houghton Mifflin

Building Skills

1. Refer to the directions in the first paragraph to answer the following questions.

   a. What materials are needed in order to follow the directions?
   b. What do the directions explain about the meaning of the numbered items?
   c. Which are you supposed to do *first*—draw and label a time line or read the items numbered 1 to 5?
   d. Why is the last sentence in this paragraph a "key" direction?

2. Refer to the directions in the second paragraph to answer the following questions.

   a. How many groups do the directions tell you are given?
   b. If you were to do this exercise, where do the directions tell you to record your answers?
   c. If you were to do this exercise, which are you supposed to write *first*—the region or the number of each group? What time word gives you the clue?

SKILLS LESSON

Finding the Main Idea of a Paragraph

Do you remember how to find the topic and main idea of a paragraph? The topic is what the paragraph is about. The main idea is the most important thing the paragraph says about the topic. What is the topic of the following paragraph? What is the main idea?

Many mammals have long life spans. The average life span of an elephant is forty years. However, some elephants have lived as long as seventy years. The great apes and most horses have twenty-year life spans. But some apes and some horses are known to have lived for more than forty years. Among the mammals, humans have the longest life spans. Some people have lived for more than one hundred years.

What is the topic of the previous paragraph?

1. Life spans of elephants
2. Life spans of mammals
3. Life spans of humans

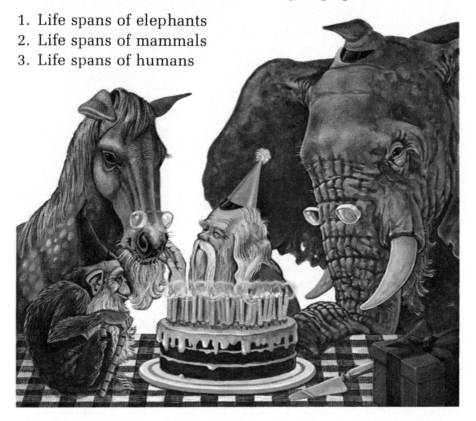

Notice that all the sentences are about the life spans of mammals. This is the topic of the paragraph. What is the most important thing the paragraph says about this topic? The main idea is stated in the first sentence: *Many mammals have long life spans.*

Duck-billed platypus.

Main Ideas That Are Stated in Two Sentences

Very often two sentences are equally important parts of the main idea of a paragraph. When this happens, you have to put together the information from both sentences to find the main idea. Read the following paragraph.

The duck-billed platypus of Australia is like a duck in many ways. It lays eggs as a duck does. Its bill and webbed feet are like a duck's. Unlike the duck, the platypus is a mammal. Like other mammals, it has hair on its body. And, just as other female mammals do, mother platypuses feed their young with their own milk.

Which of the following sentences best states the main idea of the paragraph above?

1. The duck-billed platypus of Australia is like a duck in many ways.
2. Unlike the duck, the platypus is a mammal.
3. The duck-billed platypus is like a duck in many ways, but unlike the duck, the platypus is a mammal.

Sentence 1 tells part of the main idea. But it doesn't include any of the information in the second half of the paragraph. Sentence 2 omits all the ways the platypus is like a duck. It, too, only gives part of the main idea. You need both parts to state the main idea. Therefore, sentence 3 best states the main idea.

Unstated Main Ideas

In some paragraphs, the main idea is not directly stated. But you can figure it out from the details.

In the following paragraph, the main idea is not directly stated. Find the topic of the paragraph. Then state the main idea in your own words.

Leonardo da Vinci is best known as a painter, but he was also a sculptor and a musician. He was an engineer and an inventor, too. One of his greatest interests was astronomy, the science of the stars and planets.

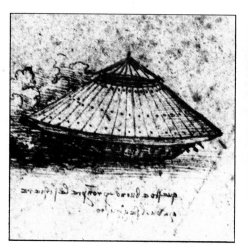 

Did you say that the topic of the paragraph is *Leonardo da Vinci*? This is the topic because each sentence is about Leonardo. How did you state the main idea of the paragraph? One way to state the main idea is: *Leonardo da Vinci worked in many fields.* You might also have said: *Leonardo da Vinci had many talents (or abilities or interests).* If you were able to see that none of his talents was presented as more important than another, you saw the main idea.

Try This

Read each of the following paragraphs. State the topic and main idea of each paragraph.

1. Before 1900, there were millions of passenger pigeons in the forests of North America. But people hunted these birds for food and sport. At the same time, the forests where these birds lived were cut down for use as lumber. By 1915, there was not even one passenger pigeon left alive.

2. If you join the drama club, you will get a chance to act in at least one play. You will also have a chance to help build sets and make costumes. The club has arranged a field trip to Minneapolis to see a performance. All club members are invited to come along!

VOCABULARY STUDY

Suffixes

Word Play

1. Use the suffix *-ful* with one of his sisters to make a word that completes each sentence below.

   a. The dancer's movements were as _____ as a butter-fly's.
   b. She really needs _____ muscles to lift that weight.
   c. A juggler must be _____ to balance water glasses.

2. Add *-ful* to *right*, *joy*, and *help*. Then use each new word in a sentence. Check the meaning of the words in a dictionary.

157

In some paragraphs, you will notice that the main idea is stated in one sentence. When the main idea is not stated, read carefully to see how the details are related. They can help you discover the main idea.

You don't have to travel thousands of miles to meet Wong Pei and Sarah Jordan. Right now, you can go on . . .

A VISIT TO HONG KONG

by Terry Shannon

Hong Kong is a British crown colony, just as certain parts of the United States were once British colonies. It lies thousands of miles across the Pacific Ocean from North America. It is one of our most distant neighbors. Hong Kong is also thousands of miles from Great Britain, to which it belongs.

Part of Hong Kong is Britain's through a permanent treaty with China, signed in the mid-1800's. Other areas of this colony were leased by China to Britain some years later. The lease expires in 1997.

Most of the people living in Hong Kong are Chinese. Sidewalks bulge with people going about their daily lives. Shops are jammed like a too-full bean bag.

New ways of doing things and new ways of living are having an effect on the lives of the people of Hong Kong. Once few children in Hong Kong went to school. Today school is a must, and nearly all children of proper age are in school.

Hong Kong is a great world trade center. Its harbor is crowded with big cargo ships and passenger liners, as well as junks, sampans, and *walla wallas*. Walla wallas are the water taxis of Hong Kong. They are so called because the first sampans to be used for that purpose were operated by an American whose home town was Walla Walla, Washington.

159

Meet Wong Pei

Life has changed for Wong Pei. Until she was eight years old, Pei had never been beyond the small village in the People's Republic of China where she was born.

Pei attended the school in her small village. Arithmetic was easy for her. But learning to read and write some of the thousands of characters used in Chinese writing was harder. Pei also worked in the fields outside the village where her mother and father worked all day.

Wong Pei and her family have since left their village in the People's Republic. They live in a new factory town in Hong Kong, one of many built by the Hong Kong government. These

towns offer shelter and a place to work to the tens of thousands of people who, like Pei's family, went to Hong Kong to seek a different way of life.

Pei's mother and father now work in one of the factories near their new home. The family has a happy time visiting with relatives who had arrived in Hong Kong before they did.

Pei and some of her brothers and sisters go to school atop the big building where they live. There are many such high-rise buildings in the new towns, each with its own school.

Schools are crowded and, like some children in America, students go to school in shifts. Some attend classes in the morning, others in the after-noon, and others in the evening.

Pei is in school from eight in the morning until one o'clock.

After school she does her homework and helps her grandmother look after the younger children. Pei also carefully tends the little garden growing in a box on the balcony outside the family apartment. The apartment is on the fourth floor of the building.

Sometimes Pei misses the quiet and the open spaces of the fields and orchards of her native village, where only a few hundred people live. She often thinks of her grandparents who remained there. She is glad that one of her grandmothers came to Hong Kong with the family. Elders are given great respect in Chinese homes, and much attention is paid to the wisdom of their years.

Gradually, Wong Pei is becoming used to the great flow of traffic in the street below her building. The automobiles of many colors are a never-ending source of wonder to her. Never had she seen anything like the big buses jammed with passengers. Pei had been used to seeing only carts pulled by oxen or by men and women. And never had Pei seen so many bicycles as in Hong Kong. There were few in her village who could afford such a luxury as a bicycle.

Meet Sarah Jordan

Sarah Jordan has never known the quiet and the open spaces of Pei's village. She had always been used to big buses and automobiles and crowds of people.

Sarah was born in England. At ten, she had been going to school in her native London for several years. Most of the subjects she studied were similar to those studied by children her

age in the United States and Canada.

Sarah, too, now lives in Hong Kong. There her father works in a government office in the city of Victoria on Hong Kong Island. Hong Kong Island is the second largest of the colony's many islands. Victoria, the seat of Hong Kong's government, is a blend of the cultures of the East and the West. The colony's emblem displays the British Lion and the Chinese Dragon side-by-side. It is a symbol of a "live-and-let-live" understanding between the British and the Chinese people of Hong Kong.

Sarah lives in an apartment in one of the modern high-rise buildings that have been built on the hillsides of Hong Kong Island. They pierce the sky on the steep slopes of Victoria where land is very scarce. There are few private houses there or anywhere in the colony.

In Hong Kong, Sarah goes to a school much like the one she attended in England. Most of the students are British. But Chinese children and children of other origins go there, too. Teaching is in English, with Chinese taught as a second language.

Sometimes Sarah and her mother do their shopping in Victoria stores that are so British they seem like shops back in London. They also enjoy the Chinese shops on the island and those across the harbor on the Kowloon Peninsula. The city of Kowloon on the Peninsula is even more crowded than Victoria. The two cities face each other across the water.

Sometimes Sarah and her mother drive through the great

underwater tunnel that links the two cities. Sometimes, more to Sarah's liking, they cross the harbors on one of the ferries.

When the government put on a drive to "Keep Hong Kong Clean," Sarah was especially busy. She joined with other children in keeping an eye out for litterbugs. All the children were very careful not to be litterbugs themselves. *Lap Sap Chung,* which is Cantonese for litterbug, was the "enemy." And the people of Hong Kong were out to destroy the "enemy."

Wong Pei and Sarah Jordan represent two of the many faces of Hong Kong. Although the majority of the people speak a language different from those spoken in the Western world, they have a common bond with people everywhere. They share the same enjoyment of learning, of developing interests and hobbies, and of participating in many different kinds of activities.

Understanding What You've Read

1. What country does Hong Kong belong to?
2. What new things did Wong Pei find when she and her family moved to Hong Kong?
3. How is Sarah Jordan's life in Hong Kong similar to her life in London?
4. What things do the people of Hong Kong share with people everywhere?

Applying the Skills Lesson

1. Read again the first paragraph of the selection on page 159. What is the topic? What is the main idea?
2. Read again the first full paragraph in the right-hand column on page 159. Find the sentence that states the main idea.
3. Read again the last paragraph on page 160, which begins, "Pei is in school. . . ." (The paragraph ends on page 161.) Note how the details are related. State the main idea.

Many paragraphs in this selection have stated main ideas. Look for details that support or explain the main ideas.

The power and majesty of "modern" dance thrilled José Limón. From the first time he saw this kind of dance, he decided that . . .

Dance Was His World

by Kathryn Hitte

"As a dancer, he was an eagle."

These words are part of a tribute to the great dancer, José Limón. They aptly describe Limón's noble appearance and his big, graceful, powerful movements on stage—his striking "stage presence." Anyone who has seen him dance would agree. Yet there was a time when even Limón himself would have laughed at such a tribute.

The time was the year 1929. The place was New York City. Young José Limón, over six feet tall and princely in appearance, did not feel at all like a prince. He felt lost. He did not know what he was going to do with his life. He had only recently come to New York to study art. He had wanted very much to be a painter. But what he found at the art school overwhelmed him and threw him into despair.

How can I be a successful painter, he thought, if I don't like the modern trends in art that everyone else admires and tries to follow? He gave away his brushes and gave up his dreams. He moped. He wandered the streets of the city. He tried to unknot the tenseness in his body and mind by running in the park.

Someone suggested that he might consider becoming a dancer. José hooted at the idea. "Dancing is for girls!" he said. For himself—never!

One day some friends lured him into a theater, but they did not tell him what they were going to see. It was a dance program performed by a man.

"What I saw," Limón wrote many years later, ". . . changed my life."

There on the stage before him was a kind of dance that was different from any he had ever seen, a dance full of power and majesty. It used the natural movements of the human body instead of formal, complicated steps. It was called "modern dance," and it reached José Limón at once.

"That's what I want to do!" he exclaimed. And the next day he enrolled in several classes.

He became one of the greatest figures and strongest influences in the modern dance world.

The way to success and greatness was not easy, of course. It rarely is. It took years of devotion and hard work—cruelly strict and demanding work. "Dancing," Limón said, "is tough."

But he was fortunate to have a teacher, Doris Humphrey, who recognized the young man's gifts almost at once and encouraged José to believe in them, too. He spent ten years learning from this great modern dancer. He learned in her classes, in performances with her dance company, and in Broadway shows she choreographed. He discovered the excitement of choreography—the art of planning the movements of a

dance. He began to compose dances and try them out in small public performances at Humphrey's studio.

Finally the time came to strike out on his own. In 1945, with a small group of dancers, he formed his own company. Almost from the start, they met with success. Critics called him the finest and the most important male dancer of his time. Audiences loved him. Schools approached him and asked him to teach.

In the 1950's and 1960's, Limón and his company became known throughout the world. They danced in Mexico City at the invitation of the Mexican government. Limón created new dances for the Mexican National Ballet. He and his company traveled abroad four times under the sponsorship of the United States government. Through their dancing they served as "cultural ambassadors" for America. They gave a special

performance at the White House in Washington. And Limón won almost every dance award that can be won.

What was José Limón like as a person? Gentle, kindly, courteous—a fine man. Through his dancing he expressed warmth, dignity, pride, and strength. He always reached out to other human beings. He put his strongest feelings into his creations. He put his love for people into many dances. He also honored his favorite composers in dance. And his masterpiece, "The Moor's Pavane," [mŏŏrz′ pə·vän′] is his expression in dance form of one of Shakespeare's great plays, *Othello* [ō·thel′ō].

Limón was greatly influenced by Mexican and Native American traditions. His deep respect for his heritage led him to create many dances. Some of these dances were inspired by Mexican history; some, by legend; and

some, by Limón's admiration for the Mexicans of today. Some of these dances were made for his own company and some for the National Ballet of Mexico.

José Limón died in 1972, but the company he founded and led still performs as the José Limón Dance Company. The José Limón Dance Foundation is devoted to continuing his work. It keeps alive not only the dances he created, but also the style of dancing he loved and taught. His former students work with the Limón company and with many other dance companies. Some of the dances he choreographed are now part of the world's "dance literature." In such ways, José Limón has left invaluable gifts to the world.

This is what he always wanted to do. "I simply want to make beauty," he once said in an interview. And that is just what he did.

Understanding What You've Read

1. Why did José Limón decide not to become a painter?
2. How did José Limón become interested in dance?
3. Who was Doris Humphrey?
4. What is the function of the José Limón Dance Foundation?

Applying the Skills Lesson

1. Read the fourth paragraph on page 167 again. Which sentence states the main idea?
2. Find the sentence that states the main idea of the first full paragraph on this page. What details help explain this main idea?

Finding Main Ideas

Paragraphs in textbooks often have main ideas stated in them. In some cases, however, the main idea may not be directly stated.

To find the main idea, first find the topic. Then look for the most important thing that is said about the topic. When the main idea is not stated, think about how the details are related. Then state the main idea in your own words. The sidenotes will help you to find and state the main ideas of the paragraphs.

Finding the Main Idea in Health

Some people get a lot of exercise each day. Some get very little. Scientists have studied both kinds of people to find out how exercise affects their health. The studies show that people who get a great deal of exercise have less heart disease. They also live longer lives. Their bodies have the strength, suppleness, and stamina they need to stay healthy.

> The main idea is not directly stated in this paragraph. Several of the details tell how exercise affects people's health.

How does exercise make your body strong and supple? Lifting, carrying, reaching, and bending make your body work harder than when you are still.

> You can use this question to help you state the main idea of this paragraph.

Your body has to build new tissues and muscles to help you work hard. As this happens, you become stronger. You can reach farther and carry more.

You also become more supple. You can reach and bend more easily.

How does exercise give your body stamina? Walking, running, and other exercises make your body work harder than usual. To do this extra work, your heart has to pump more blood. Your lungs have to take in more air. How would a stronger heart and stronger lungs help you the next time you walk or run?

—*Toward Your Future:* Brown
Harcourt Brace Jovanovich

Building Skills

1. Which of the following sentences best states the main idea of the first paragraph in the selection?

   a. Some people get a lot of exercise every day.
   b. Scientific studies show that people who exercise a lot are stronger and healthier and live longer lives.
   c. People who exercise a lot are very healthy.

2. Read again the second paragraph of the selection. What is the main idea of the paragraph?
3. Read again the last paragraph of the selection. What is the main idea of the paragraph?

Finding the Main Idea in Science

What Do You Call Them?

Every ten years the Census Bureau hires workers to count the people who live in the United States. It is a big job. But an even bigger job would be counting all the one-celled living things in the United States. There are more one-celled living things than all the other living things put together.

Notice that the topic of each of the paragraphs is *one-celled living things*.

Suppose you are hired to count just the single-celled organisms in and around your home. An **organism** is any living thing. First, you need lots of time. Since almost all single-celled organisms are invisible to the unaided eye, you need a microscope.

You can state the main idea of this paragraph by combining all the details: *To count the single-celled organisms around you, you would need lots of time and a microscope.*

Information from the first two sentences will help you state the main idea of this paragraph.

Where would you look for single-celled organisms? Almost anywhere. It would take several days to count those on your skin. It would take months or years to count those in a shovelful of soil. It would be easiest to count the single-celled organisms in the air. Since none of the single-celled organisms have wings, they are probably attached to dust particles or pieces of lint.

—Understanding Your Environment
Silver Burdett

Building Skills

1. The topic of the first paragraph of the selection is *one-celled living things*. Find the sentence that states the main idea of the paragraph.
2. What's the main idea of the third paragraph of the selection? State it in your own words.

Distinguishing Between Important and Unimportant Details

I remembered all the details this time. Pin stripes, straight legs, three buttons, wide lapels, and a vest.

What is a **detail**? A detail is a piece of information. In writing, a detail may be a word, a group of words, or a sentence. Read the following two paragraphs. Notice that they contain many details about the Conestoga wagon.

(1) The chime of the Conestoga's bells and the rumbling of its wheels were familiar sounds along the highways of America during the late 1700's and early 1800's. (2) Thousands of these brightly painted wagons, pulled by powerful horses, moved along the roads. (3) It is believed that the first of these wagons

was built in Pennsylvania's Conestoga Valley, from which they received their name. (4) These large freight carriers, with their curved bottoms and white canvas covers, were often painted red and blue. (5) They could carry five or six tons of freight.

(6) The Conestogas played an important part in American history. (7) They helped to link the East and the West when there were no other kinds of long-distance transportation. (8) During the Revolution, they carried supplies to the American forces. (9) Later they carried settlers to the West. (10) The settlers usually called the wagons "prairie schooners."

What details about the Conestoga wagon are important to a reader? The best answer you could give to this question is: "It depends on the reader's purpose."

Suppose that you want to find out what the Conestoga wagon looked like. Sentence 4 gives details that would suit your purpose. What other sentence gives details about the Conestoga's appearance? The answer is sentence 2.

Now suppose your purpose were to find out what role the

wagon played in American history. Notice that sentences 7, 8, and 9 give details about the wagon's historical importance. Does sentence 10 tell why the wagon was important? No. Although it is an interesting detail, it doesn't suit this purpose.

Not all details are important enough to try to remember. You must decide which ones are important for your purpose.

Try This

Which details in the following paragraph are important if you want to know where the cherry trees in Washington, D.C., came from? Which details are *not* important?

Washington, D.C., is most beautiful in early April. Six hundred fifty cherry trees around the Tidal Basin are in bloom. Their silky white and pale pink blossoms are a joy to visitors' eyes. Hundreds of trees showing deep pink blossoms line the Potomac River. These trees, planted in 1912, were a gift from the Mayor of Tokyo. Many of them began their lives near Tokyo's Arawaka River.

Antonyms

From the Shears Roadhog Catalogue

Check out Shears Roadhog's roller skates for all occasions. Have you ever been embarrassed when someone asked you to a **formal** skating party and you didn't have the right skates to wear? No more! Now Shears has just the skates for those elaborate occasions—solid gold roller skates with whitewall wheels. Each pair has its own AM-FM radio. For informal occasions, we still have our regular skates. When you feel casual, wear these skates and get your music by playing the free comb and tissue paper that come with each pair.

Do you work in an office? Have you ever spilled ink on your nice new clothes? As you know, **permanent** ink stays on forever. Well, Shears Roadhog's Nine to Five Department has the answer. Come see our new temporary clothes. These clothes were made to be worn for a short time only. Each suit or dress is made of newspaper, with several layers of pages. If your clothes get dirty, just rip off the top page. For evening wear, we have clothes made of magazines.

Starting this month, each Shears Roadhog store will open its own pet department. With each pet you buy, Shears will give you a **general** book on the care and feeding of all kinds of pets. Some of the specific animals it discusses are on sale. This month we're featuring these particular animals: boa constrictors, pythons, yaks, wombats, skunks, and blue whales. Come between noon and three on Saturday and watch our sales staff demonstrate how to cheer up those blue whales.

Word Play

1. For each word in Column 1, find an antonym, or word with an opposite meaning, in Column 2. Then choose the correct meaning in Column 3 of the word in Column 1.

1	2	3
formal	specific	lasting forever
general	temporary	not specialized
permanent	informal	requiring elaborate dress and manners

2. Give an antonym for these words from the story: *right, regular, new, dirty*. Use each antonym in a sentence.

**There are many details in this se-
lection. You will not want to remember all of them. Watch for
some of the important details that
tell what Madurodam is, why it
was built, and what it represents.**

THE
MINIATURE
CITY

*Where can you find an entire
"living" city reduced to one
twenty-fifth its normal size?
Look to Madurodam, . . .*

by Elinor Porter Swiger

What would happen if, one night, a whole city were magically covered with a shrinking substance so that, in the morning, all the buildings, people, and cars were reduced to one twenty-fifth their normal size? You can discover just what the result would be if you visit the miniature world of Madurodam in The Hague, capital city of The Nether- lands, or Holland. Here you can walk along two miles of pathways beside small streets lined with buildings the size of dollhouses, and past a harbor filled with tiny boats. You can see wee trucks and cars on a busy mini-highway; an airport with planes the size of toys; and a little castle with a mini-moat, surrounded by bushes the size of your fists and many

flowers as tiny as thumbtacks.

This wonderful world of supersmall structures was built about thirty years ago with funds donated by the parents of a war hero named George Maduro, who died during World War II. It is a memorial enjoyed each day by thousands of children and adults who come here from many different countries.

Madurodam was originally designed to represent, in miniature, an average Dutch city, but much has been added. You can see a small dairy farm complete with tiny cows. You can also see trees in a replica of the world's largest nursery, and scenes from the famous Dutch flower fields.

A large part of Madurodam consists of replicas of real buildings from different Dutch towns. As in most towns, some of the buildings are old and some are new. Two areas of small buildings are like those constructed centuries ago, during the Middle Ages. There is a copy of an old castle called "Voordensteyn" [vōr′dən·stän′] that stood on an island in the south of Holland 1,000 years ago.

Many of the small structures are quite modern. There are glass-walled office buildings, a motel, a shopping center, and an exhibition hall that looks like a flying saucer. One interesting "sight" is the replica of a modern

"traffic garden" like those used in some Dutch cities. A safe park with streets and signals, it is used to teach traffic rules to schoolchildren.

There is a little amusement park that can be activated by putting a coin in the proper slot. There is also a zoo with mini-animals, including an elephant with tusks the size of matches. The small sports park has an American baseball field, tennis courts, and a soccer stadium with floodlights that are tiny but bright enough to light the whole area.

In another area is a waterway where you can see small people on water skis behind tiny speedboats. This is but one of the fascinating sights on the waterway. You can see working models of nearly every type of boat, from small tugs to the great passenger ship, the *Rotterdam.* This model is twenty-seven feet long, complete with every detail needed for the 1,300 passengers the real ship carries. And don't forget to watch the fire boat send tiny streams of water to put out the fire blazing on the tanker in the harbor!

A great part of the fun at Madurodam is watching the "real life" activities. You can see chil-dren fishing with poles the size of toothpicks, mini-bands marching, a repair crew ripping up a small street, and traffic of all kinds moving back and forth.

In fact, watching all this, you will forget that you are in a make-believe world. So you may be shocked when a *real* sparrow lands on a small sailboat, and nearly sinks it—or when a power boat almost runs over a swimming duck! It is a quick reminder of the difference in size between Madurodam and the real world.

No one chases the live birds away, and you'll laugh to see them in funny places. Sitting on the grass beside the mini-bushes, they look like monsters.

If you walk over to visit the miniature railroad yard, you are likely to see a starling attacking a little train signal, pecking first at the green light, then at the red one. The bird flies away quickly, though, when the speedy trains pass through. In addition to the yards, you will see a central station, a suburban station, and several interesting bridges. Blue and yellow Dutch passenger trains and long freight trains speed over six miles of track. Crashes are avoided because of the automatic signal system.

Things are very realistic over on the small superhighway. It is filled with cars and trucks, and accidents do happen there. When there is a crash, a police jeep and an ambulance rush to the scene. Drivers in trouble can call for help at little "talking phones" by the roadside, just like those used on a large Dutch highway nearby.

There are up-to-date communications at the Madurodam airport, too. Here a working public address system relays flight information, and luggage carts move to and from planes painted with the names of all the major world airlines. The scene looks much as it does at the large Schiphol [skip′ōl] Airport near Amsterdam. Representatives of this airport and Dutch KLM Airlines helped build this mini-airport.

There is industry in miniature at Madurodam, too: a lumberyard and sawmill, an oil refinery, and a shipyard. There is a sugar-processing plant, as well as a milk company where the milk from the small farms is taken. You can see a model of a silverware factory, too.

Many of the Madurodam scenes, like the highway and the baseball field, will be familiar to you. But some of the "sights" here will be unfamiliar. For instance, have you ever heard of a "polder"? This is a land area that was once under water. Polders make up a good part of Holland because much of the country is below the level of the sea. For many years the Dutch people worked to find ways to keep their land dry and to "reclaim" land that had been under water so it could be used. All of this was done by building dikes and dams, and by pumping. In the early days, water was drained from the land by windmills. Now it is done with mechanical pumps. At Madurodam you can see models of the pumps, the polders, and the windmills.

A tour of Madurodam with its many typical Dutch scenes is an ideal beginning of a visit to Holland. After seeing the Madurodam miniatures, you probably would be anxious to see the "life-size" originals. Since Holland is a small country, this is quite easy to do.

Understanding What You've Read

1. What is Madurodam?
2. What does the author mean by saying you can see "real life" activities at Madurodam? What are some of these activities?
3. What are two old things you can see at Madurodam? What are two modern things?
4. How is Madurodam like a city you know? How is Madurodam different?

Applying the Skills Lesson

1. Read again the first three paragraphs of the selection on pages 181 and 182. Tell which sentence is important if your purpose is:

   a. to find out where Madurodam is
   b. to know why it was built
   c. to know what it represents

2. Which of the following details from the selection would you consider important if you wanted to remember some of the unusual sights in Madurodam?

   a. Madurodam is located in Holland.
   b. There is a replica of a "traffic garden"—a park with streets and signals that is used to teach traffic rules to schoolchildren.
   c. On the waterway you can see working models of nearly every type of boat, from small tugs to the great passenger ship, the *Rotterdam.*
   d. Madurodam has models of the pumps and windmills that were used to drain water from the land.
   e. Thousands of children and adults come to Madurodam from different countries.

Beatrice Medicine tells about herself in . . .

MY WORLD: PEOPLE!

by Beatrice Medicine

As an anthropologist, my work requires me to study people. On my job I travel all over the world and watch how people work, play, and get along together. I learn about people's music, art, and ideas about living.

Ever since I was a young girl, I loved hearing stories. The ones I really liked were from faraway places. My father served in World War I, and from him I learned of his experiences in England, France, and Germany. The stories he told used to delight me because I always liked to know about people in other places.

187

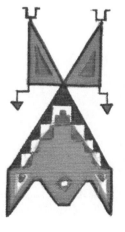

I am a Lakota Sioux, born on Standing Rock
Reservation in South Dakota. In the Lakota lan-
guage my name means Returns-Victorious-with-a-
Beautiful-Red-Horse-Woman. In English it is
Beatrice Medicine. Medicine is the name of my
father and grandfather.

My parents were very interested in learning,
and they helped all their children to enjoy the
Lakota language, as well as English. They both did
crossword puzzles, told stories in Lakota, and read
to all of us.

In public school, storytelling was my favorite

time because I liked to tell stories about my people, the Sioux. My classmates told about their families from parts of the world as far away as Russia, Germany, and Sweden. Hearing how other people lived in different parts of the world was exciting for me.

My first real knowledge about anthropology was from my mother's cousin, Ella Deloria. Almost every summer during my childhood, she came to visit my family to collect language materials and folktales and legends of the Lakota people. She was working with the well-known American anthropologist, Franz Boas [bō′az]. I already had some idea of the kind of work Aunt Ella was doing. Although anthropologists study about all people all over the world, Aunt Ella studied about one specific group of people. Aunt Ella's work was one of the things that aroused my curiosity and ambition to learn how groups of people were the same and how they were different.

A favorite high school teacher of mine encouraged us to interview our parents and grandparents and other elders living nearby. This was a good start for me to find out how a group of people living together in one area share common interests. We published an edition of our high school paper with folktales, stories, and legends about my area of Standing Rock Reservation.

In order to attend college, I had to borrow money. The government agency that lent the money advised me to study something more "practical" than anthropology. So I majored in home economics. When I went away to college, it was the first time that I was away from my family.

At college my closest friend was my roommate. Many times I spent weekends at her family's home in a nearby town. Those weekends not only were

very pleasant, but also served to help me observe
cultural differences. From these pleasant times I
began to learn about the life styles of different
people.

Upon graduation in 1945, I started teaching.
After that I accepted a job in Michigan as a health
lecturer. While teaching, I was able to continue my
education. In 1954, I received my master's degree
in sociology and anthropology. My dream was realized—I became an anthropologist.

In 1948, I married a fellow graduate student,
James Garner, whom I met at the University of
New Mexico. A son was born to us in 1957.

From 1959 until 1967, I lived with my family in
Canada. After returning to the United States, I
started work toward my Ph.D. degree. I did some
more teaching at many colleges, which I found
rewarding. I have also kept in close touch with the

community in which I was born and with several American Indian organizations.

Of all the groups of people that I studied, my own people, the American Indians, interest me the most. My work has brought me to Germany, Peru, and Italy, where I have presented professional papers. In all my professional writing, I have tried to show our life styles as they really are. My teaching and research and writing is for everyone all over the world to understand and, I hope, respect.

Understanding What You've Read

1. What does Beatrice Medicine do in her work as an anthropologist?
2. How did Beatrice first become interested in anthropology?
3. What group does Beatrice say interests her the most?

Applying the Skills Lesson

Which of the following details would be important if you wanted to remember what influenced Beatrice Medicine's choice of career?

1. Her father told stories about his experiences in other countries.
2. Her mother's cousin, Ella Deloria, collected language materials, folktales, and legends of the Lakota people.
3. In high school, she was encouraged to interview her parents and other elders.
4. She studied home economics in college.
5. She spent many weekends with her college roommate's family.

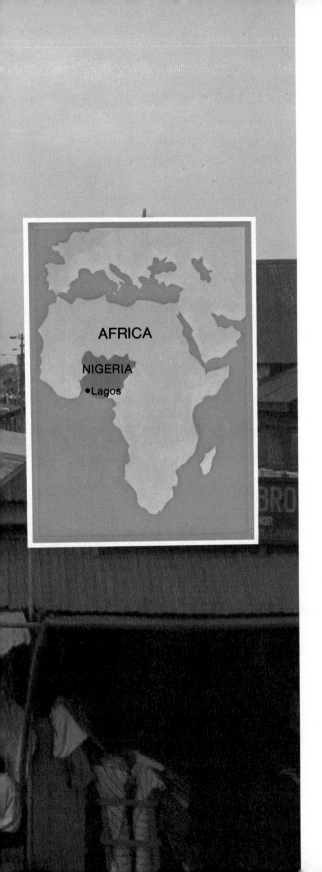

The author tells many details about events in the life of a young girl named Iyabo in Lagos, Nigeria. Look for those details that tell about school, games, and work to help you understand Iyabo's life.

Spinning cone shells in the sand, playing games with Uncle Ereko, eating Grandmother Adekunle's snacks—these are some things Iyabo did . . .

AT HOME IN LAGOS

by
Rhoda Omosunlola Johnston

Bronze head, dating from the 12th century. From Ife, Nigeria.

My family has lived a long time in Lagos, Nigeria. We are part of a group of people called Yoruba.

My parents, and their parents, were born and brought up and married in Lagos, the great capital city of Nigeria. The first child born in my family was a girl named Ibironke [ē'bē·rôn·kā'], who is two years older than I. I have two younger brothers, Olanrewa [ō'län·rā'wä] and Olayimika [ô'lī·ə·mē'kä].

My parents and family gave me many names, as is our custom, one of which is Iyabo [ē·yä'bō], meaning "Mother returns." I was named after my father's mother, whom everyone said I resembled so much.

My childhood was a happy one, with devoted parents and many wonderful relatives, friends, and neighbors. Those years were pleasant, fun, and work-filled ones.

My father was a teacher in one of the primary schools in the city. I was used to seeing him read, write, and study long before I was old enough to start school. My sister, Ibironke, taught me nursery rhymes and songs, and my mother taught me her rich store of Yoruba proverbs and wise sayings.

Mother was self-employed as a small trader. She set her wares in a sort of cupboard with shelves in it. This was built at the front of our house. I used to enjoy helping her arrange her soap, salt, and other things on the shelves in the morning and pack them away every evening.

School and Friends and Uncle Ereko

I made many friends in school. We had many subjects and I learned a lot. After the third year of school, great importance was attached to learning the English language. I liked studying history and geography and literature. I enjoyed reading for pleasure in both Yoruba and English. From my many teachers and friends, I learned important lessons, which I still cherish today.

Uncle Ereko [ā'rā·kō'], a younger brother of my father's, was a kind-hearted man. He had lived all his life in the Ereko area of Lagos, which is in the commercial part of the city. Uncle Ereko would join us in our games or take time to tell us fascinating stories, endless jokes, riddles, and old Nigerian tales.

Uncle Ereko first introduced us to some of the traditional games of Yorubaland. "Spinning the Cone Shell" was one of the popular ones. The cone-shaped shell of one kind of snail found in Nigeria was used. Uncle Ereko showed us how to give it a sharp twist and set it in motion so the shell would spin on its point. This game was usually played in the sand.

Bronze leopard, dating from the 16th century. From the Kingdom of Benin, situated in what is now Nigeria.

Grandmother Adekunle

My mother's mother was quite a remarkable woman. Her name was Hannah Olufummilayo Adekunle [ô·lōō′fuom·mē′lä·yō ä′dē·kun′lā]. She was quite old when I knew her, but she was still strong, smart, and charming.

Grandmother Adekunle was a trader in Lagos. Her stall was in the market near her home, and every morning she carried her wares there and arranged them attractively. She spent all day at the market, selling and visiting with people. Then at night she packed her items into boxes and carried them home—a half mile away.

Grandmother Adekunle was president of the local Bead Seller Association. In her stall she sold more beads than anything else. However, she also offered sewing thread, needles, sponges, soap, tinned goods, laundry bluing, and other items.

There was always a great deal of activity in the market, and we enjoyed visiting Grandmother Adekunle there. Yoruba markets are established for buying and selling, but they are also social centers where advertisements are announced.

Special Times

In our school system, qualifying tests and examinations were given free before promotion. Our class teacher warned us that we would not be allowed to take the School Leaving Certificate Examination if we failed the qualifying test. The certificate opened the gates to good jobs and higher education. Much praise and honor awaited the fortunate candidates. I was studying one night for this important examination when my father's relatives from a village twenty-five miles from Lagos came to visit us. They were tired and hungry. Mother had an idea. She would buy cooked bean stew from a seller who worked nearby and sold her product piping hot. Mother asked me to go out and buy stew for each of the cousins. She handed me a coin.

As I was about to pay the bean seller, I discovered the coin was missing. I became upset. I just couldn't return home and tell Mother that the coin was lost. The tears began to flow, and I felt very sorry for myself.

I was searching for the coin under the dim electric street light when I heard the sound of a bicycle bell. I looked up and saw a young man watching me search, so I explained what I was looking for. He offered his help, which I accepted. With his bicycle lamp we were able to find the coin. I was most grateful and thanked him sincerely for his help.

I paid for the bean stew and brought it back home. Our relatives enjoyed the stew and were very appreciative. I tried to return to my studies, but I could not concentrate. I kept wondering about the helpful stranger. Finally, I went to sleep.

Two weeks later I received a letter from Olufemi Ajayi [ô·lōō′fä·mē ä·jä·yē′], the young man who had helped me find the coin. The letter explained how he had met someone who knew me and that that person gave him my name and address. In the letter he asked if he could come to the house to see me. We finally met and became good friends.

I studied very hard for the school examination. I passed this lengthy test and was awarded the important School Leaving Certificate. At that time I was eighteen years old. I then went to work in an office.

Later on, I married Olufemi. From then on, Olufemi and I were on our own. Both of our parents had done their best for us. We could not ask for more. They left us to ourselves to make the best and the most of our lives together.

Understanding What You've Read

1. What were some of the things Iyabo learned as a young child from her sister and from her mother?
2. What is "Spinning the Cone Shell"?
3. Why does Iyabo say that Grandmother Adekunle was a remarkable woman?
4. What was the importance of the School Leaving Certificate?

Applying the Skills Lesson

Which of the following details would be important if you wanted to remember some things about Yoruba life?

1. It is a custom to give children many names.
2. History, geography, and literature are taught in school.
3. One of the traditional games of the Yoruba people is "Spinning the Cone Shell."
4. Yoruba markets were established for buying and selling.

Recognizing Important Details

Which details in textbooks are important? The answer depends on your purpose in reading. If you have specific questions to answer, you will need to pay close attention to details that will help you answer those questions. If your purpose is to remember generally what a textbook selection is about, you will need to look for main ideas. The important details, then, would be those that can help you understand the main ideas.

As you read the following selections, refer to the sidenotes. They will help you focus on main ideas and important details.

Recognizing Important Details in Social Studies

Tame animals work for people. The ox and the donkey may have been the first animals trained to carry and pull loads in northern Africa and western Asia. In India and China, people tamed water buffalo at a very early time. These slow, gentle animals still give much of the animal power in India and Southeast Asia. The water buffalo have sometimes been called the "living tractors of the East."

This is the main idea. The next two sentences give important details about which animals were tamed and where.

This is the main idea. Which detail is *most* important if you want to remember the result of people's using animal power?

The taming of the ox, donkey, and water buffalo gave people extra power. No longer did people have to depend on their own muscles only. An ox or a water buffalo could be hitched to a plow. It could take the place of a person with a hoe. By using animal power, people could do more work.

In time, horses became one of the most useful of the working animals. But the first tame horses were used for war rather than work. The earliest horse tamers lived in Central Asia. They hitched their horses to light, two-wheeled chariots. In these they charged their enemies on the field of battle. It is easy to understand why men on foot would run when a thundering team of horses pulling a chariot bore down on them.

Which detail will help you remember this main idea?

The horse was not used much in the fields or for pulling heavy carts. People had no way of harnessing a horse's full strength. A horse cannot pull with yokes like those used for an ox. A horse's shoulders are not broad enough. Straps fastened about its neck tend to choke it when it pulls a heavy load. When someone invented the padded horse collar, people had a way of using horses for heavy work.

—People and Change
Silver Burdett

Building Skills

1. Read again the third paragraph of the selection. Which details are important if your purpose is to learn:

    a. what tame horses were first used for
    b. where the first horse tamers lived
    c. how people used horses for war

2. Suppose you were only interested in what made it possible for people to use horses for heavy work. What detail from the selection would be important to you?

Recognizing Important Details in Science

A female snake lays her eggs in a hole in the ground or in between rocks. These eggs are covered with a leathery shell. The shell helps protect the growing snake embryos from other animals and the weather. Why do you think growing snake embryos need to be protected from these things?

Which detail will help you remember this main idea?

Though the embryos of many kinds of snakes grow inside eggs, the embryos of some kinds of snakes grow inside the body of their mother. Snakes which grow inside their mother are born live.

The details in this paragraph tell how snakes get out of a shell.

In about two months, the growing snakes become too big for their shell. This causes the shell to crack. The snakes break their shell further with a small egg tooth which sticks out from their jaw. Once the young snakes are out of their shell, they shed the egg tooth.

After young snakes shed their egg tooth, they look very much like adult snakes. The young snakes also do many things that adult snakes do. For example, young snakes find their own food and protect themselves from enemies. During very hot days, snakes sleep in dens under rocks or under the ground. During the winter, snakes hibernate.

Look for details that tell about the behavior of young snakes.

Though young snakes are able to do many of the same things adult snakes do, very few young snakes live to be adults. Those young snakes that do live become adults when they are about two to three years old. Adult snakes may live to be about twenty years old. Why do you think few young snakes live to become adults?

—*Exploring Science:* Red Book
Laidlaw Brothers

Building Skills

1. Suppose that you were only interested in the *behavior of snakes.* Which of the following details would be important to your purpose?

   a. Young snakes look like adult snakes.
   b. Young snakes find their own food and protect themselves from enemies.
   c. During very hot days, snakes sleep in dens under rocks or under the ground.
   d. Snakes hibernate during the winter.
   e. Snake eggs are covered with a leathery shell.

2. Suppose you were only interested in *how long snakes live.* Which detail from the selection would be important to your purpose?

203

SKILLS LESSON

Topical Organization and Outlining

ZOO

If you were the zookeeper, how would you organize the zoo? You'd most likely have a section for all the big cats. And you'd probably plan to use one section of the zoo for birds and another for snakes and other reptiles.

Authors, like smart zookeepers, also organize their work. Sometimes, they organize articles according to topics. Suppose an author wanted to write about winged animals. He or she might organize the topics as the following outline shows:

Winged Creatures

I. Flying insects
   A. Two-winged insects
      1. Houseflies
      2. Mosquitoes
   B. Four-winged insects
      1. Dragonflies
      2. Beetles
      3. Bees and wasps
II. Birds
   A. Flying birds
   B. Flightless birds
      1. Ostriches
      2. Penguins
      3. Emus
III. Flying mammals
   A. Bats
   B. Squirrels

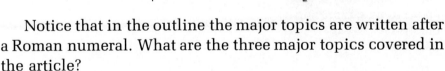

Notice that in the outline the major topics are written after a Roman numeral. What are the three major topics covered in the article?

Two subtopics are included under the major topic *Flying insects: Two-winged insects* and *Four-winged insects*. Before each is a capital letter. What subtopics are covered under the major topic *Birds*? Under *Flying mammals*?

Look at *Flightless birds* in part II of the outline. Under this subtopic, the author gives three examples of flightless birds: *Ostriches, Penguins,* and *Emus.* An Arabic numeral on an outline generally shows an example or a detail. What examples of two-winged insects are given under subtopic A of part I? What examples of four-winged insects are given under subtopic B of part I? Are any examples of flying birds given under subtopic A of part II?

Making Your Own Outline

When you read an article or a chapter of a book, a good way to remember what you've read is to make an outline from it. Read the following article. It is organized by topics. The sidenotes will help you to see this organization. Once you understand the organization of ideas, you can make an outline.

Stinging Insects: Friends or Foes?

The first two paragraphs introduce the article.

You're happily sitting at a picnic table, munching a hot dog. Suddenly you hear a loud buzzing noise. Oh oh. Uninvited guests—yellow jackets!

This paragraph gives you an idea of the major topics that are about to be covered in the article—*wasps* and *bees*.

Yellow jackets are one kind of wasp. Wasps are stinging insects. Bees are another kind of stinging insect. Most people fear these tiny creatures. They don't know that many stinging insects help us.

This paragraph and the next three are about wasps. What kind of wasp is covered in the first two paragraphs? What details are given?

Yellow jackets are about the size of a paper clip. Like their larger cousins, the bumblebees, they have yellow and black stripes. Yellow jackets' bodies, however, are smooth, while bumblebees' bodies are fuzzy.

The yellow jackets that ruined

Yellow jacket wasp.

Paper wasps and nest.

Bumblebee.

your picnic were attracted by odors. Perhaps they liked the smell of your hot dog or the sweet soda in the open bottle on your table. Watch out! Don't hit at them or move quickly. Yellow jackets are quick to defend themselves by stinging.

Another kind of wasp is sometimes mistakenly called a "queen yellow jacket" because it is twice the size of a yellow jacket. This is the European hornet. It is really yellow and *brown* — not black.

Paper wasps are another of the stinging insects you have probably seen. Paper wasps often live under the eaves of buildings. Like yellow jackets

Yellow jacket wasp.

What kind of wasp is covered in this paragraph? What details are given?

Worker honeybee.

The third kind of wasp is described in this paragraph. What details about paper wasps are given?

Notice that the topic has changed from wasps to bees. How many kinds of bees are mentioned?

Honeybee.

and European hornets, paper wasps make nests from wood mixed with their own saliva. These little brown and black insects are very useful to farmers and gardeners. They eat many harmful insects.

The yellow and black bumblebee is the largest of the bees. Like the yellow jacket and European hornet, it makes its nest underground. The bumblebee has an important place in nature. It carries pollen from one flower to another. In this way, it helps flowers to reproduce. Many flowers—like red clover—would not be around at all if it weren't for the bumblebee.

Smaller than the bumblebee, the honeybee is also a good pollen carrier. But it is best known because it makes honey. Honeybees make more honey than they could ever use themselves. In wooded areas, honeybees make their homes in hollow trees. Bears often find the hives and eat the honey. On honey "farms," beekeepers keep many wooden boxes that the bees use as hives. Beekeepers sell their honey.

Making an outline of the article you just read can help you remember the information in it. What is the topic of the whole article? The topic is *stinging insects.* This is your outline's title. What major topics are covered in the article? What are the subtopics? What details are given?

Try This

Use the following partly filled-in outline to help you make your own outline. You can also refer back to the sidenotes that go with the article, if you need to.

Stinging Insects

I. Wasps
   A. _____
      1. Yellow and black stripes
      2. Smooth bodies the size of a paper clip
      3. _____
      4. _____
   B. European hornet
      1. Mistakenly called "queen yellow jacket"
      2. Twice the size of a yellow jacket
   C. _____
      1. _____
      2. _____
      3. _____
      4. _____

II. _____
   A. _____
      1. Largest of the bees
      2. Yellow and black
      3. Nest underground (like yellow jacket and European hornet)
      4. _____
   B. _____
      1. Smaller than bumblebees
      2. Good pollen carriers
      3. Make great amounts of honey
      4. Make hives in hollow trees
      5. Kept by beekeepers on honey "farms"

VOCABULARY STUDY

Getting Meaning from Context Clues

PLINKER'S BUILDING INSTALLS STATUE

by Claudia Sanchez

HANKSVILLE, December 20—Crowds gathered despite heavy rain yesterday to witness the placement of the new sculpture in front of the Plinker's Building on Main Street.

At 4 P.M., a huge crane drove up next to the **pedestal**, or base, that will support the statue. The huge pedestal, which was placed here two weeks ago, is an exact copy of one from ancient Greece. This **replica** so exactly matches its Greek model, and is so large, that the crowd was breathless as it awaited the appearance of a **gigantic** Greek sculpture. The people watched with wonder as workers gathered around the crane. What was the object they attached to the hook? Cries of amazement went up as a **miniature** elephant was lifted into place. The tiny sculpture was no more than twenty centimeters high.

Word Play

A context clue is a word or phrase that hints at the meaning of a word. Use context clues to help you select the correct definition for each word below. Then use each word in a sentence.

1. **pedestal:** (a) a crane (b) a base for a statue (c) a machine with pedals
2. **replica:** (a) an exact copy (b) an outdoor monument (c) a large, ancient building
3. **gigantic:** (a) small (b) beautiful (c) large
4. **miniature:** (a) large (b) very small (c) manufactured

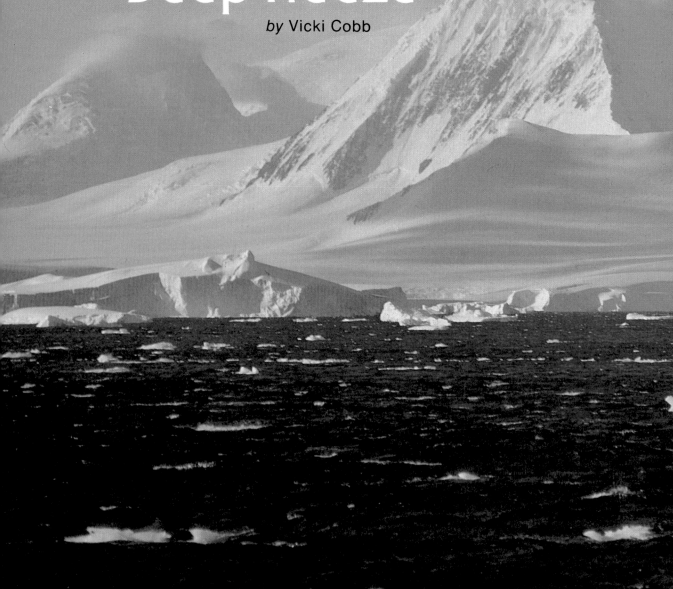

As you read, notice how the author has organized her information. Look for changes in major topics. The subheadings will help you.

For some people, the coldest parts of the Earth are an invitation to adventure and new knowledge. Find out why people would want to go to . . .

The Earth's Deep Freeze

by Vicki Cobb

Your winter clothes won't keep you warm very long at the coldest place on Earth—Antarctica. It's so cold there that it's hard to tell whether today is colder or warmer than yesterday.

The Climate

In 1960, an alcohol thermometer was used to record the lowest temperature ever found anywhere on Earth: 127°F below zero. It was recorded about one thousand miles from the South Pole in the heart of Antarctica. At such low temperatures, rubber breaks like glass and a steel bar can snap in two.

Antarctica is famous for its winds as well as its cold. The wind there usually blows at about fifty miles an hour. That's strong enough to lift the tops off some chimneys. Buildings in Antarctica are built close to the ground to prevent damage by high winds.

Of course, the South Pole is never spoiled by rain. In fact, it hardly ever snows there. Only about two inches of snow fall every year. That's not even enough for good sledding! But wait. It never gets warm enough for snow to melt. For millions of years snow has piled up. As the weight of new snow presses on snowfalls of the past, old snow changes into ice. Today, Antarctica is covered with a pile of ice—topped with snow—that is almost two miles high in many places. No wonder scientists and Navy personnel who work here call the Antarctic continent "the ice."

The Seasons

At the South Pole, "the bottom of the world," there are really only two seasons, a long winter and a short summer. They are not like the seasons you probably know. There are no trees to blossom and lose their leaves. And it is always cold.

Winter and summer at the South Pole are as different as night and day. In fact, they *are* night and day. The end of winter comes around September 21 when the sun rises. For six months the sun never sets.

People there think of November, December, and January as

summer. That's the working season when, day by day, the sun gets higher in the sky until it's high enough to warm things up a bit. The nine-month winter begins as the sun gets lower. Around March 21 the sun sets, bringing the heart of the Antarctic winter. For six long months there is only night at the South Pole. Bitter cold and howling winds rule the ice. It's not the time many dare make a visit.

If you visited the South Pole, you would probably come on an Antarctic summer day. It feels almost like another world here, not a part of the Earth we call home. The cloudless summer sky is very blue. You are surrounded by a bright field of snow that stretches as far as you can see, like a frozen desert. The sunlight looks as it does at three in the afternoon at home. But here the height of the sun doesn't give you a clue to

what time it is. It never gets any higher or lower in the sky all day. It simply moves around the sky in a circle, as bright at midnight as it is at noon.

On this day it is about 19°F below zero, about average for summer. As you look around, you see a cloud of ice crystals suddenly appear in the air and sparkle like diamonds in the sunlight. This happens only in very cold, dry air.

Air where you live has water in it. You can't see this water because it is in the form of a gas. Extra water in air can be "squeezed out" as droplets in the form of dew or fog. Warm air can hold a great deal of water vapor before droplets form. But at Antarctic temperatures, air can hardly hold any water at all. Moisture that escapes into the air from the surface of the snow is squeezed out and frozen instantly in clouds of glittering ice crystals. Moisture from your breath also crackles and freezes the instant it meets the cold, dry polar air.

The "Call" of Antarctica: Glaciers

It is not beautiful scenery that brings people to Antarctica. It is not ice crystals in the air. It is not the hotels. (There are none.) And it is certainly not the weather. People come to Antarctica to learn. Many nations have agreed to share Antarctica peacefully. Scientists come here from all over the world to unlock the mysteries of nature's deep freeze.

There are secrets in the ice. Great masses of ice, called glaciers, once covered much of the Earth. Glaciers creep over land like heavy, slow-moving rivers. They drag along rocks that scratch the land like giant fingernails. They push soil around like monster bulldozers. When they melt, they leave behind hills of rock and soil.

Most of the glaciers that once covered the Earth are gone. We know of them from scars and rocks they left behind. But these scars can teach us only a small amount about the ways of glaciers, just as footprints can only teach us a little about the animals that left them. To

understand how glaciers change the face of the Earth, scientists want to study the real thing. Antarctica is one of the few places left on Earth where they can see a glacier in action.

The glaciers of Antarctica also hold a key to Earth's history. Layers of ice, laid down year after year, have a message scientists can read. They can tell scientists when the Earth was warm and when it grew colder. Air from millions of years ago is trapped in the ice. Scientists drill into the glaciers for ice samples to study the past.

Under the ice, if you drill deep enough, there is land. It is the Antarctic continent, which is as large as the United States and Mexico together. Scientists have found the preserved remains of tropical

215

plants and animals in Antarctic soil. This discovery can only mean that once, millions of years ago, Antarctica was warm. Scientists believe that somehow the Antarctic land mass drifted to the bottom of the Earth from a place farther north. They know that other land masses on Earth have moved and are still moving. (But they are moving so slowly you would never notice it.) By learning more about the movement of Antarctica, we add to our knowledge of the shifting positions of other parts of the Earth.

Other "Calls" of Antarctica

Scientists also come to the South Pole to study the strange lights that glow overhead during the Antarctic night. (It's a cold and lonely world for the few hardy people who "winter over" the polar night.) These "southern lights" are caused by the Earth acting like a magnet on electrical particles in the air. They are clues that may help us understand the Earth's core and the upper edges of its blanket of air.

Even pollution is a reason for scientists to come to Antarctica. Air and water pollution from other parts of the world come here in

wind and ocean currents. By measuring pollution here, scientists can see how fast it is spreading around the world.

Although Antarctica is bitterly cold and dry, it is not lifeless. Penguins and seals raise families on its rocky shores. Fish and small plants live in its icy seas. Perhaps their secrets of survival can help us survive better. It's something some scientists are looking into.

Scientists come to learn. But they need housing, heat, food, and contact with the rest of the world. So others come to provide these services. Cargo ships arrive with supplies. Planes bring visitors and supplies to inland areas. People from newspapers and magazines come to do stories about the work going on here.

But everyone who comes, from scientist to radio operator to cook, has another reason deep inside. Going to Antarctica is an adventure. It is dangerous. Many of the first voyagers to come here died. Visitors—and everyone here is only a visitor—feel that they are following in the footsteps of the first brave explorers. Deep inside, everyone has a question that waits for an answer. You too may wonder, "Can I face danger and handle it well?" Antarctica is one place where an answer can be found.

Understanding What You've Read

1. Why is there so much snow in Antarctica?
2. Why does the author say that the two seasons in Antarctica are probably not like the seasons you know?
3. What are some of the reasons why scientists go to Antarctica?
4. Why do scientists want to study glaciers?
5. How do scientists know that Antarctica was once warm?

Applying the Skills Lesson

1. Which of the following titles is best for an outline of the selection you just read?

   Antarctica   The Cold Continent
   The Earth's Deep Freeze

2. Below is a list of the four major topics in the selection. Put them in the order in which they occurred.

   Glaciers   Why People Come to Antarctica
   Seasons   Climate

3. Choose *one* of the major topics above and make an outline for it. Use capital letters to list subtopics. Use numerals to list details.

Topical Organization and Outlining

Textbook authors usually organize their information by topics. Making an outline of the important ideas and details can help you understand an author's organization and remember the information. The outline helps you to see major topics, subtopics, and details.

As you read the following selection, refer to the sidenotes. They will help you understand the author's organization so that you can make an outline.

Topical Organization and Outlining in Social Studies

A Human Being's Third Greatest Need

As you know, human beings around the world do things very differently. Preparing food is one such thing. Foods around the world look, smell, and taste different. Human beings also call their foods by different names. How many of the following names of foods do you recognize? What are they made of?

> **Why is this *not* a good title for your outline? Read to find out what a human being's third greatest need is.**

> **This paragraph introduces the topic of food. The important ideas about why people need food are covered in later sections of this selection.**

pasta	sauerkraut
tortilla	filet mignon
borscht	sukiyaki
salami	bagel
curd	pemmican
poi	cassava

This paragraph tells you two important ideas: (1) that food can be broken down into three kinds of food or nourishment, and (2) that people need *all* three kinds of food.

Look at each sub-heading in italics. What do foods do for people?

This paragraph tells about *two* of the three kinds of food — *carbohydrates* and *fats.* What are some of the sources of these substances? Look for details in this paragraph and the next one.

If you were able to analyze these foods, you'd find that they broke down into three basic kinds of **nourishment.** Just as all people need oxygen and water, they all need three kinds of food.

Foods for Energy

Human beings get **energy** from substances called **carbohydrates** and **fats.** When you eat grains, such as rice and wheat, you get carbohydrates. They are also provided by starchy roots like potatoes or cassava. Cassava is called "the staff of life" in parts of Africa. Sugar is another source of carbohydrates. The white stuff you sprinkle on cereal comes from sugar cane or sugar beets. But you also get sugar from many other foods. For example, raisins, honey, and even onions all give you sugar.

Here you see a few of the ways in which people around the world prepare food.

Fats have the highest energy value. Americans get most of their fats from meat, cream, butter, margarine, and nuts. In the body, fats are changed to fatty tissue. About 15 percent of a healthy body is fatty tissue. It helps keep you warm and protects delicate parts of the body.

Foods for Growth and Repair of Body Cells

The foods called **proteins** build bones, muscles, and skin. Meat, fish, poultry, cheese, and milk give you protein. So do beans, peas, and nuts. Even after a person is fully grown, he or she still needs protein. Can you guess why?

> **What is the third kind of food people need? What are some of the sources of *protein*?**

Vitamins and Minerals

Foods also give you **vitamins** and **minerals.** These perform important jobs in the body. Such minerals as iron and copper help form red blood cells. Another mineral, calcium, is needed for healthy bones and teeth.

> **Notice that this paragraph is *not* about another kind of food. It tells what foods do for people.**

— The Way People Live
Houghton Mifflin

Building Skills

Using the sidenotes in this selection as a guide, make an outline of the major topics, subtopics, and important details. Remember to use Roman numerals.

Books About the World Around Us

Margaret Mead: Student of the Global Village by Carol B. Church. Greenhaven, 1976. The life, work, and adventures of this great anthropologist are told about in this book.

Children Are Children Are Children: An Activity Approach to Exploring Brazil, France, Iran, Japan, Nigeria, and the U.S.S.R. by Ann Cole and others. Atlantic-Monthly Press — Little, 1978. You'll find out what it's like to be a child growing up in another part of the world.

In Our Carib Indian Village by Faustulus Joseph Frederick and Elizabeth Shepherd. Lothrop, 1971. Faustulus is a Dominican boy. He tells how the people of the West Indies live, work, and play.

The Boy Who Sailed Around the World Alone by Robin L. Graham and Derek Gill. Golden Press, Western Pub., 1973. When he was sixteen years old, Robin sailed around the world alone. This book tells of his adventures.

It's a Model World by Suzanne Hilton. Westminster, 1972. You'll find out how scale models are used for both scientific research and pleasure.

We All Come from Puerto Rico Too by Julia Singer. Atheneum, 1977. You'll get a special view of the many different things people do in Puerto Rico.

The New Moon by Herbert S. Zim. Morrow, 1980. Findings from materials collected on the moon are presented and fitted into an overall picture of the moon as scientists now know it.

Part 4

Flights of Fantasy

UNDERSTANDING AND APPRECIATING LITERATURE

Fantasy

The man in the cartoon has a problem. Look at picture 1. A bad driver has hit the man's car from behind. Look at picture 2. What surprises you? The driver of the car isn't a person — it's a giraffe.

Cartoons and stories both have characters, a plot, and a setting. Both are fiction. What does this cartoon have that many stories do not? One character in the cartoon is an animal. A giraffe driving a car is not real; it is fantasy. The cartoon deals with fantasy, or make-believe.

Understanding Fantasy

Look at the cartoon again. What things are real, or true-to-life, in the story? Two cars, two drivers, a stop sign, and an intersection are all real objects, characters, or places. What is make-believe in the story? A giraffe driving a car is something you would see only in fantasy. A fictional story that involves people or animals, objects, places, and events, some of which are real and some of which are make-believe, is called a **fantasy.**

Read the following fantasy.

> In the wintertime the Rat slept a great deal, retiring early and rising late. During his short day he sometimes scribbled poetry or did other small, domestic jobs about the house; and, of course, there were always other animals dropping in for a chat, and consequently, there was a good deal of story-telling and comparing notes on the past summer and all its doings.

How do you know that this story is a fantasy? The character, a rat, and the activities the rat takes part in — scribbling poetry, doing chores around the house, and exchanging stories and talking with his animal friends — are unrealistic and tell you the story is a fantasy.

A story setting can also be a clue to fantasy. What clues in the story below, from Lewis Carroll's *Alice in Wonderland*, tell you that it is a fantasy?

> To punish the kitten, Alice held it up to the looking glass. "If you're not good directly," she added, "I'll put you through into Looking-Glass House. Oh Kitty!" Alice exclaimed. "How nice it could be if only we could get through into Looking-Glass House! Let's pretend the glass has got all soft, like gauze, so we can get through. Why, it's turning into a sort of

mist now, I declare! It'll be easy to get through." And certainly the glass *was* beginning to melt away, just like a bright silvery mist. In another moment Alice was through the glass and had jumped down lightly into the Looking-Glass room.

How can you tell the story is a fantasy? The setting — the Looking-Glass room — is a clue. Another clue is the way in which Alice gets through the mirror into the Looking-Glass room. The author simply has the mirror turn into a mist, and Alice passes through it. The setting and the way Alice gets through the mirror tell you that this story is a fantasy.

The plot of a story can be another clue that the story is a fantasy. Even when the characters or setting seems real, what happens in the story can be pure fantasy. Some fantasies have plots about flights through space, voyages underground, or journeys backward or forward in time. Look for the make-believe parts in the following paragraph.

Sue and Bill ran through the galaxy chasing the rocket-thief. Their laser gear wouldn't work in this time warp. What could they do? Suddenly, Sue had an idea. She activated their magnetic field-finder. The rocket-thief stopped in his tracks, unable to move past the magnetic cage.

What tells you that this paragraph is a fantasy? The setting is one clue. It is in outer space — a galaxy. The plot is another clue. Sue and Bill are trying to stop the rocket-thief, but their laser gear will not work, so Sue activates a magnetic field-finder. The thief can't move.

Remember, fantasy is a special kind of fiction whose characters, setting, or plot is make-believe. In fantasy, you can meet strange characters, step into strange worlds, and listen in on strange conversations. Perhaps even more importantly, you learn new things about the real world.

Try This

Read the following story. Then answer the questions.

Alice was beginning to get tired of sitting. Suddenly a White Rabbit with pink eyes ran by her.

There was nothing so *very* remarkable in that nor did Alice think it so *very* much out of the way to hear the Rabbit say to itself, "Oh dear! I shall be too late!" (When she thought it over, it occurred to her that she ought to have wondered at this, but at the time it seemed quite natural.) But when the Rabbit actually *took a watch out of its waistcoat-pocket* and looked at it, and then hurried on, Alice jumped up. It crossed her mind that she had never seen a rabbit with either a waistcoat-pocket, or a watch to take out of it. Full of curiosity, she ran after it, only to see it pop down a large rabbit-hole. In another moment, Alice followed it, never once considering how she would get out again.

1. What parts of the story are make-believe—the characters? the setting? the plot?
2. Explain how these parts are fantasy.

Writing

1. Imagine that you could step through the Looking-Glass. In a sentence, tell about a fantastic ability you might have in Looking-Glass House.
2. In *Alice in Wonderland*, Alice was surprised to see a rabbit that talked to itself and wore a waistcoat. Think of a pet or an animal like the rabbit. Write a sentence or paragraph telling something make-believe about the animal.

As you read the stories in "Flights of Fantasy," look for clues to fantasy: make-believe characters, settings, and plots.

Pod is an old hand at borrowing. He and his wife Homily have made a comfortable home for their daughter Arrietty. Now that Arrietty has learned to read and write, Pod and Homily decide to tell her some of the family history. Just before this story begins, Pod had told Homily about a happening that could spell disaster for the whole family. While on a borrowing expedition for a teacup that Homily wanted from the old nursery, Pod was "seen" by the boy Oliver. Pod and Homily decide it is time to tell Arrietty about this situation—for being seen is the greatest threat that exists for Borrowers.

Upstairs and Downstairs

by MARY NORTON

Arrietty had not been asleep. She had been lying under her knitted coverlet staring up at the ceiling. It was an interesting ceiling. Pod had built Arrietty's bedroom out of two cigar boxes, and on the ceiling lovely painted ladies dressed in swirls of chiffon blew long trumpets against a background of blue sky; below there were feathery palm trees and small white houses set about a square. It was a glamorous scene, above all by candle-light, but tonight Arrietty had stared without seeing. The wood of a cigar box is thin and Arrietty, lying straight and still under the quilt, had heard the rise and fall of worried voices. She had heard her own name; she had heard Homily exclaim: "Nuts and berries, that's what they eat!" and she had heard, after a while, the heart-felt cry of "What shall we do?"

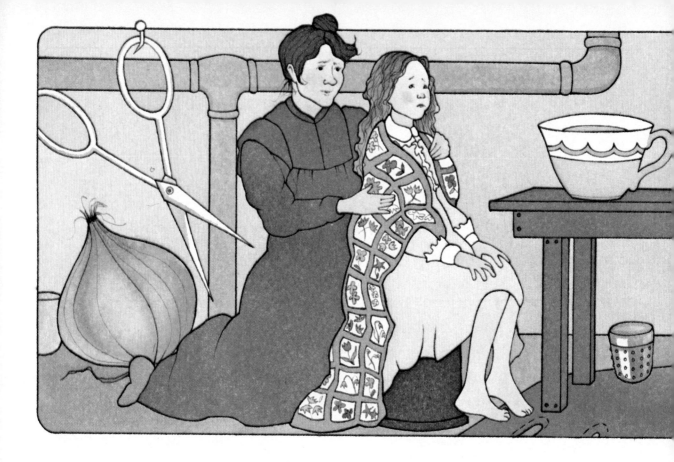

So when Homily appeared beside her bed, she wrapped herself obediently in her quilt and, padding in her bare feet along the dusty passage, she joined her parents in the warmth of the kitchen. Crouched on her little stool she sat clasping her knees, shivering a little, looking from one face to another.

Homily came beside her and, kneeling on the floor, she placed an arm round Arrietty's skinny shoulders. "Arrietty," she said gravely, "you know about upstairs?"

"What about it?" asked Arrietty.

"You know there are two giants?"

"Yes," said Arrietty, "Great-Aunt Sophy and Mrs. Driver."

"That's right," said Homily, "and Crampfurl in the garden." She laid a roughened hand on Arrietty's clasped ones. "You know about Uncle Hendreary?"

Arrietty thought awhile. "He went abroad?" she said.

"Emigrated," corrected Homily, "to the other side of the world. With Aunt Lupy and all the children. To a badger's set — a hole in a bank under a hawthorn hedge. Now why do you think he did this?"

"Oh," said Arrietty, her face alight, "to be out of doors . . . to lie in the sun . . . to run in the grass . . . to swing on twigs like the birds do . . . to suck honey . . ."

"Nonsense, Arrietty," exclaimed Homily sharply, "that's a nasty habit! And your Uncle Hendreary's a rheumatic sort of man. He emigrated," she went on, stressing the word, "because he was 'seen.'"

"Oh," said Arrietty.

"He was 'seen' on the 23rd of April 1892, by Rosa Pickhatchet, on the drawing-room mantelpiece. Of all places . . ." she added suddenly in a wondering aside.

"Oh," said Arrietty.

"I have never heard nor no one has never seen fit to tell why he went on the drawing-room mantelpiece in the first place. There's nothing on it, your father assures me, which cannot be seen from the floor or by standing sideways on the handle of the bureau and steadying yourself on the key. That's what your father does if he ever goes into the drawing room —"

"They said it was a liver pill," put in Pod.

"How do you mean?" asked Homily, startled.

"A liver pill for Lupy." Pod spoke wearily. "Someone started a rumor," he went on, "that there were liver pills on the drawing-room mantelpiece. . . ."

"Oh," said Homily and looked thoughtful, "I never heard that. All the same," she exclaimed, "it was stupid and foolhardy. There's no way down except by the bell-pull. She dusted him, they say, with a feather duster, and he stood so still, alongside a cupid, that she might never have noticed him if he hadn't sneezed. She was new, you see, and didn't know the ornaments. We heard her screeching right here under the kitchen. And they could never get her to clean anything much after that that wasn't chairs or tables—least of all the tiger-skin rug."

"I don't hardly never bother with the drawing room," said Pod. "Everything's got its place like and they see what goes. There might be a little something left on a table or down the side of a chair, but not without there's been company, and there never is no company—not for the last ten or twelve years. Sitting here in this chair, I can tell you by heart every blessed thing that's in that drawing room, working round from the cabinet by the window to the—"

"There's a mint of things in that cabinet," interrupted Homily, "solid silver some of them. A solid silver violin, they got there, strings and all—just right for our Arrietty."

"What's the good," asked Pod, "of things behind glass?"

"Couldn't you break it?" suggested Arrietty. "Just a corner, just a little tap, just a . . ." Her voice faltered as she saw the shocked amazement on her father's face.

"Listen here, Arrietty," began Homily angrily, and then she controlled herself and patted Arrietty's clasped hands. "She don't know much about borrowing," she explained to Pod. "You can't blame her." She turned again to Arrietty. "Borrowing's a skilled job, an art like. Of all the families who've been in this house, there's only us left, and do you know for why? Because your father, Arrietty, is the best borrower that's been known in these parts since—well, before your granddad's time. Even

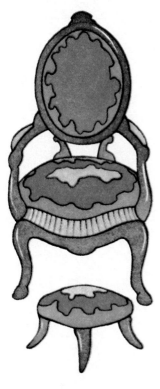

your Aunt Lupy admitted that much. When he was younger I've seen your father walk the length of a laid dinner table, after the gong was rung, taking a nut or sweet from every dish, and down by a fold in the table-cloth as the first people came in at the door. He'd do it just for fun, wouldn't you, Pod?"

Pod smiled wanly. "There weren't no sense in it," he said.

"Maybe," said Homily, "but you did it! Who else would dare?"

"I were younger then," said Pod. He sighed and turned to Arrietty. "You don't break things, lass. That's not the way to do it. That's not borrowing. . . ."

"We were rich then," said Homily. "Oh, we did have some lovely things! You were only a tot, Arrietty, and wouldn't remember. We had a whole suite of walnut furniture out of the doll's house and a set of wineglasses in green glass, and a musical snuffbox, and the cousins would come and we'd have parties. Do you remember, Pod? Not only the cousins. The Harpsichords came. Everybody came—except those Overmantels from the morning room. And we'd dance and dance and the young people would sit out by the grating. Three tunes that snuffbox played—*Clementine,* *God Save the Queen,* and the *Post-Chaise Gallop.* We were the envy of everybody—even the Overmantels. . . ."

"Who were the Overmantels?" asked Arrietty.

"Oh, you must've heard me talk of the Overmantels," exclaimed Homily, "that stuck-up lot who lived in the wall high up—among the lath and plaster behind the mantelpiece in the morning room. And a queer lot they were. They'd climb about and in and out the carvings of the overmantel, sliding down pillars and showing off. They were a conceited lot too, always admiring themselves in all those bits of overmantel looking glass. They never asked anyone up there and I, for one, never wanted to go. I've no head for heights, and your father never liked the men. He's always lived steady, your father has."

"Now, Homily," protested Pod, who did not like gossip, "I never said I didn't like 'em."

"But Pod, you said yourself when I married you not to call on the Overmantels."

"They lived so high," said Pod, "that's all."

"Well, they were a lazy lot—that much you can't deny. They never had no kind of home life. Kept themselves warm in winter by the heat of the morning-room fire and ate nothing but breakfast food; breakfast, of course, was the only meal served in the morning room."

"What happened to them?" asked Arrietty.

"Well, when the Master died and She took to her bed, there was no more use for the morning room. So the Overmantels had to go. What else could they do? No food, no fire. It's a bitter cold room in winter."

"And the Harpsichords?" asked Arrietty.

Homily looked thoughtful. "Well, they were different. I'm not saying they weren't stuck-up too, because they were. Your Aunt Lupy, who married your Uncle Hendreary, was a Harpsichord by marriage and we all know the airs she gave herself."

"Now, Homily—" began Pod.

"Well, she'd no right to. She was only a Rain-Pipe from the stables before she married Harpsichord."

"Didn't she marry Uncle Hendreary?" asked Arrietty.

"Yes, later. She was a widow with two children and he was a widower with three. It's no good looking at me like that, Pod. You can't deny she took it out of poor Hendreary: she thought it was a come-down to marry a Clock."

"Why?" asked Arrietty.

"Because we Clocks live under the kitchen, that's why. Because we don't talk fancy grammar and eat anchovy toast. But to live under the kitchen doesn't say we aren't educated. The Clocks are just as old a family as the Harpsichords. You remember that, Arrietty, and don't let anyone tell you different. Your grandfather could count and write down the numbers up to—what was it, Pod?"

"Fifty-seven," said Pod.

"There," said Homily, "fifty-seven! And your father can count, as you know, Arrietty; he can count and write down the numbers, on and on, as far as it goes. How far does it go, Pod?"

"Close on a thousand," said Pod.

"There!" exclaimed Homily. "And he knows the alphabet because he taught you, Arrietty, didn't he? And he would have been able to read—wouldn't you, Pod?—if he hadn't had to start borrowing so young. Your Uncle Hendreary and your father had to go out borrowing at thirteen—your age, Arrietty, think of it!"

"But I should like—" began Arrietty.

"So he didn't have your advantages," went on Homily breathlessly, "and just because the Harpsichords lived in the drawing room—they moved in there, in 1837, to a hole in the wainscot just behind where the harpsichord used to stand, if ever there was one, which I doubt—and were really a family called Linen-Press or some such name and changed it to Harpsichord—"

"What did they live on," asked Arrietty, "in the drawing room?"

"Afternoon tea," said Homily, "nothing but afternoon tea. No wonder the children grew up peaky. Of course, in the old days it was better—muffins and crumpets and such, and good rich cake and jams and jellies. And there was one old Harpsichord who could remember sillabub of an evening. But they had to do their borrowing in such a rush, poor things. On wet days, when the human beings sat all afternoon in the drawing room, the tea would be brought in and taken away again without a chance of the

Harpsichords getting near it—and on fine days it might be taken out into the garden. Lupy has told me that, sometimes, there were days and days when they lived on crumbs and on water out of the flower vases. So you can't be too hard on them; their only comfort, poor things, was to show off a bit and wear evening dress and talk like ladies and gentlemen. Did you ever hear your Aunt Lupy talk?"

"Yes. No. I can't remember."

"Oh, you should have heard her say 'Parquet'—that's the stuff the drawing-room floor's made of—'Parkay . . . Parr-r-kay,' she'd say. Oh, it was lovely. Come to think of it, your Aunt Lupy was the most stuck-up of them all. . . ."

"Arrietty's shivering," said Pod. "We didn't get the little maid up to talk about Aunt Lupy."

"No, we didn't," cried Homily, suddenly contrite. "You should've stopped me, Pod. There, my lamb, tuck this quilt right round you and I'll get you a nice drop of piping hot soup!"

"And yet," said Pod as Homily, fussing at the stove, ladled soup into the teacup, "we did in a way."

"Did what?" asked Homily.

"Get her here to talk about Aunt Lupy. Aunt Lupy, Uncle Hendreary, and"—he paused—"Eggletina."

"Let her drink up her soup first," said Homily.

"There's no call for her to stop drinking," said Pod.

"Your mother and I got you up," said Pod, "to tell you about upstairs."

Arrietty, holding the great cup in both hands, looked at him over the edge.

Pod coughed. "You said a while back that the sky was dark brown with cracks in it. Well, it isn't." He looked at her almost accusingly. "It's blue."

"I know," said Arrietty.

"You know!" exclaimed Pod.

"Yes, of course I know. I've got the grating."

"Can you see the sky through the grating?"

"Go on," interrupted Homily, "tell her about the gates."

"Well," said Pod ponderously, "if you go outside this room, what do you see?"

"A dark passage," said Arrietty.

"And what else?"

"Other rooms."

"And if you go farther?"

"More passages."

"And, if you go walking on and on, in all the passages under the floor, however they twist and turn, what do you find?"

"Gates," said Arrietty.

"Strong gates," said Pod, "gates you can't open. What are they there for?"

"Against the mice?" said Arrietty.

"Yes," agreed Pod uncertainly, as though he gave her half a mark, "but mice never hurt no one. What else?"

"Rats?" suggested Arrietty.

"We don't have rats," said Pod. "What about cats?"

"Cats?" echoed Arrietty, surprised.

"Or to keep you in?" suggested Pod.

"To keep me in?" repeated Arrietty, dismayed.

"Upstairs is a dangerous place," said Pod. "And you, Arrietty, you're all we've got, see? It isn't like Hendreary — he still has two of his own and two of hers. Once," said Pod, "Hendreary had three — three of his own."

"Your father's thinking of Eggletina," said Homily.

"Yes," said Pod, "Eggletina. They never told her about upstairs. And they hadn't got no grating. They told her the sky was nailed up, like, with cracks in it —"

"A foolish way to bring up a child," murmured Homily. She sniffed slightly and touched Arrietty's hair.

"But Eggletina was no fool," said Pod; "she didn't believe them. So one day," he went on, "she went upstairs to see for herself."

"How did she get out?" asked Arrietty, interested.

"Well, we didn't have so many gates then. Just the one under the clock. Hendreary must have left it unlocked or something. Anyway, Eggletina went out . . ."

"In a blue dress," said Homily, "and a pair of button-boots your father made her, yellow kid with jet beads for buttons. Lovely, they were."

"Well," said Pod, "any other time it might have been all right. She'd have gone out, had a look around, had a bit of a fright, maybe, and come back—none the worse and no one the wiser . . ."

"But things had been happening," said Homily.

"Yes," said Pod, "she didn't know, as they never told

her, that her father had been 'seen' and that upstairs they had got in the cat and—"

"They waited a week," said Homily, "and they waited a month and they hoped for a year but no one ever saw Eggletina no more."

"And that," said Pod after a pause and eyeing Arrietty, "is what happened to Eggletina."

There was silence except for Pod's breathing and the faint bubble of the soup.

"It just broke up your Uncle Hendreary," said Homily at last. "He never went upstairs again—in case, he said, he found the button-boots. Their only future was to emigrate."

Arrietty was silent a moment, then she raised her head. "Why did you tell me?" she asked. "Now? Tonight?"

Homily got up. She moved restlessly toward the stove. "We don't never talk of it," she said, "at least, not much, but, tonight, we felt—" She turned suddenly. "Well, we'll just say it straight out: your father's been 'seen,' Arrietty!"

"Oh," said Arrietty, "who by?"

"Well, by a—something you've never heard of. But that's not the point: the point is—"

"You think they'll get a cat?"

"They may," said Homily.

Arrietty set down the soup for a moment; she stared into the cup as it stood beside her almost knee high on the floor; there was a dreamy, secret something about her lowered face. "Couldn't we emigrate?" she ventured at last, very softly.

Homily gasped and clasped her hands and swung away toward the wall. "You don't know what you're talking about," she cried, addressing a frying pan which hung there. "Worms and weasels and cold and damp and—"

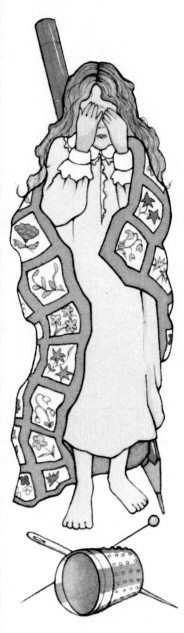

"But supposing," said Arrietty, "that *I* went out, like Eggletina did, and the cat ate *me*. Then you and Papa would emigrate. Wouldn't you?" she asked, and her voice faltered. "Wouldn't you?"

Homily swung round again, this time toward Arrietty; her face looked very angry. "I shall smack you, Arrietty Clock, if you don't behave yourself this minute!"

Arrietty's eyes filled with tears. "I was only thinking," she said, "that I'd like to be there—to emigrate too. Uneaten," she added softly and the tears fell.

"Now," said Pod, "this is enough! You get off to bed, Arrietty, uneaten and unbeaten both—and we'll talk about it in the morning."

"It's not that I'm afraid," cried Arrietty angrily; "I like cats. I bet the cat didn't eat Eggletina. I bet she just ran away because she hated being cooped up . . . day after day . . . week after week . . . year after year. . . . Like I do!" she added in a sob.

"Cooped up!" repeated Homily, astounded.

Arrietty put her face into her hands. "Gates, . . ." she gasped, "gates, gates, gates. . . ."

Pod and Homily stared at each other across Arrietty's bowed shoulders. "You didn't ought to have brought it up," he said unhappily, "not so late at night . . ."

Arrietty raised her tear-streaked face. "Late or early, what's the difference?" she cried. "Oh, I know Papa is a wonderful borrower. I know we've managed to stay when all the others have gone. But what has it done for us, in the end? I don't think it's so clever to live on alone, for ever and ever, in a great, big, half-empty house, under the floor, with no one to talk to, no one to play with, nothing to see but dust and passages, no light but candlelight and firelight and what comes through the cracks. Eggletina had brothers and Eggletina had half-brothers; Eggletina had a tame mouse; Eggletina had yellow boots with jet buttons, and Eggletina did get out—just once!"

"Shush," said Pod gently, "not so loud." Above their heads the floor creaked and heavy footfalls heaved deliberately to and fro. They heard Mrs. Driver's grumbling voice and the clatter of the fire irons. "Drat this stove," they heard her say, "wind's in the east again." Then they heard her raise her voice and call, "Crampfurl!"

Pod sat staring glumly at the floor; Arrietty shivered a little and hugged herself more tightly into the knitted quilt, and Homily drew a long, slow breath. Suddenly she raised her head.

"The child is right," she announced firmly.

Arrietty's eyes grew big. "Oh, no—" she began. It shocked her to be right. Parents were right, not children. Children could say anything, Arrietty knew, and enjoy saying it—knowing always they were safe and wrong.

"You see, Pod," went on Homily, "it was different for you and me. There was other families, other children . . . the Sinks in the scullery, you remember? And those people who lived behind the knife machine—I forget their names now. And the Broom-Cupboard boys. And there was that underground passage from the stables—you know, that the Rain-Pipes used. We had more, as you might say, freedom."

"Ah, yes," said Pod, "in a way. But where does freedom take you?" He looked up uncertainly. "Where are they all now?"

"Some of them may have bettered themselves, I shouldn't wonder," said Homily sharply. "Times have changed in the whole house. Pickings aren't what they were. There were those that went, you remember, when they dug a trench for the gas pipe. Over the fields, and through the wood, and all. A kind of tunnel it gave them, all the way to Leighton Buzzard."

"And what did they find there?" said Pod unkindly. "A mountain of coke!"

Homily turned away. "Arrietty," she said, in the same firm voice, "supposing one day—we'd pick a special day when there was no one about, and providing they don't get a cat which I have my reasons for thinking they won't —supposing, one day, your father took you out borrowing, you'd be a good girl, wouldn't you? You'd do just what he said, quickly and quietly and no arguing?"

Arrietty turned quite pink; she clasped her hands together. "Oh—" she began in an ecstatic voice, but Pod cut in quickly:

"Now, Homily, we got to think. You can't just say things like that without thinking it out proper. I been 'seen,' remember. This is no kind of time for taking a child upstairs."

"There won't be no cat," said Homily; "there wasn't no screeching. It's not like that time with Rosa Pickhatchet."

"All the same," said Pod uncertainly, "the risk's there.

"The way I look at it," said Homily, "and it's only now it's come to me: suppose anything happened to you or me, where would Arrietty be—if she hadn't learned to borrow?"

Pod stared down at his knees. "Yes," he said after a moment, "I see what you mean."

"And it'll give her a bit of interest like and stop her hankering."

"Hankering for what?"

"For blue sky and grass and suchlike." Arrietty caught her breath and Homily turned on her swiftly: "It's no good, Arrietty, I'm not going to emigrate—not for you nor anyone else!"

"Ah," said Pod and began to laugh, "so that's it!"

"Shush!" said Homily, annoyed, and glanced quickly at the ceiling. "Not so loud! Now kiss your father, Arrietty," she went on briskly, "and pop off back to bed."

Understanding What You've Read

1. In "Upstairs and Downstairs," it is the characters who make the story a fantasy. In what ways are the characters fantastic?
2. Why do the characters in "Upstairs and Downstairs" seem like real people?
3. What might the "upstairs people" have thought when household objects disappeared?
4. Why did a Borrower sometimes have to "emigrate"?
5. Why was it such a serious event for a Borrower to be "seen"?
6. In explaining borrowing to Arrietty, Homily says, "Borrowing is a skilled job, an art like." Why was this so?
7. Arrietty had said that "the sky was dark brown with cracks in it." Why was this true for her?
8. What was so exciting for Arrietty about becoming a Borrower?

Writing

1. Think of an object you have recently lost that might have been "borrowed" by the Borrowers. In a few sentences, describe the lost object and tell what use you think the Borrowers might have made of the object.
2. Imagine that you are a Borrower. What might happen if you were "seen"? Write at least one paragraph describing how, when, and where you were seen. If you wish, tell what happened when you were seen.

The Phoenix and the Carpet

by E. NESBIT
and adapted as a radio play
by MADELINE SUNSHINE

Cast

CYRIL	SALESMAN
ANTHEA	MOTHER
ROBERT	THE PHOENIX
JANE	

Setting: England;
November, 1904

SCENE 1

A Friday afternoon, in an English country home

(SOUND EFFECTS: *Morning sounds. A doorbell rings. Door opens.*)

SALESMAN: 'ello, Mum. 'ere's your carpet, all spick-and-span. Shall I lay it out for you?

MOTHER: No, that won't be necessary. Children? (*Calling louder*) Children? Come give me a hand.

(SOUND EFFECTS: *We hear footsteps of four children running down a flight of stairs.*)

SALESMAN: Well then, . . .

MOTHER: Wait; before you go, I will say this: I've never bought a second-hand carpet before and if this one isn't in good condition, I'll expect you to exchange it right away.

SALESMAN: There ain't a thread gone in it nowhere, Mum. It's a bargain if ever there was one, and I'm more'n 'arf sorry I let it go so cheap.

MOTHER: Humph!

SALESMAN: Well, that'll be that then. Good day, Mum. You and your kiddies enjoy the carpet.

(SOUND EFFECTS: *Door closes.*)

MOTHER: Okay, children, let's get this down to the playroom.

(SOUND EFFECTS: *Door opens and shuts. Five pairs of footsteps on stairs.*)

Here, each of you grab an end and let's get this thing laid out.

(SOUND EFFECTS: *Stone object thumps to ground. It makes three distinct thumps.*)

CYRIL: Hey, look at this! It feels like stone but it looks just like an egg.

ANTHEA: Yes, but it's yellow and eggs aren't yellow.

ROBERT: Hey, Cyril, doesn't it look like it has a light inside it?

CYRIL: Yes, but watch—when I turn it, the light kind of changes.

JANE: Well, I don't think it has a light, I think it has a fire inside it.

CYRIL: Can we keep it, Mother, please?

MOTHER: Certainly not! You'll take it right back to the man I bought the carpet from. I paid for a carpet, not a stone egg with a light inside. You'll find the shop on Kentish Town Road—that's right near the Bull and Gate Hotel. You know the one. Now, put on your coats and get along.

(SOUND EFFECTS: *Footsteps of kids. Door opens and closes. We fade out and then in again, indicating the passage of time. Street noises. Shop bell clangs as a door shuts.*)

SALESMAN: (*Shouting angrily*) Oh no you don't, you kids. I ain't a'goin' to take back no carpets, and don't you make no mistake about that! A bargain's a bargain, and the carpet's perfect throughout.

CYRIL: We don't want you to take it back. It's just that we found something in it.

SALESMAN: Well, it must 'ave gotten into it up at your place. There ain't nothing in nothing what I sell. It's all clean as a whistle.

CYRIL: I never said it wasn't clean, but. . . .

SALESMAN: I tell you the carpet's good through and through. It 'adn't got no moths when it left my 'ands—not so much as an egg.

JANE: But that's just it. There *was* so much as an egg.

SALESMAN: (*Shouting*) Well, I never! Clear out I say! Clear out or I'll call for the police. A nice thing for customers to 'ear—you a'coming in 'ere a'charging me with finding things in goods I sell. Be off afore I send you off with a flea in your ears. Out; out! Constable, Constable!!!

(SOUND EFFECTS: *Store doorbell rings as the door opens and slams shut. We hear kids' running footsteps.*)

CYRIL: *(Out of breath)* Whew! I'm glad we're out of there!

JANE: *(Out of breath)* And that means we can keep the egg!

ROBERT: *(Out of breath)* Hey, that's right! Mother can't refuse now!

ANTHEA: Home! I'm tired!

(SOUND EFFECTS: *Door opens and closes. Footsteps stop.*)

ROBERT: Well, there's not much to do now.

ANTHEA: We could talk about the Psammead.

CYRIL: What's the good of *talking*? It's gone. What I want is for something to happen. I'm getting bored with just school and home, eating and sleeping. We need something exciting to happen again.

ANTHEA: Still, we're luckier than anyone else I know. No one else has ever found a Psammead . . . I think. Anyway, we ought to be happy that once something exciting happened to us.

CYRIL: Yes. The Psammead is a wonderful, magical creature and it did grant wishes, but it's gone away now. Why does it all always have to end?

ANTHEA: Cheer up, Squirrel. Perhaps something will happen. I mean, I sometimes think we're just the sort of people things *do* happen to.

JANE: Oh, I wish they taught us magic at school. I'm sure if we could do even a little magic it would make something happen.

ANTHEA: I've read tons of books about magic. Here's what we'll do: First we must light a magic fire in the fireplace and then recite all sorts of strange chants. We'll have to put all sorts of sweet-smelling woods and herbs in the fire. Cyril is allowed to light matches; he's the oldest.

CYRIL: I'll get some from the kitchen.

ANTHEA: (Getting into the spirit) And we can get the spices there, too. Wait, what about the sweet-smelling wood? Where will we get that?

JANE: I know! Our pencils say they're made of cedar wood. That's a sweet-smelling wood.

ANTHEA: Then it's set. Let's get everything ready.

SCENE 2
Later the same evening

(SOUND EFFECTS: *We hear a crackling fire and children chanting.*)

ANTHEA: Well, the fire *looks* pretty magical.

ROBERT: Yes, but nothing's happening.

CYRIL: I know! Let's add some flower petals.

JANE: We haven't any.

CYRIL: Yes we do. Right there—in the vase. Look— Robert, it's on the mantelpiece. (Annoyed) No, to the left, right near where you put our stone egg.

ROBERT: Okay, I've got it.

(SOUND EFFECTS: *We hear stone egg as it falls into fireplace.*)

Oooooh! The egg! Is it smashed?!!

ANTHEA: No, but look at it! It's absolutely glowing!

ROBERT: I dropped it; I'll get it. Ow! It's burning hot! How could it have gotten that hot so fast? I'd better get the tongs from the upstairs fireplace.

ANTHEA: No wait! Look at it! Something's moving inside the egg!!

(SOUND EFFECTS: *Amplified cracking as of a large eggshell.*)

ROBERT: It's a bird!

(SOUND EFFECTS: *Flutter of wings.*)

CYRIL: I'll get it. Come here, birdie—here, birdie. . . .
(*He makes chirping noises to attract bird.*)

PHOENIX: Be careful—don't touch me yet. I'm not nearly cool. May I inquire which of you put the egg into the fire?

ANTHEA, JANE, *and* CYRIL: Robert did!

PHOENIX: My dear master Robert, I am your grateful debtor!

ROBERT: I know who you are. You're *The Phoenix!* I've a picture. It's right here in this book on the second shelf.

PHOENIX: Ah yes, my fame has lived for two thousand years then. Good to know, good to know. Allow me to look at my portrait.

ROBERT: Here. . . .

PHOENIX: Not a flattering likeness. No, not flattering at all. And what are these doodlings?

ROBERT: Doodlings? Oh, you mean the words. Nothing really. It's all pretty dullish and not much about you. But, uh, you are in lots of books—

PHOENIX: *(Excitedly)* With portraits?

CYRIL: I'm afraid not. In fact, I don't think I ever saw any portrait of you but that one Robert has. But, if you like, I can read you something about yourself. Janey, please get the *P* volume of the encyclopedia. It's on the shelf beside you.

JANE: Here, Cyril.

(SOUND EFFECTS: *We hear pages being turned.*)

CYRIL: Okay—"Phoenix." A fabulous bird of antiquity.

PHOENIX: Antiquity is quite correct. *(With false modesty)* But fabulous—well, I *do* look it.

CYRIL: Shall I go on?

PHOENIX: Yes, do.

CYRIL: The ancients speak of this bird as single, or the only one of its kind.

PHOENIX: That's right enough.

CYRIL: They describe it as about the size of an eagle.

PHOENIX: Not at all a good description. Eagles are all different sizes. *(Slight pause)* Oh dear—I'm afraid I've gotten too close to your tablecloth and scorched it.

ANTHEA: Never mind. It will come out in the wash.

PHOENIX: Oh good, I'm so relieved. Do go ahead reading.

CYRIL: Uh *(Mumbling as he finds the place)* the size of an. . . . They say that it lives about five hundred years in the wilderness, and when advanced in age, it builds itself a pile of sweet wood and herbs, lights it with its wings, and thus burns itself. And, that from its ashes arises a worm which, in time, grows up to be a Phoenix. Hence the. . . .

PHOENIX: (*Interrupting*) Hence nothing! That book ought to be destroyed! That part about the worm is just a vulgar insult! The Phoenix has an egg, like any respectable bird. It makes a pile of sweet-smelling woods and herbs—that part's all right—and it lays an egg, and it burns itself; and it goes to sleep and wakes up in its egg and comes out and goes on living again, and so on, for ever and ever.

ANTHEA: But, I don't understand something: How did your egg get here?

PHOENIX: I had resided, just as your book says, for many thousands of years in the wilderness, which is a large, quiet place with very little really good company. I was becoming more and more bored as each thousand years passed by. But I had acquired the habit of laying my egg and burning myself every five hundred years—and you know how hard it is to break a habit.

CYRIL: Oh yes. Jane used to bite her nails.

JANE: *(Annoyed)* But I broke myself of it, you know.

CYRIL: Not till Mother put iodine on them.

PHOENIX: I doubt whether even iodine could have cured me. But then one day something happened. There I was, just about ready to build that tiresome fire and lay that tedious egg upon it, when suddenly I saw two people—a man and a woman. They were sitting on a magic carpet. (You've heard of magic carpets, I imagine.) Anyway, it seems they had decided to live forever in the wilderness. They had no more need for the carpet that brought them there. So, I asked them whether I might not have it. And, wonder of wonders, they said yes.

JANE: I don't see what you wanted with a carpet when you've got such lovely wings.

PHOENIX: They are nice wings, aren't they? Well, I got the woman and the man to help me spread out the carpet and I laid my egg on it. What a nice change that was, too. Then I said to the carpet— "Take my egg somewhere where it can't be hatched for two thousand years and where, when that time's up, someone will light a fire of sweet wood and herbs and put the egg in to hatch." And you see, everything's come out exactly as I said. I knew of nothing else until I awoke just now on yonder altar.

ANTHEA: Altar?!! Oh, you mean our fireplace.

ROBERT: But the carpet, I mean the magic one that takes you anywhere you wish—what became of that?

PHOENIX: *(Disdainfully)* Oh that. I should say that the one beneath your feet *is* that very carpet. I remember the pattern precisely.

(SOUND EFFECTS: *Door opening upstairs.*)

CYRIL: *(Whispering)* Shush! I hear something.

(SOUND EFFECTS: *Door closes.*)

(Whispering) It's got to be Mother and Father. And it's late; we'll catch it for not being in bed by now.

PHOENIX: *(Whispering)* Wish yourselves there and then wish the carpet back in its place.

ANTHEA: Really?!!

PHOENIX: *(Whispering)* Yes, but hurry! Go on—all of you stand on it and then wish!

ROBERT: *(Whispering)* Shall I say it?

PHOENIX: *(Whispering)* Yes, yes—just hurry!

ROBERT: *(Whispering; rushing his words)* I wish this carpet would get us up to bed and then go back to its own place in the playroom.

(SOUND EFFECTS: *Whooshing sound of carpet taking off.*)

JANE: It worked! It worked!

ANTHEA: *(Whispering)* Not so loud.

PHOENIX: *(Softly)* Robert, my dear friend, I think I shall sleep on that ledge above your curtains. And please, don't mention me to anyone.

ROBERT: *(Whispering)* Don't worry; no one would ever believe us even if we did.

Understanding What You've Read

1. At what point in the play do you learn that "The Phoenix and the Carpet" is a fantasy?
2. A fantasy, like any story, has characters, a setting, and a plot. Which elements tell you that "The Phoenix and the Carpet" is a fantasy?
3. You know that fantasy combines realistic details with imaginary ones. On pages 255–256, find three examples of realistic details and three examples of fantastic details.
4. At the end of the play, the author lets you in on a secret that you may have already figured out. Edith Nesbit tells you that the play is really a fantasy. It is not a true story. What does Robert say on page 259 that tells you this?
5. The play ends with the children in bed. What do you think will happen to the characters on the next day and in the days that follow?

Writing

1. Complete the following sentences to make them fantasy.

   a. As Martha approached the high jump, a marvelous change came over her. She . . .
   b. George stepped to the departure gate and his eyes widened. The plane at the ramp was . . .
   c. Sue walked nervously to the microphone. As she opened her mouth to speak, she . . .

2. Write two groups of sentences. In the first group of sentences, describe real people, objects, or events. In the second group of sentences, include some fantasy. Read the sample sentences on page 261 for ideas.

a. Sandy loved visiting the pandas at Cityside Zoo. The bears were almost human. They looked as though they wanted to speak to you.

b. As Sandy was walking past the panda pen at Cityside Zoo, she heard a soft voice. She turned, and the panda spoke again. "How would you like to be locked up in a pen?"

Danger or Not?

by ISAAC ASIMOV

Jonathan Derodin looked about the new planet curiously. It was named Anderson Two and it really was a new planet, at least for human beings. There was just a small area where humans lived and where the land had been made to turn green with Earth plants.

It looked as though he and his mother would be here for a while. There was no help for it. His mother was a planetary inspector. It was her job to decide whether certain planets were fit for human life or not. She had to go where her job called her.

They had been heading for Earth, which Jonathan had never seen, although he had read about it many times in his twelve years of life. His father, a mining engineer, was already there, and Jonathan and his mother were to meet him there.

Then the message reached them that she had to go to Anderson Two. Emergency, it said. Inspector Derodin had changed her plans at once.

"You can go on to Earth by yourself, Jonathan," she had said. "You're old enough to make the trip, and a vacation on Earth is really special."

Jonathan had been tempted, but the thought of an emergency on a brand-new planet, with his mother having to make important decisions, tempted him also.

"Would it be all right if I came with you, Mother?" he asked. "Or are you going to tell me there's danger?"

His mother smiled. "I don't think there's danger. And there'll be room for you on the space-cruiser that's coming to take me there. It's just that your vacation won't be quite the same on a young world like Anderson Two."

"That's all right," answered Jonathan. "I'll visit Earth another time."

She was packing all the new smooth foam-fabric clothing she had bought for the vacation on Earth. Jonathan wondered if she was disappointed, too. If she was, she did not show it. Her face remained calm, and her hair was all in place. She acted as though it were a job she had to do and that was all there was to it.

When Jonathan was younger, she had once said, "You know, Jonathan, there was once a time when all human beings lived only on Earth. It was the only world with people on it. Now we're spreading out through hundreds and thousands of worlds, and someone has to decide whether certain worlds are fit for human beings or not. Such decisions are important."

Jonathan wondered why a world might not be fit for human beings, but he wasn't sure he ought to ask. It might be a foolish question, and he didn't want his mother to think he was foolish.

He was born on the planet Ceti Four, a planet that circled another sun far from Earth. It seemed perfectly fine to him—friendly and homelike. It never had snow, though, and he sometimes wondered what snow was like. He had seen pictures of it on other worlds and on Earth.

He wondered if there would be snow on Anderson Two. He read a folder about the planet as the space-cruiser took them there, and he decided there wouldn't be. At least not in the one place where human beings were living.

Once he was on the surface of Anderson Two, Jonathan was sure there wouldn't be. It felt warm and pleasant and it had to be cold for it to snow. He knew that.

He was curious about the new planet. He and his mother had arrived the day before, and all that time they had been in quarantine. They had to stay in a certain building away from everyone else while they were examined. This was to make sure they didn't bring dangerous germs to the planet. Now he was out of quarantine and he could wander about.

His mother had said, "Stay close to the Base, Jonathan, please." She was going into a conference with the leaders of the colony of the planet. She would have to see the Mayor, who seemed a short, cheerful man, and various councilmen.

Jonathan was glad he'd be left alone because he wanted to explore. The folder he had read said it was not a dangerous world. It certainly didn't seem so from what he could see.

He and his mother had been given a cabin near the spaceport. All the land around it looked very friendly and homelike. The houses were made of a kind of shiny rock that glittered a bit in the yellow sunlight (which seemed a little bit brighter than the sun back home at Ceti Four). Between the houses and all around them, it was green. There were grass and shrubs and, farther off, fields of grain on low, rolling hills. When he climbed to the top of one of them, he could see a river in the distance.

In the other direction, the green human world stopped. Jon took a road in that direction, and when it stopped, he found the land beyond was made up of rocky ridges.

Some of the rocks were lined with grey-brown crystals that made the edges sharp and glittery. He walked slowly out onto a ridge and stooped to look at the sharp edges more carefully. He put on his thin collagenite gloves and then, with a cautious finger, touched one of the rocks. The gloves protected his hands but did not interfere with the sensation of touch. He found that what looked like hard, brittle crystal was rather tough and rubbery.

He pinched along the edge and, with a little glassy sound, some of it broke off and fell. Jonathan snatched his hand away. He had not meant to do that. The folder had said that the crystals were like Earth plants. They absorbed carbon dioxide from the air and liberated oxygen just the way Earth plants did.

He saw that certain tan-colored rocks seemed to flow slowly until they reached the fallen crystals and covered them. He had read that those rocks were like earthly animals that live on the plants. Only they didn't have to eat plants for food. They could also absorb the energy they needed from the sun.

He walked cautiously onward, trying not to jar any of the crystal edgings, or to step on any of the tan rocks. Once, when he did step on some of the rocks, they didn't seem changed in any way, and after that he walked more confidently.

He turned and could still see the patch of green human world clearly. He didn't want to get out of sight of that.

It was then that he saw his first Wheel, one of the native inhabitants of Anderson Two.

He didn't know it was a Wheel, of course, even though the folder had described them. What he saw was just a slab of rock about eight feet high, standing on its narrow edge in the sunlight, like a big figure 1. There didn't seem anything alive about it, but there was nothing else like it anywhere.

He was making up his mind to go closer and see what it was like, when from behind a rock there came another human being. He was looking at the big slab, too, looking so hard he didn't see Jonathan.

The man was inching forward slowly, and then his right arm started to rise and Jonathan saw that he had a blaster in it. It was then that it occurred to Jonathan that the slab must be one of the Wheels he had read about, and before he even thought about it, he was shouting, "Don't shoot it, mister!"

The man with the blaster whirled, his face twisting in surprise. He had a ruddy complexion and fiery red hair. He seemed so astonished at seeing Jonathan that for a moment he simply froze.

In that moment the slab of rock came to life. It broke into a series of bright, flashing lights of various colors coming and going very rapidly. The top third and the bottom third of the slab each split into six parts. It seemed suddenly a large hand with six thick fingers at each end. The fingers spread wide, and then it went whirling away like a twelve-spoked wheel, turning end over end so rapidly that it blurred. Jonathan could see now why they were called Wheels.

The red-haired man turned back only in time to see the Wheel vanish. His hand was still tight about his blaster. He walked toward Jonathan with long strides, heedlessly cracking and breaking off the rock-crystal plants under foot. Jonathan kept his eye on the blaster a little nervously. The man looked very angry.

The red-haired man called out, "Who are you? What are you doing here?"

Jonathan felt the urge to run, but he fought it down. There was no reason to run; he had done nothing wrong. He said, "I'm Jonathan Derodin. I'm just looking around."

The red-haired man's eyes narrowed. Some of the anger went out of his face. He looked cautious instead. "Are you with the Inspector?"

"She's my mother," said Jonathan.

"Why aren't you with her, then?"

"She's in conference, and I'm looking around. No one told me I couldn't."

"In conference?" The red-haired man suddenly turned and hurried off toward the patch of green that Jonathan could still make out.

Jonathan thought that perhaps he ought to go back to the Base, too. He wasn't sure what the red-haired man might say about what had happened. He turned to start going back, when his eye caught a movement. It was another Wheel, but a little one. It was not more than three feet high, with delicate spokes that turned slowly. It sparkled with lights, mostly in different shades of orange.

"I greet you."

Jonathan heard the words. But it was as though he had not really heard them, but thought them. They seemed to be in his mind at first, but then it was as if he had somehow heard them from outside. He looked about wildly. Was there another human being somewhere?

Then he looked at the little Wheel, and it sparkled in different oranges again and Jonathan heard "I greet you" once more. He heard it two more times and each time there were those sparkles on the little Wheel.

Jonathan asked, "Are you saying something to me, Little Wheel?" He felt foolish saying this.

But he heard, "Yes. When you make the funny noises I hear you in my mind. I heard you before when you were speaking to the Red-top."

Jonathan said, "When you make the funny colors, I hear you in my mind."

They came closer together, slowly, almost fearfully.

The little Wheel said, "Old Brown-Blue heard your noise. That's why he whirled. I heard you tell Red-top not to use his Exploder. You are a friend."

Jonathan said, "Was Brown-Blue the big Wheel that went away?"

"Yes. He can't hear the thoughts of you Sound-things. I can, though."

"You can?"

"Because I'm still little. I can hear your thoughts better than I can hear the others. Maybe because you're little."

"My name is Jonathan."

"I don't understand that," said the little Wheel.

"Jonathan," said Jonathan.

Slowly the little Wheel shone in spots of blue and purple, and Jon heard the sound inside his head, "Jon-eethin."

"That's pretty good," said Jonathan.

The little Wheel said, "My name is Yellger."

That was what the name sounded like in Jonathan's head, when one of the spokes of the little Wheel shone in two shades of yellow followed by a deep sea-green.

Jonathan said doubtfully, "Yellger?"

The little Wheel sparkled with rapid white flashes and there was the sound of laughter in Jonathan's head. "You say it very oddly," he heard, "but I understand."

They had gradually come closer to each other. They were so close now, they were almost touching. To Jonathan, this new way of talking was starting to seem like the most natural thing in the world.

They talked of many things. Jonathan was not afraid when he saw the large Wheel come whirling in. Yellger told him, "That's my mother. She's worried about me, I guess."

Jonathan just moved away slowly, and said out loud, "I'm not doing any harm, Mrs. Wheel."

He heard Yellger say, "Mother, do not drive him away," and then the big Wheel stopped. Jon could not understand her flashes. He just heard confused sounds. It seemed as though messages went from mind to mind only in young people and young Wheels.

He turned to leave now, and then he saw the man with red hair coming toward them in the distance – and his mother, too.

"You see him," the man said, "and you saw the Wheels."

Jonathan turned to look, but the Wheels were leaving rapidly.

The man with the red hair said, "Your son has no business here. He was in danger. Those Wheels are large and can kill."

Jonathan was running toward them now. He cried out, "There was no danger, Mother. The Wheels were doing no harm at all. This man tried to shoot one that was just standing there, doing nothing."

Inspector Derodin was calm. Her smooth hair, drawn backward, was completely unruffled and her dark eyes showed no anger. She held out an arm toward Jonathan and placed it on his shoulder.

She said, "I appreciate your concern, Councilman Caradoc, but Jonathan is a sensible boy and the reports I have on this world of Anderson Two stress that it is a calm world. It has an oxygen atmosphere, a terrain that is not dangerous, no large animal forms—"

"The Wheels are large," said Caradoc angrily. "You saw it for yourself. You saw it charging the boy."

The Inspector turned to her son. "What have you to say about this, Jonathan?"

"The Wheel was *not* trying to harm me, Mother."

Caradoc said, "It was charging you, boy. We saw that from the distance."

"She was his mother," Jonathan said, "the little Wheel's mother. She was just worried about Yellger— about her child. I backed away and she just went off with him. That's all."

"There *was* a smaller Wheel present, Councilman. I saw it," the Inspector added.

"What's that got to do with it?" asked Caradoc. "And what makes the boy think the big Wheel was the little one's mother? It's just a story he tells himself. We don't have to listen to that."

The Inspector said, "I don't think my son makes up stories. He is both intelligent and honest. Jonathan, what makes you say that the big Wheel is the mother of the little Wheel?"

Jonathan hesitated, then said, "Yellger told me so."

"Who's Yellger, Jonathan?"

"The little Wheel. That's his name."

Caradoc laughed.

Jonathan said angrily, "He *told* me so. Yellger told me so. That was what I heard when he made the light-flashes that are his name."

Caradoc shook his head and said, "Inspector Derodin, aren't we wasting our time? I don't want to say anything against your son, but I'm afraid he has a galloping imagination. These things are just rolling rocks. They don't have names except for those some youngster might make up for them."

"They are *not* just rolling rocks," said Jonathan, a little wildly. "Yellger talked to me all right. I understood him and he understood me."

Caradoc looked annoyed, but then he managed to smile and say, "Well, I won't argue with the boy. Just the same, it is not right for him to break the rules governing behavior on this planet. Our young people are not allowed to pass beyond the boundaries of the green plant life, and they do not do so. Your son set a bad example and it was dangerous besides. I don't think it should happen again."

The Inspector's cheeks flushed a little, but she said evenly, "Jonathan was not aware of the rule. He was not told. Naturally, he will not do it again. Shall we go back to the council-room now and continue our discussion?"

She walked slowly back toward the green Base with her arm still on Jonathan's shoulder. She said, "Anderson Two seems an interesting planet."

Caradoc nodded. "The soil will grow anything and it could be made into a paradise. The trouble is that we can't attract immigrants as long as we don't have a final classification as a Human World. No one wants to start making a home for themselves if there's a possibility they'll have to leave. If we don't get the classification soon, the colony will fail."

"Yes," said Inspector Derodin, "I quite understand why you should be anxious. Your Mayor has explained the situation to the Colonization Board and they sent me here on an emergency call. You see we understand your situation."

"May we have the necessary classification, then?"

"Ah, but there is some question as to the presence of native intelligent life here on Anderson Two. You surely understand that the basic rule by which we are colonizing the stars of the Galaxy is that we must never settle ourselves on a world that already has an intelligent life-form. We would wish to be treated the same if some other intelligence tried to colonize one of our worlds."

Caradoc said, "There is no intelligent life-form on this world except for human beings."

"Might not the Wheels be intelligent?"

"Because your son claims he has talked to them?" Caradoc's voice became angry and his face grew almost as red as his hair.

"No, no. There are some reports that the Wheels *do* communicate. They flash lights in varying colors and at varying intervals."

"So do fireflies on Earth," said Caradoc.

"Not in nearly so complicated a fashion. The flashing *could* be a communication device. If so, they may be intelligent. This planet must then be left to them."

"I've heard this before," said Caradoc impatiently. "For years now, someone mentions this every once in a while. But no one has ever proved it. No one has ever shown that the flashing lights are really a communication device. How long must this world wait?"

"Well, there's something to that," said the Inspector pleasantly, "but let us have a few days to think about it. Our holidays will soon be here and there's no reason why we can't wait till after that."

Caradoc shook his head. "There's no reason you can't give us an answer right now."

"We might find ourselves making a hasty decision we would all regret. No, Councilman, give us three days, and then you'll have my decision."

Understanding What You've Read

1. You know that "Danger or Not?" is science fiction. It takes place on another planet. What is the name of the planet? What is the weather like on the planet? Find details on pages 263–264 that support your answers.

2. Why were Jonathan and his mother on Anderson Two? Find the paragraph on page 263 that tells you.

3. Who were the native inhabitants of Anderson Two? Give two or three sentences that describe their *fantastic* characteristics.

4. In a fantasy, the realistic details that describe fantastic characters can make the characters seem real. What details do you learn about Yellger's mother on page 272 that make her seem like a person?

5. In Isaac Asimov's description of the world of the future, what details are different from the world as you know it today?

Writing

1. Imagine that you could get into a time machine and journey one hundred years into the future. Choose a place with which you are familiar, such as your school or your town. Write some sentences or paragraphs describing what this place might be like one hundred years from now.

2. Write a report of one or more paragraphs that Inspector Derodin might have made after reaching her decision on the suitability of Anderson Two for colonization. In your report, consider what the weather is like; whether the land is mountainous, flat, wet, or dry; what kind of housing you would find; what the people who live there are like; and what your recommendation is for future settlement by outsiders.

More Stories of Strange Worlds

The Mortal Instruments by T. Ernesto Bethancourt. Holiday, 1977. Eddie Rodriguez, Olympic-caliber athlete and top student, disappears . . .

Can I Get There by Candlelight? by Jean Slaughter Doty. Illustrated by Ted Lewin. Macmillan, 1980. A horse story and fantasy about a friendship that crosses the barriers of time.

Enchantress from the Stars by Sylvia Engdahl. Atheneum, 1970. A young scientist visits another planet where civilization is not as advanced as it is on her home planet.

The Cry of the Crow by Jean Craighead George. Harper & Row, 1980. A youngster rescues and trains a talking crow but can't control its dangerous instincts.

A Wrinkle in Time by Madeleine L'Engle. Farrar, Straus & Giroux, 1962. Meg, Charles Wallace, and Calvin find themselves involved in a rescue attempt that takes them across time and space.

Caves of Fire and Ice by Shirley Rousseau Murphy. Atheneum, 1980. The fourth book in the science fiction series about the planet Ere.

Star Ka'at World by André Norton and Dorothy Madlee. Walker and Co., 1976. Two human children, Jim and Elly Mae, find themselves transported to a world ruled by cats.

Part 5
Seeing It Through

SKILLS LESSON

Understanding Qualifying Ideas in Sentences

The young boy might not be in trouble if he had paid attention to one little word—*some*. Missing that one word changed the whole idea of his father's statement. Words like *some* are very important when you read. They **qualify** or **limit** ideas in sentences.

Words and Word Groups That Limit the Main Thought of a Sentence

Look at the sentences below. See how one small word changes the meaning of each one.

All of my friends play baseball.
Most of my friends play baseball.
Some of my friends play baseball.
None of my friends plays baseball.

You can see how important it is to pay attention to words like the ones in italics in these sentences. Watching for them when you read can save you from getting incorrect information.

Groups of words can also limit the main thought of a sentence. The main thought in each of the following sentences is the same: "We play baseball."

1. We play baseball.
2. We play baseball *every Saturday.*

See how the words in italics in sentence 2 limit the main thought. They tell when "We play baseball." Read sentences 3 and 4 below. Notice that the words in italics further limit the main thought, "We play baseball."

3. We play baseball every Saturday *during July and August.*
4. We play baseball every Saturday during July and August *except when it rains.*

The words *during July and August* tell you that sentence 3 isn't about every Saturday in the year. When the words *except when it rains* are added, the sentence is about even fewer Saturdays.

Here are two more sentences. See how the words in italics in each one limit the meaning of the main thought.

Richard is the only one on the team *who has never struck out.*

We'll get our picture in the paper *if we win the championship.*

The first sentence would be silly without the qualifying idea *who has never struck out.* There can't be just one player on the team. The main thought of the second sentence is, "We'll get our picture in the paper." This makes sense, but it isn't true. The team will *only* get its picture in the paper if it wins. If you want to be sure of your facts, pay attention to qualifying ideas when you read.

Word Groups That Add Information

Study the two sentences below. The first is like the sentences in the previous section. It contains words that limit the main thought. How is the second sentence different?

Suzanne Lenglen had never been defeated *in her native France.*
Suzanne Lenglen, *who won her first championship at fifteen,* was a great tennis player.

In the first sentence, the words in italics *limit* the main thought. Without the words *in her native France,* the sentence would not be true. What is the main thought of the second sentence? Is it true without the words *who won her first championship at fifteen?* The idea that she was a great tennis player remains the same with or without these words. These words have another purpose. They give you additional information about Suzanne Lenglen.

Pay attention to words that add information. The ideas you get if you miss them *may* be correct. But you may miss important or interesting facts. Read the following pair of sentences. What information is added in the second sentence?

"Babe" Didrikson Zaharias was a great athlete.
"Babe" Didrikson Zaharias was a great athlete who excelled in baseball, bowling, tennis, golf, and track.

You can see that the added information can be as important as the main thought of the sentence. The statement that "Babe" Didrikson Zaharias was a great athlete means more when you know how many sports she excelled in.

Try This

Read each of the sentences below. Study the qualifying words in italics. Do they limit the main thought of each sentence or add information to the main thought?

1. *One* of the girls brought skis.
2. We'll go to the movies *on Saturday if it rains.*
3. Judy spent three weeks in Africa *during January.*
4. *At the age of eight,* Nadia Comaneci won the gymnastic competition *in the Romanian National Junior Championships.*
5. Arturo Toscanini became famous as a conductor, *although he began his career as a cellist.*

Synonyms

Rachel Curewell, M.D.

"Doc, you've got to call an ambulance. I'm very sick."

"Now, Mr. Verbosity. Try to stay **serene**. Be calm. What are your **symptoms**? What signs make you think you're so sick?"

"Oh, it isn't a sign, Doc. It was a conversation I had with my neighbor when she came to visit. She told me that I'm **hospitable**. How long do you think I'll have to be off work?"

"I don't understand. You are hospitable. You are a welcoming sort of person. But that doesn't mean you're sick."

"Do you mean you won't have to give me a subscription? I hate to take those pills and cough stirrups."

"Mr. Verbosity, I don't send out magazines. But wait. I think I know what your problem is now. And I do have a prescription for you. Get yourself one of these."

"A dictionary? All right, but it'll be tough to swallow."

Word Play

1. Synonyms are words with the same or nearly the same meanings. Find a synonym for each boldfaced word in the story. Then use each synonym in a sentence.
2. Look up *subscription* and *prescription* in a dictionary. Find a synonym for each word. Use the synonyms in sentences.

Pay attention to words that qualify or limit the main thought of a sentence. If you are not aware of them, you may get incorrect information.

Roberto Clemente didn't want to be an ordinary baseball player. He wanted to be . . .

The Very Best

by Kenneth Rudeen

When Roberto Clemente was a small boy in Puerto Rico—long before he ever dreamed of becoming a great baseball player—just having a baseball was important. Not many boys had real baseballs, white and round and firm with neat stitches along the seams. Roberto and his friends made their own baseballs. They would find an old golf ball. They'd use that for the center. Then they would get some string and wind it around the golf ball and tape it all together.

In Puerto Rico baseball was the favorite sport. Baseball players were heroes to Roberto.

Roberto Clemente was born in the town of Carolina [kä′rō·lē′nä], Puerto Rico, on August 18, 1934, not far from the big city of San Juan. There were other boys much better at baseball than he was. People did not say, "Roberto is going to be a great ballplayer." He was small and thin. He could not hit the ball as hard or throw it as far as the bigger boys of his age.

Roberto and his friends played a game that was more like softball than baseball. They did not have the gloves or catching masks and pads to handle the hard, stinging baseball the big-

leaguers use. But they saw the real game played in the park in Carolina—and they longed to play there, too, someday.

When time came for Roberto to go to high school, he was happy. The high school had a real baseball field. It had real baseballs, gloves, and masks. Roberto played the outfield. He had to run fast to get the balls that were hit in his direction and

throw hard to keep the hitter from running to extra bases.

Roberto had always been a fast runner. Now he worked hard to become a good thrower and a good hitter. Roberto's high school had a track team. Besides running on the team, Roberto also threw the javelin, which is like a spear. When you throw it, the javelin sails through the air and then comes down and sticks in the ground.

Roberto threw the javelin to

make his arm strong for baseball. In time he became one of the best throwers on his baseball team.

In high school Roberto was a quiet and serious boy. "He did not want to be just an ordinary person—he wanted to be the best," one of his friends said.

Just before Roberto was graduated from high school, he was chosen to play for the team in Santurce [sän·tōōr′sā], a town near Carolina. Roberto was paid to play baseball for this town. He did not make a great deal of money, but now he was *somebody.* People turned their heads to look at him when he walked in the plaza. He was the new young ballplayer, **Roberto Clemente.**

Roberto wanted to be the best. He wanted to play in the major leagues. Men who look for new players for the major leagues came to see him in Puerto Rico. They saw him hit the ball hard. They saw him catch it in the outfield with sure hands. They saw him throw the ball fast and true. They saw him run swiftly.

In 1954, when Roberto was nineteen years old, he was chosen by one of the most famous teams in the National League, the Brooklyn Dodgers. He was very happy to have this chance. The Dodgers were the team of Jackie Robinson. Jackie was the first black man to play in the major leagues. He was a wonderful player, but he had many problems with white people who did not accept black people as equals.

So while Roberto was happy, he was also scared. He was going far from home for the first time in his life, and to places where black people still were not always treated fairly.

First, Roberto was sent to Montreal in Canada to play for a farm team of the Dodgers. A farm team helps prepare young players for the major leagues.

The Dodgers had a problem. They wanted to keep Roberto for the future, but on a farm team, scouts for other teams might discover him. One of these teams might take him.

The Dodgers did not want that to happen. They wanted to hide Roberto from these scouts. But how were they to do it? They had to try to hide him by making it look as if Roberto were not as good a player as he really was.

It was not easy to hide Roberto. The manager of the Montreal team did his best. When Roberto was doing fine in a game, the manager would take him out. When Roberto was having just an ordinary day, the manager would leave him in.

Roberto did not know why he was being treated this way. He became confused and angry. He was lonely, anyway, living among strangers so far from home. But his desire to play, and

to be the best, was stronger than his loneliness and his anger. He kept on playing.

The Dodgers just could not make him look bad enough. Other teams could see that he was a fine player. Scouts for the Pittsburgh Pirates, another team in the National League, watched Roberto closely. They decided to take him and have him play for them.

Right from the start the people of Pittsburgh loved Roberto. He was tremendous as a fielder. He had a trick of catching a fly ball way up in the air, with both of his feet off the ground, and then whirling to throw the ball back to the infield before his feet came down to Earth. He thought nothing of crashing into walls and fences if he had to do that to catch a ball. He also became an excellent hitter.

More and more black men, more and more Spanish-speaking players like Roberto were coming into major league baseball. But still there were times when Roberto felt that he and other Spanish-speaking players were treated unfairly. He believed that they were not given as much praise and publicity as the others, even when they were just

as good. Roberto was the kind of man who could make people listen to him. He asked for equal treatment for Spanish-speaking players. Whenever he could help one of them, he did.

By 1960 Roberto's Pirates were strong enough to win the championship of the National League. They played the American League champions, the New York Yankees, in the World Series. There were seven games in that World Series. Roberto made a hit in every game and the Pirates won.

Roberto went on to win four batting championships in the National League. Nearly every year he was a member of the All-Star team—the best players from all the teams in the National League.

Every winter, after the major league baseball season ended in the United States, Roberto went home to Puerto Rico. On one return trip he met Vera Zabala, the woman he later married. They built a beautiful house in the town of Rio Piedras [rē′ō pē·ā′ dräs], which is near Carolina, and in time had three boys.

When Roberto talked to young Puerto Ricans, he remembered the rough playing field of his boyhood and he began to dream of a sports city for the island. There young people could be able to play baseball, basketball, tennis, and soccer with the best equipment.

Each spring he returned to the United States to play for the Pirates. But not until 1971 did he and the Pirates win another National League championship and go into another World Series. In this World Series, the Pirates faced the Baltimore Orioles. Nearly everybody thought Baltimore was a better team than Pittsburgh.

The score was 0–0 in the fourth inning of the last game of the Series when Roberto stepped up to bat. The ball floated in toward Roberto. Crack! went the bat. The ball flew over the outfield and into the seats beyond. It was a home run! Pittsburgh was ahead in the game, 1–0.

In the eighth inning the Pirates scored another run. Baltimore scored a run in the eighth inning, too, but the Orioles could do nothing after that to even the score. The Pirates won the Series in the last possible game by the score of 2–1. Without Roberto's

home run, who knows what might have happened?

Just as he had in 1960, Roberto made a hit in every game of the World Series. He was voted the most valuable player of the Series by the reporters who wrote about it. Of all the players on both teams, Roberto Clemente was the very best.

There was just one more thing left in baseball for Roberto to do. That was to make 3,000 hits. He would soon be thirty-eight years old—very old for a ballplayer. Only ten men in the entire history of baseball had ever played long enough or well enough to make 3,000 hits. These were special heroes.

At the very end of the 1972 season, on September 30 in Pittsburgh, Roberto hit Number 3,000. He was a special hero. He was the very best.

On December 31, 1972, Roberto Clemente was killed in an airplane crash. He was on his way from San Juan to bring supplies to earthquake victims in Managua [mä·nä'gwä], a city in the Central American country of Nicaragua [nik·ə·rä'gwə].

Shortly after his death, Roberto was elected to Baseball's

Hall of Fame—the greatest honor a baseball player can receive. The Hall of Fame is in Cooperstown, New York. In it there are pictures of the best players, along with things such as their bats and caps.

Before Roberto died, he worked hard to see his dream of a sports city realized. The building of it, however, began after his death. It is called Ciudad Deportiva Roberto Clemente—The Roberto Clemente Sports City.

Understanding What You've Read

1. How were the conditions when Roberto played baseball as a young boy different from when he played in high school?
2. How did Roberto get to play for the Pittsburgh Pirates?
3. What was the one thing in baseball that Roberto felt he had to do after winning the 1971 World Series? What was so special about doing this?
4. How was Roberto honored even after his death?

Applying the Skills Lesson

Read each sentence below. Study the words in italics. Do they limit or add information to the main thought?

1. *Every winter,* after the major league baseball season ended in the United States, Roberto went home to Puerto Rico.
2. Nearly every year he was a member of the All-Star team—*the best players from all the teams in the National League.*
3. *Nearly* everybody thought Baltimore was a better team than Pittsburgh.
4. Shortly after his death, Roberto was elected to baseball's Hall of Fame—*the greatest honor a baseball player can receive.*

As you read, look for words that add information to or limit the main thought of a sentence. Such qualifying ideas can often help you to better understand what you read.

Nadia Comaneci received the first perfect mark, the first 10, ever scored in gymnastics at the Olympics. Her dedication and hard work led her to become a . . .

Young Olympic Star

by Frank Deford

There are so many athletes and so many winners, but in the first week of the 1976 Olympics in Montreal, Canada, there was only one star. That star was a child named Nadia Comaneci. Every bit of her was poured out every night: over the vault, on top of the beam, on the bars, and upon the mat of the Montreal Forum. All eighty-six pounds of her was graceful.

In 1976 Nadia was fourteen years old. She and her family lived in Onesti, a factory town in the mountains of Romania. Her father worked as an automobile mechanic and her mother worked in a hospital.

Nadia's precision and daring in gymnastics had never been seen before in an Olympics. And few women in any sport had ever so charmed the Games. Nadia burst upon the world with the first perfect Olympic gymnastic score, a 10, on the first day of competition.

Nadia was in every final gymnastic event. She won gold medals for all-around, for the balancing beam, and for the bars. She led Romania to a silver medal in the team competition. She also took a bronze medal for floor exercises, and just missed

another bronze medal with a fourth place in the vault. Eyes never strayed from her.

As a very young child, Nadia had shown signs of athletic skill. She always beat her friends in running and playing and jumping. When Nadia entered kindergarten, gymnastics was part of the school athletic program. Her coach, Bela Karolyi [kä′rō·yē], found Nadia in kindergarten.

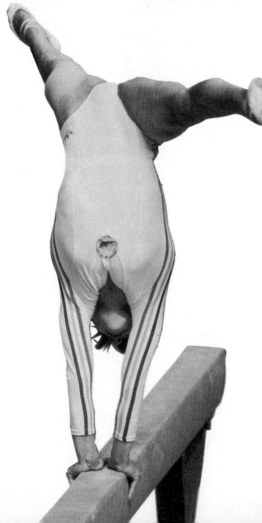

From that time Bela Karolyi and his wife Marta trained Nadia. For four hours every day Nadia worked out in the gym. Within a year, at age seven, Nadia placed thirteenth in her first meet. She was number one the very next year, in 1971, when she competed in the Romanian National Junior Championships.

At the 1976 Olympics in Montreal, Nadia's hard work paid off. She received four of her seven 10's on the uneven bars. But it was on the beam that she seemed to show more of her unbelievable skill. She scored her three other 10's on the beam. Her pace and poise hushed the crowd.

"Everyone is scared on the beam," said a Canadian coach.

"It is the most difficult. No matter how good they are, they are all shaking inside." But Nadia was very sure of herself.

The beam is four inches wide. In the ninety seconds that was allowed, Nadia did a handstand, twirled and skipped, did many fancy dance steps, a back walk-over, cartwheels, split leaps into the air, and a double somersault to get off. No one had ever given such a show as this one.

Nadia received a gold medal for being the best all-around gymnast in the world. She came back to Romania with three gold medals, a bronze, and seven perfect scores. She had truly been the star of the 1976 Olympics.

Understanding What You've Read

1. What is a gymnast?
2. What was so amazing about many of Nadia's scores in the 1976 Olympics?
3. Why is the beam considered so difficult? How did Nadia's performance on the beam show her great skill?

Applying the Skills Lesson

Read each sentence below. Study the qualifying ideas in italics. Do they limit the main thought of each sentence or add information to the main thought?

1. Every bit of her [Nadia] was poured out every night: *over the vault, on top of the beam, on the bars, and upon the mat of the Montreal Forum.*
2. Nadia's precision and daring in gymnastics had never been seen before *in an Olympics.*
3. Nadia burst upon the world with the first perfect Olympic gymnastic score, *a 10,* on the first day of competition.

Understanding Qualifying Ideas in Sentences

Sentences in textbooks often have words or groups of words that qualify or limit the main thought or that add information to the main thought. It is important to pay attention to these words to get the correct information.

As you read the following selections, look for the main thought of a sentence. Then see how a word or a group of words qualifies that main thought. The sidenotes will help you in the first selection.

Understanding Qualifying Ideas in Sentences in Language Arts

How Our Language Grows
Ups and Downs

Just as people change all during their lives, words frequently change in meaning over a period of time.

These words qualify the main thought of the sentence. They tell you that *words don't change all at once.*

Often these changes are simple alterations of a word's original meaning. *Hospital* once meant a "guest room" or "inn." *Host, hospitality,* and *hospital* still show the meaning.

In the course of change, however, many words have become more dignified. *Nice,* an often overworked compliment today, wasn't always such. It originally meant "foolish or ignorant." *Minister* once meant "servant." The word still carries the

These words add information. What do they tell you about the word *nice*?

meaning that a minister serves the people. However, over the centuries the word has moved up in status. So has *respect*, which at one time meant "to spy."

Many other words have taken on less respectable meanings. When we refer to someone today as being *sly*, we're hardly paying a compliment. At one time we would have been, however, for *sly* once meant "wise." The word *bribe* once simply meant "a piece of bread." How might its original meaning be related to what it means today?

Our language is constantly changing. Even words we take for granted have been involved in the process.

— *Language for Daily Use:* Brown
Harcourt Brace Jovanovich

How do these words qualify the main thought of the sentence?

Building Skills

Read each sentence below. Study the qualifying words in italics. Do they limit the main thought in each sentence or do they add information to the main thought?

1. *Often* these changes are simple alterations of a word's original meaning.
2. In the course of change, however, *many* words have become more dignified.
3. *Just as people change during their lives*, words frequently change in meaning over a period of time.

Understanding Qualifying Ideas in Sentences in Mathematics

There are no sidenotes for this selection. Read it and then answer the questions that follow.

Pirate Pete must walk the plank. But he can go free if he can solve three problems correctly.

He can use this division exercise for all the problems, but he must give different answers.

$$
\begin{array}{r}
17\text{ R5} \\
25\overline{)430} \\
-25 \\
\hline
180 \\
-175 \\
\hline
5
\end{array}
$$

What should Pete's answers be?

A. A pair of boots costs 25 pesos. How many pairs of boots can be bought with 430 pesos?
Answer: ☐ pairs of boots

B. If 25 pirates equally share 430 gold coins, how many coins will each pirate receive?
How many coins will be left over?
Answer: ☐ coins for each pirate
☐ coins left over

C. How many 25-gallon barrels are needed to store 430 gallons of water?
Answer: ☐ barrels

— Mathematics Around Us
Scott, Foresman

Building Skills

Read each sentence below. Study the qualifying words in italics. Do they limit the main thought of each sentence or add information to the main thought?

1. But he [Pirate Pete] can go free *if he can solve three problems correctly.*
2. He can use this division exercise for all the problems, *but he must give different answers.*
3. If 25 pirates *equally* share 430 gold coins, how many coins will each pirate receive?

SKILLS LESSON

Understanding Cause-and-Effect Relationships

Why did the real estate developer build a giant elephant in New Jersey? Read the sentence below to find out.

In 1881 James V. Lafferty built a giant elephant in South Atlantic City because he thought the elephant would bring people to the area.

Do you think Lafferty had a sensible reason? Silly or sensible, the reason why something happens can be as interesting or important as the thing that happened. You can find the

304

answer to the question "Why?" when you read carefully.

Remember that *why things happen* is called the **cause.** *What happened* is called the **effect.** Sometimes word clues help make cause-and-effect relationships clear. *Because* in the example on page 304 is such a clue. Other word clues are *therefore, as a result,* and *so.*

Sometimes authors don't use word clues to show cause-and-effect relationships. When they don't, you can ask yourself "What happened?" to find the effect and "Why did it happen?" to find the cause. If the example on page 304 didn't have the word *because* in it, would you still know why Lafferty built the elephant?

In 1881 James V. Lafferty built a giant elephant in South Atlantic City. He thought the elephant would bring people to the area.

Try out the *why* and *what* questions. What did James Lafferty do? He built a giant elephant. Why did he do it? He thought it would bring people to the area. It's like a riddle, isn't it? But you don't have to think up the answer. It's right there in what you're reading. See if you can find the cause and effect in the next sentences.

People began to buy land and build houses near the elephant. The area grew into a town that was called Margate.

Each of the sentences tells one thing that happened. One of the things caused the other to happen. If people hadn't bought land and built houses, the area wouldn't have become a town. So the cause was *People began to buy land and build houses near the elephant.* The effect was *The area grew into a town that was called Margate.*

One Effect from Several Causes

Some things have more than one cause for happening. The paragraph below gives more than one cause for one effect. See if you can find all the causes.

People who visited the elephant were very impressed. The elephant was almost twenty meters high at the tallest point. The body was over eleven meters long and over six meters wide. When visitors climbed the stairs to the top, they had a great view of the surrounding area.

The effect in this paragraph is given in the first sentence: "People who visited the elephant were very impressed." The causes for this are given in the sentences that follow it. Can you find them? One is the size of the elephant. The other is the view from the top of the elephant. Each of these things caused the visitors to be impressed.

One Cause Leading to Several Effects

Just as one effect can be the result of a number of causes, one cause may lead to a number of effects.

The elephant was so impressive that it attracted thousands of visitors. Even very important people came to see it. One woman made news by dancing on the elephant's head.

The paragraph above tells the effects of one cause. The cause is that the elephant was impressive. The first effect is in the same sentence as the cause. The fact that the elephant was impressive led to (1) thousands of people visiting it, (2) very important people visiting it, and (3) a woman making news by dancing on its head.

Try This

1. The following paragraph tells some other things about what happened to the elephant at Margate since it was built in 1881. Find the effect and tell the causes of this effect.

    In time, the elephant's toes had rotted from the salt air. A storm had blown off the howdah, or covered seat, on its back. The elephant had been repainted a dull black. People in Margate began to dislike having such an ugly elephant in their town.

2. Let's not leave our elephant friend in such an unhappy state. Here is the happy ending. There are two effects in this paragraph. One is that *the elephant survived*. What were the causes? What was the final related effect?

    But the elephant survived. It was given to the city of Margate in 1970. A committee raised money to restore it. The government matched the funds the committee raised. When the restoration was complete, the city turned the elephant over to a museum.

VOCABULARY STUDY

Etymologies

BRUTUS (YOUR HOST): Good evening, folks. And welcome to *Run for Your Life,* the first Latin TV quiz show. Tonight's first contestant is from far-off Gaul. Let's have a big hand for Pierre LaBouche. Pierre, I understand you're just learning Latin.

PIERRE: How's that again?

BRUTUS: How does it feel to be on Latin **television**, Pierre?

PIERRE: Television. Isn't that from the Greek *tēle-*, meaning "far off," and the Latin *vision,* from a word meaning "to see"? It's nice to be seen from far off.

BRUTUS: You'll know the **benefit** if you answer the next question correctly.

PIERRE: Benefit? The Latin *bene* means "good." I get something good if I answer correctly?

BRUTUS: Right! You'll win a prize. The question is: Is Rome **inhabited**?

PIERRE: That's easy. The Latin *in* means "in." *Habitare* means "to dwell." Of course Rome is inhabited. Lots of people live in Rome.

BRUTUS: Congratulations! You've won the prize!

PIERRE: Thanks, Brutus. There's just one thing I've been wondering. Why is this show called *Run for Your Life*?

BRUTUS: Oh, that refers to the prize. Bring Leo out, please. (STAGEHAND brings out a ferocious-looking lion. PIERRE screams and runs the opposite way.) Funny.... Nobody ever stays to collect the prize.

Word Play

1. Tell what the word in boldface means in each sentence below. The etymologies, or the Greek and Latin word parts from which these words come, will help you decide.

   a. A bear's place of **habitation** is a cave.

   b. Exercise is **beneficial** to one's health.

   c. The baseball game was **televised**.

2. *Uni-* is a prefix that comes from the Latin word *unus*, which means "one." *Cycle* comes from the Greek word *kyklos*, which means "wheel." What do you think *unicycle* means? Check your answer in a dictionary.

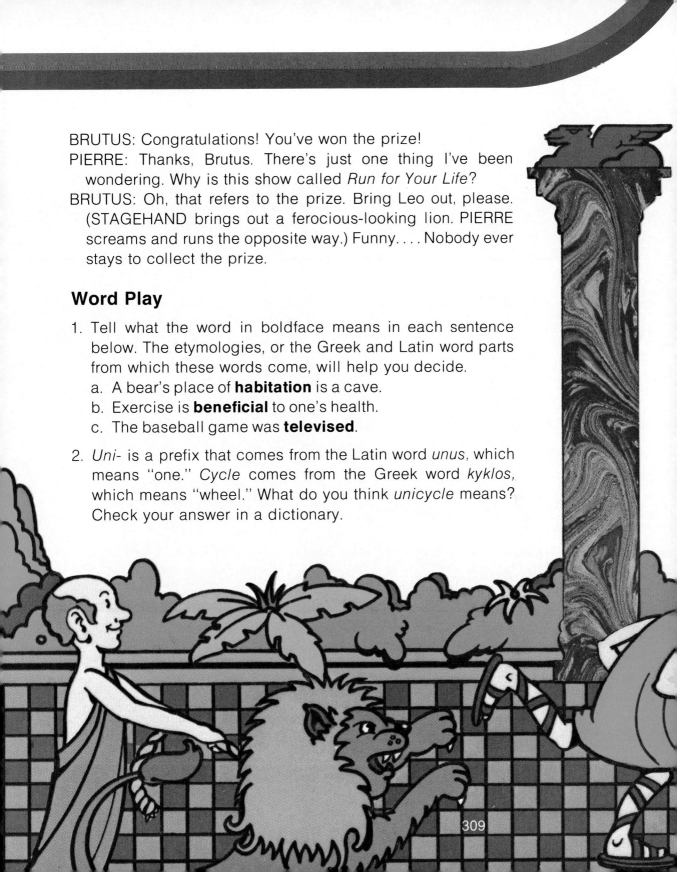

309

To understand cause-and-effect relationships when no clue words are given, ask yourself: "What happened? Why did it happen?"

Isamu Noguchi's sculptures are seen and admired all over the world. They were created with a variety of materials, and appear in numerous shapes and forms, because to Isamu Noguchi . . .

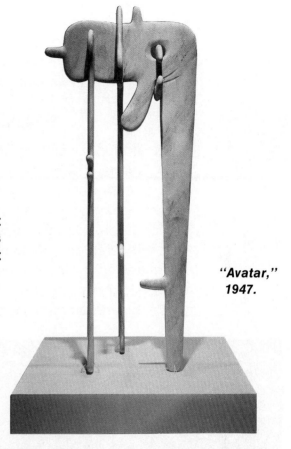

*"Avatar,"
1947.*

SCULPTURE IS EVERYTHING

by Nicholas Pease

311

Ask most people what a sculpture is, and probably they will answer, "a statue." But ask that question of Isamu Noguchi, the world-famous artist, and his reply might very well be, "Sculpture? Why, almost anything can be a sculpture!" Noguchi's many works bear that opinion out.

Sculpture is gardens. . . .

Noguchi was born in 1904 to an American mother and a Japanese father. At the age of two, he was brought from the United States to Japan, where he grew up among the serene and lovely stone-filled gardens that are a traditional form of Japanese art. "My regard for stone as the basic element of sculpture," he would later write, "is related to my involvement with gardens. . . ." Out of earth, stone, grass, and trees Noguchi has sculpted elegant gardens such as the UNESCO center in Paris.

Sculpture is the human form. . . .

When Isamu was thirteen, it was decided that he should get an American education. He spent his high school years in Indiana and then went to Connecticut to study with the sculptor Gutzon Borglum. The boy was determined to become an artist. To Isamu's dismay, Borglum said that sculpture was the wrong field for him.

In a way, the man was right, for Borglum was the creator of Mount Rushmore and other huge public monuments. Noguchi's talent ran to other forms—more personal and experimental kinds of sculpture. He went to study in New York, where he developed a style that soon brought him recognition.

In 1929, at the age of twenty-five, the young artist had one of his dreams come true. He won a fellowship that took him to Paris, where he began working with the man who was his idol—the sculptural genius Constantin Brancusi. Here was Noguchi's chance to learn about new forms, new materials for his creative urge.

At about this time he began two important lifelong friendships. One was with the well-known architect R. Buckminster Fuller. The other was with the choreographer Martha Graham. Both friends influenced Noguchi in his work.

Noguchi sculpted both Fuller's and Graham's heads. This form of sculpture, called *busts,* was very realistic.

"Bird in Space," 1919, by Constantin Brancusi.
Bronze; height, 54"

313

Sculpture is a stage design. . . .

Martha Graham was a pioneer in the art of modern dance. She created dances that were abstract, suggesting ideas and feelings through gesture without acting them out in the ordinary way. Noguchi began designing stage settings for her that helped bring out these ideas and feelings. With a few pieces of wood, stone, metal, or wire, he created a world for the dancers to move in. One example is *Night Journey,* a dance based on a Greek myth. The objects Noguchi created for it suggest rocks, steps, bones, and other things important to the tale.

Stage set for Martha Graham's production of "Alcestis."

Sculpture is heavy—or light. . . .

Over the years, Noguchi has explored a wide range of possibilities in sculpture. He has made pieces that show extremes in lightness and in heaviness. This was his way of expressing his own wonder and delight at the shapes in the world around him. At two extremes are the massive, rounded hulk called "Mountain" and the almost weight-less piece called "Bird's Nest."

Noguchi coined the word *akari* to describe the paper lanterns he designed. He wanted to suggest both light as illumination and lightness as opposed to weight. "Looking more fragile than they are," he says, "the *akari* seem to float, casting their light as in passing. . . . They perch light as a feather, some pinned to the wall, others clipped to a cord, and all may be moved with the thought." Noguchi's *akari* grew out of an ancient Japanese tradition of lantern-making.

An example of akari.

"Mountain," 1964.

Sculpture is water. . . .

Always seeking new forms of expression, Noguchi turned to fountain design. He devised ways of making sculptures that appear both solid and liquid at the same time. One example is the Fountains at Expo '70 in Osaka, Japan, 1970.

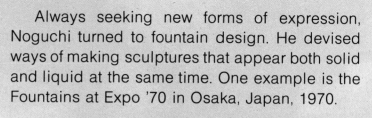

Sculpture is the outside, inside. . . .

Noguchi also designed "inside landscapes"—metal arranged along walls and ceilings and shaped to resemble rolling hills. One sculpture even has its own "river"—a flow of water down a stone and metal wall. Seeing and hearing the water, it is easy to forget that one is standing in the building at 666 Fifth Avenue, New York City!

Sculpture is a part of life. . . .

For a time, Noguchi turned to designing furniture. He wanted to make things that might become part of people's lives. So he created objects that were both attractive and completely practical.

It may seem surprising, but Noguchi has one interest that many would not think of as "art" at all: playgrounds. Noguchi created a plaster model of a playground he proposed for the United Nations Building. You can see climbing bars, a seesaw, slides, hills, tunnels, caves, and other exciting places to play.

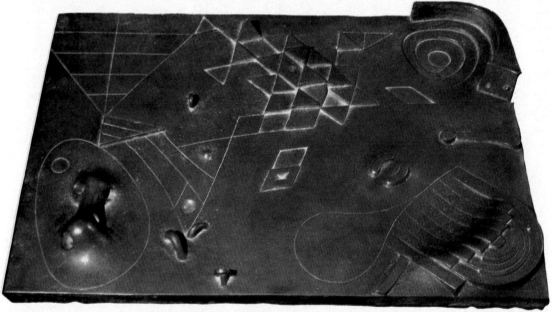

Most of Noguchi's sculptures are abstract designs that simply *suggest* familiar objects. But they are also lines and shapes that realistically depict the world. His sculptures are to be viewed — but they are also to be felt, climbed, listened to, and played upon. To Noguchi, sculpture is water, stone, paper, wood, and metal. It reflects yesterday's traditions while pointing the way to tomorrow. For all these reasons, to Isamu Noguchi, sculpture is everything.

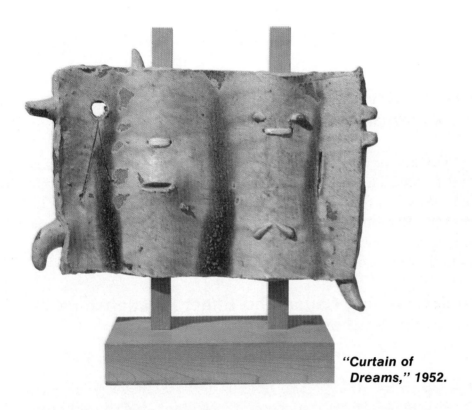

"Curtain of Dreams," 1952.

Understanding What You've Read

1. Name three kinds of sculptures that Noguchi created.
2. Why did Gutzon Borglum say that sculpture was the wrong field for Noguchi?
3. What kinds of materials did Noguchi use in his sculptures?
4. Look at the photographs of Noguchi's sculptures. Do you like the sculptures? Why or why not?

Applying the Skills Lesson

1. Read the first paragraph on page 315. Why did Noguchi make pieces that showed extremes in lightness and in heaviness?
2. Read the first paragraph on page 318. What caused Noguchi to turn to designing furniture?

Understanding Cause-and-Effect Relationships

Textbooks often explain events in terms of their causes and effects. The authors will tell you *what happened* (an effect). Read to find out *why* an event happened (the cause or causes). Remember that words such as *so* and *because* may signal a cause-and-effect relationship. Refer to the sidenotes to help you understand causes and effects.

Understanding Cause-and-Effect Relationships in Social Studies

Technology Helps Pests Too

This is an *effect*. The causes are explained in the next two sentences.

This sentence further explains the effect stated in the first sentence.

The people of Israel have been very successful in making their desert land bloom. They drill deep wells and use power pumps. They pipe water long distances to where it can best be used. They now grow two or three crops a year on land that used to be desert.

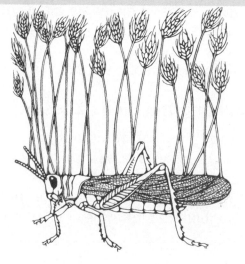

But there are problems as well as benefits. Water helps insect pests as well as crops. And new crops have meant new kinds of insect pests. Some of the pests attack more than one crop. Since the land is planted all year, the pests have food all year.

Land is irrigated to grow crops, not insects. People do not intend to grow both, but they do. Technology may create new problems even as it helps solve old ones.

—People and Change
Silver Burdett

> **This paragraph describes several *effects* of water being piped into the desert. What are those effects?**

Building Skills

1. Read the first paragraph of the selection again. Why have the people of Israel been successful in making their desert land bloom?
2. Read the last paragraph of the selection again. What are two effects of irrigating land?

Understanding Cause-and-Effect Relationships in Science

The Lively Mouse

About 200 years ago an investigator named Joseph Priestley was trying to find out what living things did to air.

> **The causes and effects that follow are all connected to this cause.**

Sometimes an effect is told before the cause. Why did Priestley place a mouse under a glass jar?

Priestley placed a mouse under a glass jar so that the mouse would have only the air in the jar to breathe. Then he watched what happened. For a while the mouse in the jar ran and jumped about, washed its fur, and sniffed the air. It was as lively as a mouse can be. Then it began to get drowsy. It seemed to be going to sleep.

What caused this to happen? The next paragraph will help you figure out the answer.

1

Like all animals, the mouse was breathing in air and taking oxygen from it. The oxygen helped to give the mouse energy. Each time the mouse breathed out, it gave up carbon dioxide and water. As the mouse breathed, the air in the jar held less oxygen—and more carbon dioxide. Why do you think the mouse became drowsy?

The author asks you to state a cause. It is explained in the last sentence of this selection.

Then Priestley put a green plant under the jar with the mouse. In a while the mouse was lively and scampering about again. Joseph Priestley saw that the air in the jar had become "good air" again. But he was not sure why.

Again, the author is asking you to state a cause. Try to answer the question.

Can you explain why Priestley's mouse became lively again after the

322

2

green plant was put in the jar? The green plant was giving off oxygen, as green plants do. Oxygen was just what the mouse needed. It had become drowsy because there was too little oxygen and too much carbon dioxide in the air.

The effect is explained before the cause. Why had the mouse become drowsy?

—*Concepts in Science:* Brown
Harcourt Brace Jovanovich

Building Skills

1. Study the two pictures that go with the selection. Which of the following sets of "labels" describes picture 1?

   a. Effect: The mouse is drowsy.
      Cause: It is not getting enough oxygen to give it energy.
   b. Effect: The mouse is lively.
      Cause: The mouse is getting oxygen from the green plant.

2. The following two sentences are from the selection you have just read. What word or words are clues that a cause and effect are being described?

   a. Priestley placed a mouse under a glass jar so that the mouse would have only the air in the jar to breathe.
   b. It had become drowsy because there was too little oxygen and too much carbon dioxide in the air.

SKILLS LESSON

Drawing Conclusions

The woman in the cartoon has drawn a conclusion about the car she and her friend have built. Her conclusion, ". . . we left something out," is based on what the home-built car looks like. It is also based on her knowledge of what a car *should* look like. In other words, the woman used the available facts and her own experience to help her draw the conclusion.

In your reading, you will have many opportunities to draw conclusions from the facts presented. For example, read the paragraph below. What conclusion can you draw?

Roberta wrote a short poem about her favorite outdoor sport. The poem was not about a sport in which a ball is used. The sports Roberta enjoys most are bowling, golf, and water skiing.

You know that the poem is about an *outdoor* sport that doesn't involve the use of a ball. Which sports mentioned are outdoor sports? Golf and water skiing. Of these two sports, which does not involve the use of a ball? Notice that *Roberta's poem is about water skiing* is the only conclusion you can draw based on the facts.

Drawing More Than One Conclusion

Sometimes you can draw more than one conclusion from a given set of facts. Read the following paragraphs.

For her science project, Beth decided to study the eating habits of three animals: horses, rabbits, and cats. She knew that a herbivore is an animal that eats only plants. A carnivore eats mostly other animals. An omnivore eats both plants and animals.

After several months of gathering information, Beth learned that horses will eat oats, hay, sugar, leaves, and grasses. They do not eat meat. Rabbits eat only lettuce, carrots, and a few other kinds of vegetables. Generally, cats do not eat much vegetable matter. They like fish, liver, beef, and poultry.

On the night she finished her report, Beth made dinner. She made lamb chops, a baked potato, and a green salad.

What conclusions can you draw from the information given in the paragraphs?

1. Horses and rabbits are herbivores.
2. Cats are mostly carnivorous.
3. Horses eat twice as much as rabbits.
4. Beth is an omnivore.
5. All people are omnivores.

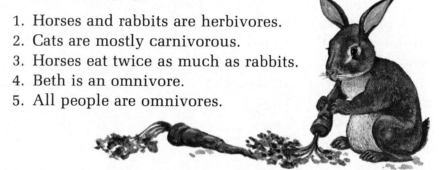

How many conclusions were you able to draw? There are three correct conclusions: 1, 2, and 4. What facts in the paragraphs support conclusion 1: *Horses and rabbits are herbivores?* You are told that a herbivore is an animal that eats only plants. Notice that plants are the only kinds of foods eaten by horses and rabbits. What facts support conclusion 2: *Cats are mostly carnivorous?* Most foods eaten by cats are meats. What facts lead you to draw conclusion 4: *Beth is an omnivore?* The last sentence tells you that she eats both plants (the potato and the salad) and animals (the lamb chop).

You have no way of concluding that horses eat twice as much as rabbits (conclusion 3) because the *amount* of food each animal eats is never mentioned. You also cannot conclude that all people are omnivores. The only person mentioned in the paragraphs is Beth.

Drawing Conclusions from Graphic Aids

You can draw conclusions from facts that are presented in graphic aids. Study the graph below. What conclusion can you draw?

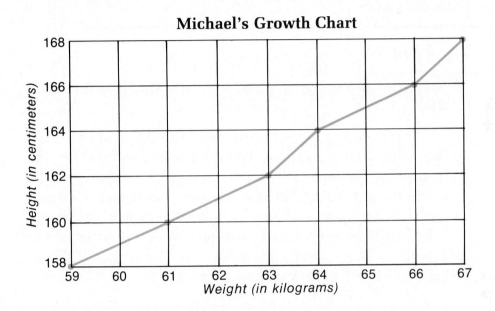

Michael's Growth Chart

Which of the following conclusions can you draw?

1. Michael gained 5 kilograms in one year.
2. Michael gained weight as he grew taller.
3. Michael weighed more when he was 158 centimeters than when he was 168 centimeters.

Look at the information given in the graph. How much did Michael weigh when he was 158 centimeters? How much did he weigh when he was 162 centimeters? When he was 166 centimeters? Notice that the graph shows a steady *trend*, or direction, upward. These facts support conclusion 2: *Michael gained weight as he grew taller.*

Conclusion 1 is incorrect because the graph does not tell you anything about how long it took Michael to reach a certain height and weight. The graph shows that conclusion 3 is incorrect. Michael weighed 59 kilograms when he was 158 centimeters tall. He weighed 67 kilograms when he was 168 centimeters tall.

Try This

Read the paragraph below. Answer the question that follows.

Anita wanted to grow flowers in the shape of a smiling face. She planted crocus bulbs in a large circle for the head. She put marigold seeds around the outside of the circle for the hair. She planted two small rows of tulip bulbs for the eyes, and hyacinths for the nose. Last but not least, Anita planted a long curving row of daffodils for the mouth. When spring arrived, Anita was very disappointed. Her flower face had no hair!

Based on the information in the paragraph, what conclusion can you draw?

a. Anita didn't water any of her flowers.
b. The marigolds did not bloom.
c. The bulbs that Anita planted did not bloom.

VOCABULARY STUDY

Antonyms

VON ETCH
PAINTINGS PUZZLING

by Claudia Sanchez

HANKSVILLE, March 25—I've been reviewing art shows for years, and many of them seem alike. But I've never seen anything like the Samson Von Etch Show at the Mortimer Gallery. Each painting is so **different**, it's hard to believe they're all by one artist. Some are **tremendous**. Others are quite small.

"Picnic" is one of the big ones. All the food is as large as life. The banana sticking out of the basket looks so real that you feel as though you could eat it.

"Jungle," which hangs next to "Picnic," is not realistic. "Jungle" is a bunch of **abstract** blobs. It's a **drab** painting. The blobs are all **dull** gray against a muddy brown background. But another painting, "Morning Flowers," is very colorful. It shows three big red, yellow, and blue flowers. They sparkle against a bright green background.

You can see why I had a **difficult** time deciding what to say about this artist. When I saw his self-portrait, however, the job became easy. It's not bad work for a monkey.

Word Play

Find the antonyms, or opposite meanings, for the words in boldface above. Then use each boldfaced word in a sentence.

As you read, think about the things that Margaret Bourke-White accomplished. What conclusions can you draw about the kind of person she was?

Margaret Bourke-White was a great photographer. Many times she risked her life to get the picture she wanted. But her hardest assignment came when crippling illness struck the . . .

WOMAN WITHOUT FEAR

by Harry Gersh

Margaret Bourke-White wanted to take important pictures, pictures that would record the world of her time. Two of the most significant symbols were factories and their machines, and the skylines of our great cities. So Margaret Bourke-White became an industrial photographer.

Margaret had an artist's eye and a scientist's sense. She could look at a drab building or a dirty machine and see a picture of light

"Hydro-Generators," 1928. ▶

and shadow that would give meaning to the subject. She could see the exact angle at which a picture had to be taken. She could figure, almost without thinking, the right distance, light, lens opening, and shutter speed. And her pictures showed it.

She was no braver than most people, but when a picture was involved she forgot to be afraid — or she didn't have time to fear. Once, she needed a particular picture of the New York City skyline. There are thousands of good pictures of the skyline, but Margaret Bourke-White wanted another one, a different one.

Margaret could have shot it from the bay or from across the river. Or she could have shot it from one of the bridges entering the city, or from the ground, looking up at the roofs of the city. But these were ordinary to Margaret. She wanted a new angle — and found it on top of the Chrysler Building. This building was, at that time, the city's tallest structure.

The Chrysler Building, however, had no roof on which a person could stand. It came to a point. Just below the thick spire, a thousand feet over the city streets, Margaret found her best position. That was the picture she wanted, and that's where she went to take it.

In the 1930's, Margaret entered a new field with her camera — that of *photojournalism*. The use of a series of photographs to tell a story had become popular. More and more newspapers and magazines used photographs to report important events (a photo story). Words identifying people and places and times were also used, but the pictures told what happened. Margaret Bourke-White felt right at home in this field and eventually became one of its leaders.

In 1936 Margaret joined the staff of *Life*, the first picture news magazine. The cover photograph on *Life*'s first issue was taken by Margaret Bourke-White. Thirty

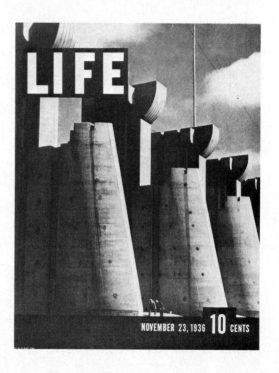

years later, she was still that magazine's star photographer-reporter.

When World War II began in 1939, *Life* sent Margaret to Europe. The editors felt that the faces of people and buildings could often tell more than words could.

In 1942 Margaret flew to China. Then, when the GI's landed in Europe, Margaret went back to Europe and covered our armies. Under direct orders from General Eisenhower, she was flown to every combat zone. She went wherever she thought there was a picture or a story.

Margaret covered all the major battles of World War II, and every major person in them.

She lived off the country like the soldiers, and she had many close calls. While she covered a story on board a ship in the Mediterranean Sea, the ship was torpedoed. Margaret escaped in a lifeboat. While she was flying over the front lines in Italy, a group of German fighters swooped down on her small plane. Her pilot dove until they were only twenty feet above ground. They stayed at that height, up hill and down, as if they were on a road rather than in the air, all the way home.

The Toughest Battle

Some years after the war, when she was at the height of her career, Margaret Bourke-White contracted a disease. There was no defense against it—except courage and a determination not to give in.

A friend took her to a special hospital in New York City. It wasn't easy for her to go there. For Margaret, it meant admitting she was really ill. Yet she faced this decision as she had faced many others. This was where she had to go to accomplish a mission, so she went.

The doctors finally discovered that Margaret had Parkinson's disease—a crippling, incurable disease. The doctors didn't tell

"Famine in India."

"Hudson Coal Co.," 1930.

her, however. They wanted her to think about trying to get stronger.

For a few days, Margaret was very scared. Then the fear passed. She was afraid of only one thing—that the editors of *Life* would find out what was wrong with her and make her stop working. She took care of that with a little story.

"The doctors say I have to exercise," she told the editors of *Life*. "They insist that I walk at least four miles a day."

The editors saw to it that Margaret got all the walking, traveling assignments they could find.

At a meeting of photographers, there was a speech about one of America's greatest photographers, Edward Weston. The speaker described how Weston had grown stiffer and stiffer until he couldn't hold a camera, until he couldn't walk. He had had Parkinson's disease.

As the speaker told of Weston's symptoms. Margaret compared them with her own. They were so alike. She knew she had the same thing. But she couldn't give up—she had never learned how.

Walking is such a simple thing. No one stops to think how to walk or of what's needed to put

"Contour plowing," 1954.

one foot in front of the other. Yet walking involves a certain combination of movements of the arms and legs, of balancing, and of changing the weight at just the right time.

Margaret continued to walk four miles every morning when each step needed tens of decisions and judgments: When do I swing my left arm forward, and at what point do I swing it back? Do I begin to pick up the right leg when the left toe hits the ground, or when the whole foot is on the ground? Do I move my body forward now, or a half-second later? And if I make a mistake, will it send me falling forward?

Then Margaret heard of a surgeon in New York City. He performed operations on the brains of persons with Parkinson's disease. She went to him.

The doctor explained the operation, its chances of success, its dangers. Margaret really heard only one fact: It had been successful in hundreds of cases. She wanted to have the operation. Once she made the decision, she did not change her mind.

Margaret awoke from the operation to find flowers, books, and messages from friends. There were other "gifts," too, but they came a few days later. Margaret's left arm swung loose one day. Her back straightened up on another. Walking once again became simple for her.

That was only the beginning. The rest was hard, patient work. Margaret went back to the hospital to learn to reuse the muscles that had become so weak. She had to relearn how to speak clearly, because the muscles of her throat had been weakened. She tossed and caught a heavy ball for hours every day. She did deep knee bends. She danced.

And she worked with her cameras. She went back to work as a reporter of the world. Margaret Bourke-White just couldn't quit.

Understanding What You've Read

1. What was unusual about how Margaret Bourke-White got her picture of the New York skyline?
2. What is photojournalism? When did this field begin?
3. What was the biggest fear that Margaret had to face?
4. After her surgery, how did Margaret fight her "battle" against Parkinson's disease?

Applying the Skills Lesson

What conclusions can you draw about Margaret Bourke-White from the selection you just read?

1. She was afraid of taking chances of any kind.
2. She was a courageous person, facing challenges, not willing to give up.
3. She had fears, but dealt with them by thinking them through and making decisions.
4. She wasn't a very successful person.

As you read paragraphs in the selection, you can draw conclusions about what has happened and about Toscanini himself. Think about the facts presented and what you know from your own experience.

The regular conductor refuses to work with the orchestra. The audience doesn't want the assistant conductor or the chorus master. In desperation, the manager asks a young, unknown cello player to take over. This is how . . .

TOSCANINI GETS HIS START

by Russell Freedman

The Imperial Theatre in Rio de Janeiro was Brazil's grandest opera house, but on the evening of June 25, 1886, sounds of shouting and stamping could be heard coming from within. Yells and nasty remarks bombarded the stage like exploding firecrackers.

The crowd was furious because Leopoldo Miguez [mē·gās′], the Brazilian conductor, had refused to direct the opera. Miguez and members of the guest Italian Opera Company had disagreed about the production of the operas on the Brazilian tour.

Claudio Rossi, the manager who had arranged the tour, decided to go ahead with *Aïda* [ä·ē′də] as though nothing had happened. He asked the assistant conductor to direct the opera. But Rossi hadn't realized how strong the feelings of the Rio audience were. They had come to the theater not to hear *Aïda* but to honor Leopoldo Miguez.

Even the assistant conductor was drowned out by the noise. Finally, he threw down his baton and went backstage.

Rossi, however, refused to give up. He called the chorus master and ordered him to

conduct. But, surrounded by angry shouts, he too raised his baton only once before leaping off the podium.

"What else can I do?" asked the puzzled Rossi. "There is no one left to conduct the opera."

One of the singers went over to Rossi. She hesitated for a moment, then in a low voice said, "You know Arturo Toscanini — the chorus master's young assistant. He knows the opera well enough to conduct it. He has rehearsed the chorus several times."

339

Rossi looked up. "Toscanini? The first cellist? Do you think this is a music school? Toscanini is not old enough to conduct a village band! He is too young. They'd laugh him out of Rio."

"They have almost laughed all of us out of Rio already. What harm can be done?" asked the singer.

Rossi answered, "They will shout him off the stage. But you are right. Nothing more can be lost."

Rossi walked over to Toscanini and glared at him. "So! You know *Aïda,* do you? So you are our last hope, are you? Well, don't just stand there. Tonight you are going to conduct *Aïda*!"

Toscanini opened his mouth to speak, but the words wouldn't come out. As he stood there, one of the singers helped him out of his jacket and slipped his arms into the assistant conductor's tailcoat. It was several sizes too big. Another singer put a baton into his hand. He scarcely knew what was happening. Why, this whole idea was crazy! He had never in his life conducted a professional orchestra!

Yet for some reason he felt he could conduct *Aïda.* He was

the only member of the group who had memorized the score. And now the manager had suddenly placed the future of the company in his hands.

Toscanini stepped into the orchestra pit, hesitated, and looked across at the podium. It seemed miles away. He held his baton tightly and faced the waiting crowd.

Once more, the noise shook the opera house. But silence gradually fell over the theater as the audience took a good look at Toscanini. He was a thin youth, barely five feet tall. His coat hung from his shoulders like a sack, the sleeves almost

covering his fingers. He didn't look like a conductor. He mounted the podium, looked at the crowd, and then slammed shut the score.

Everyone in the house leaned forward a bit. Was he going to conduct without even following the score? What foolishness! He still belonged in music school.

Toscanini stood there for a moment, staring at the audience. There wasn't a whisper in the opera house.

Toscanini turned to the orchestra. Suddenly, his baton shot up in the air. The orchestra exploded with the opening bars of *Aïda*. The music was filled with life, fire, and strength, and the people listened. Toscanini had already forgotten all about them. Nothing existed for him except the music. His enthusiasm seemed to leap out at the orchestra from the tip of his baton. Singers and musicians performed as they had never performed before.

By the end of the first act, people were cheering. By the final scene, the opera house shook with bravos, wild applause, and stamping feet. Each time Toscanini tried to leave the podium, the audience called him back. The unknown cellist had suddenly become a maestro [mī′strō].

The next day, Rio newspapers praised the nineteen-year-old conductor. And when the company was ready to return to Europe, the people of Rio gave parties in his honor. The critics praised his ability, enthusiasm, and energy.

Toscanini returned to Italy and began practicing the cello again. He expected to find another job playing with an orchestra.

In the meantime, members of the Rio opera were spreading his name all over Italy. They spoke

ter it he did. He was a great
success at the Turin Opera
House on November 4, 1886.
"He has the sureness and energy
of an experienced maestro,"
wrote one critic.

For the next twelve years
Toscanini conducted in opera
houses throughout Italy. Each
year his reputation grew, until
he stood as the country's finest
conductor. In 1898 he was asked
to take over the conductor's post
at La Scala in Milan, the world's
most famous opera house.

Most people would have felt
that the conductor's post at La
Scala was the greatest success of
a lifetime of work. For Toscanini
it was only the beginning. For
years thereafter, he brought
audiences to their feet
throughout Europe and the
United States. He filled long
engagements as a conductor of
the Metropolitan Opera
Company, the New York
Philharmonic, and the NBC
Symphony. He raised his baton
at great music festivals and
toured the cities of four
continents.

During his long career,
Toscanini's desire for musical
perfection became known
throughout the musical world.

of nothing but the young
musician who had saved them
from disaster. Before long,
Toscanini was being talked
about in opera houses from
Milan to Palermo.

Within a few weeks, he
signed a contract to make his
first appearance in his own
country. He was to conduct a
new opera, *Edmea* [ed·mē'ə], in
the city of Turin. But the Turin
newspapers laughed at the idea.
Toscanini was still nineteen
years old, and *Edmea* was an
important work.

Toscanini spent all his time
mastering the opera. And mas-

He wanted the music performed exactly the way the composer had intended. Nothing less would do. He drove himself and his musicians without mercy to achieve the perfect performance.

Toscanini returned to Rio in 1940 during a tour of South America. The maestro hadn't forgotten the night fifty-four years earlier when, at the age of nineteen, he began his career in the Imperial Theatre. "It seems it took place yesterday," he said. "I can still remember the smell of the opera house." He paused for a moment, then added: "And I can still hear the crowd."

Understanding What You've Read

1. How did Toscanini get to conduct the opera *Aïda* on the evening of June 25, 1886?
2. What happened as a result of Toscanini's performance?
3. Where did Toscanini conduct after he became famous?
4. Do you think Toscanini would have been less successful as a cellist than as a conductor? Why or why not?

Applying the Skills Lesson

1. Read the first paragraph of the selection again. What conclusion were you able to draw about the mood of the audience at the opera?

   a. The people were happy and excited.
   b. The people were angry and impatient.
   c. Everybody hated opera in 1886.

2. What conclusions can you draw about Toscanini from reading this selection?

   a. He was a perfectionist who worked continually to achieve what he wanted.
   b. He was a lazy person but knew he had talent.
   c. He loved conducting and spent great amounts of time in rehearsals.

Drawing Conclusions

Sometimes textbook authors present facts and draw conclusions for you from these facts. Sometimes the authors present facts and ask you to draw conclusions. As you read the following textbook selections, keep in mind what you already know about the subjects. Be ready to draw conclusions based on the facts and your own experience.

Drawing Conclusions in Science

The sidenotes for this selection point out questions in which the authors ask you to draw conclusions.

The author asks you to draw a conclusion. The picture or your own experience may help you.

As tadpoles get older, hind legs begin to grow out of their bodies. Soon, front legs begin to grow out, and lungs develop inside the tadpoles. During this time, the tail of each tadpole starts to shrink.

Tadpoles enter youth once their tail has disappeared. During youth, which usually begins in the summer, most young frogs are able to climb out of the water. But they do not go far from the pond. Frogs must keep their skin moist. They are also safer in water than they are on land. Why do you think this is so?

When winter comes, young frogs swim to the bottom of the pond along with adult frogs. There, each frog buries itself in the mud to wait for spring. While the frogs are under the mud, they *hibernate.* That is, they do not move. Their heart slows down until they almost seem dead. When frogs hibernate, they use stored fat from their bodies for food. They take oxygen from the water through their skin. Why do you think frogs spend the winter in this way?

The author asks you to draw a conclusion based on something you may already know.

— *Exploring Science:* Red Book
Laidlaw Brothers

Building Skills

Read each of the following questions. Then choose the statement that shows the best conclusion.

1. Why are frogs safer in the water than they are on land?

   a. Frogs can move faster in water than they can on land and can therefore escape enemies better.
   b. Frogs are safer in water because water is warmer than land.
   c. Frogs find it very difficult to move at all on land.

2. Why do frogs hibernate in winter?

   a. Frogs hibernate in winter because, unlike birds that fly south in winter, frogs cannot move long distances.
   b. Frogs need lots of food to protect their bodies from the cold weather, and food is hard to find during the winter.
   c. Frogs like cold mud better than warm mud.

Drawing Conclusions in Social Studies

There are no sidenotes for this selection. Read it and then answer the questions that follow.

Twenty-eight years is a long time to search for a missing person. This is true even if the person has been missing for more than a million years. But that made it all the more exciting when Dr. Louis Leakey and his wife, Mary, found some bones and teeth of the missing person. Mary Leakey first spotted the bones among the rocks of dry Olduvai Gorge in Tanzania in East Africa. She found them on a hot day in July 1959. That was twenty-eight years after Dr. Leakey's first search of the gorge in 1931.

At first glance, Olduvai Gorge seemed a strange place to search for human remains. No one lived there in 1931. This was because there was no water nearby during the dry season. But Dr. Leakey was certain that some trace of ancient people must lie buried among the rocks. Why did he think so? He knew that the gorge cut through what had once been the shore of a lake. Earlier searchers had found many *fossil* animal bones there. Early people had been hunters. Where there were the bones of many animals, there should be signs of the people who had hunted them.

— People and Change
Silver Burdett

Building Skills

1. Below are conclusions you could draw about the Leakeys. What facts from the selection support these conclusions?

   a. The Leakeys are anthropologists. (Look in the glossary for the meaning of this word.)
   b. The Leakeys are willing to work for a long time to prove something they believe in.

2. On which of the following facts did the Leakeys base their conclusion that ancient people had once lived in Olduvai Gorge?

   a. There was a lake nearby in ancient times.
   b. Earlier searchers had found the remains of people there.
   c. Earlier searchers had found animal bones there.
   d. Where there were bones of animals, there should be signs of the people who had hunted them.
   e. Someone had told the Leakeys to look there.

SKILLS LESSON

Predicting Outcomes

Some years ago, many movie theaters showed *cliff-hangers*. A cliff-hanger was one small episode from a full-length adventure film. These cliff-hangers were very popular because the episode often ended with the main character trapped in a dangerous situation. People had to return the following week to find out what happened. But the people didn't mind the wait. It gave them a chance to predict the outcome of the episode.

When you predict an outcome, you make a guess about what you think might happen as a result of several events. For example, what do you think might happen as a result of the events described in the paragraph below?

Juana decided to enter the Winslow Valley Kite Flying Contest. She chose the materials for her kite wisely. She used very light wood for the crossbar. She covered the crossbar with one layer of lightweight paper. She then attached a long tail made from thin strips of cotton. When she was finished, she had a strong, well-built kite. On the day of the contest, the sky was clear and the winds were light. Juana was confident as the breeze lifted her kite high into the air.

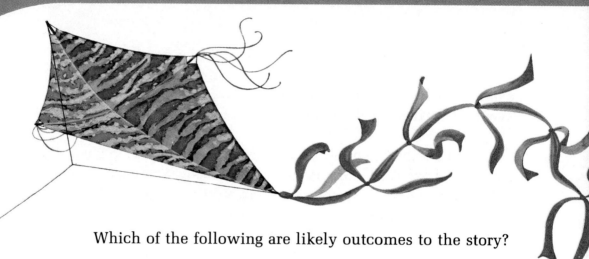

Which of the following are likely outcomes to the story?

1. Juana won the contest.
2. The howling winds tore Juana's kite.
3. The contest was canceled because of a snowstorm.
4. Juana's kite became tangled in a tree.
5. Juana won a prize for the best-built kite.

There are three *likely* outcomes to the story. Choice 1 states that Juana won the contest. Is this likely? Yes, because the paragraph tells you that the breeze carried Juana's kite high into the air. Perhaps it was high enough to win the contest. Choice 4 is also a likely outcome. Juana's kite could have become tangled in a tree. Choice 5 is a likely outcome because the paragraph states that Juana made a strong, well-built kite.

Why isn't outcome 2 likely? The paragraph states that on the day of the contest the sky was clear and the winds were *light*. Outcome 3 is also unlikely because kite-flying contests usually are not held during the winter months.

There are three things to keep in mind when predicting an outcome. First, a set of events can have several *likely* outcomes, but only one *real* outcome. Second, a predicted outcome states only what *might* happen, not what *will* happen. Third, when you predict an outcome you should consider all the facts in the selection as well as your own experience.

Try This

Read the paragraphs below. Then answer the questions.

Many volcanoes are hidden beneath the ocean. They are called underwater volcanoes. Sometimes, when this kind of volcano erupts, it forms a small island. If the volcano continues to erupt over the years, the island grows in size. However, the constant pounding of the waves can also eat away at the island, and it may disappear as quickly as it formed.

Some years ago the small island Surtsey was born after a volcano in the North Atlantic Ocean erupted. So far, Surtsey has remained, but its existence might be threatened unless the volcano erupts again.

Based on the information in the paragraphs above, which of the following are likely outcomes? Why is one outcome *not likely?*

1. The volcano will not erupt, and Surtsey will disappear.
2. The volcano will erupt again, and Surtsey will grow larger.
3. The volcano will not erupt, but Surtsey will continually grow in size.

VOCABULARY STUDY

Homophones

Mr. Verbiage's New Apartment

LANDLORD: I hope you like the apartment I'm going to show you, Mr. Verbiage. But I have to warn you. No pets are **allowed** in this building.

VERBIAGE: That's good. I like quiet pets. In my old building there is this dog that thinks it can sing. That hound practices aloud all night long. I haven't slept in weeks!

LANDLORD: No, Mr. Verbiage, I don't think you understand. . . .

VERBIAGE: Good grief, what is that awful noise?

LANDLORD: That's Ms. O'Toole in apartment 3–F. She plays cymbals. But only during the day, I assure you. At night she puts her instruments away.

VERBIAGE: That's strange. I never heard of playing **symbols**. Well, I suppose I can put up with a few plus signs and such. But if any American eagles come into this building, I leave.

LANDLORD: Mr. Verbiage, that's not what I meant. . . . Oh, never mind. Tell me more about what you do for a living. I believe you said you have a leading **role**. Are you the star of a play?

VERBIAGE: No, I'm an acrobat in the circus. I do the leading roll in a tumbling act. I hope this is a big apartment. I need lots of space to do my somersaults.

LANDLORD: Here are the keys, Mr. Verbiage. You can show yourself the apartment. I'm going to go lie down for a while. I suddenly seem to have a terrible headache. . . .

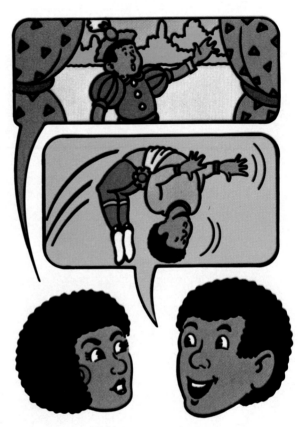

Word Play

1. Homophones are words that are pronounced the same but have different meanings. Find a homophone for each bold-faced word in the story. Then use each homophone in a sentence.

2. Which meaning is correct for each word below?

   allowed: a. permitted by rules
              b. loud enough to be heard
   symbols: a. round metal musical instruments
              b. signs standing for something else
   role: a. part played by an actor
              b. movement by turning over and over

As you read the selection, think about the facts given about Renee Harris. What do you think might happen to her career?

When Renee Harris starred as Dorothy in the show "The Wiz," she found out that . . .

DREAMS REALLY DO COME TRUE

by Karen Odom Gray

Believe that you can go home.
Believe you can float on air.
Then click your heels three times,
If you believe, then you'll be there.

These are the words that Glinda, the good witch from the North, sang to Dorothy in the musical show "The Wiz." Glinda was telling Dorothy how she could return home to Kansas. What Glinda had to say helped Dorothy get back home all right, but the message also had a special meaning for Renee Harris, who played Dorothy on stage.

Renee had always wanted to be a singer and actress. Because she believed in herself, she was able to succeed. Of course, it took more than just believing to make her dream come true. It didn't just happen overnight. Renee had been preparing all her life. She started singing when she was very young and sang in

several gospel choirs while she was growing up.

And even though Renee had been singing for a long time, it didn't mean that she would be right for the part. She had to audition to be in the show.

"My father heard about the auditions for 'The Wiz' on TV and radio," Renee remembers. "He took me down to them because he knew I could do it."

Renee went to audition one Sunday and had to sing and read lines for the director, along with about 100 other young aspiring actresses who wanted to be Dorothy. The director called Renee back two weeks later for another audition. She started going to rehearsals in the third

week, and during the fourth week, she made her Broadway debut as an understudy to Stephanie Mills.

When Stephanie Mills went on vacation, Renee got a chance to star on Broadway.

Making her dream come true also took a lot of hard work. "I thought they were working me to death," Renee said. "I had one week to learn all the lines, steps, and whatever else I needed to know."

After so much practice, Renee felt ready when her chance came. In fact, on her opening night in New York, everyone was nervous except the star herself. Her mother kept asking Renee, "Are you okay?" Renee finally had to ask her relatives and friends to leave her dressing room so she wouldn't get nervous, too!

As a successful actress, Renee had to spend much time away from her family and friends. But she didn't get too lonely because her family would visit her wherever she was performing.

Although Renee didn't have to worry too much about being nervous, she did worry about getting tired. Imagine doing eight performances every week!

Wouldn't you be tired after all that? Renee had to be sure to get enough rest because, even if she was tired, the show had to go on!

Sometimes, when Renee was very tired, she would give herself a pep talk. "I would tell myself, 'This is your life. This is your show. Go on and do the show. There's no time to be tired,'" she said. Then she would go on stage and perform.

Renee enjoyed doing the whole play, but one of her favorite scenes was when Dorothy first meets the Wiz in Emerald City.

"It fascinates me when the Wiz first comes out," Renee said. "He frightens Dorothy, but she has the courage to stand up to him. He's one of the few characters in the story who's human besides Dorothy. He knows what it's like to want something really badly."

The shows didn't always run smoothly. Renee remembers having problems in the play, like when she was afraid of the dog that played Toto in the New York City performance. But after she played with him, they became good friends. Then when she was performing in California, the dog that played Toto was almost as big as Renee. When she picked him up, she almost fell over! Since Renee had seven cats and three dogs of her own, it is hard to imagine that she would have had any problems with animals at all.

In spite of the hard work and long hours, Renee was glad to play the leading role in "The Wiz." She had finally experienced one of her dreams—being a singer and actress. She said that she has other dreams she would like to make come true.

"I'm fascinated by movies," she said. "I would like to act in films and even direct a movie of my own one day."

Renee really believes in the advice Glinda gives Dorothy in "The Wiz." Renee Harris said, "If you believe you can do it, you really *can* do it."

Understanding What You've Read

1. How did Renee get to play the part of Dorothy on Broadway?
2. What were some of the problems Renee faced while performing in "The Wiz"?
3. What other dreams would Renee like to come true?

Applying the Skills Lesson

Which of the following outcomes are likely for Renee and her career? (There is more than one.)

1. She will act in a movie or direct a movie.
2. She will become a doctor.
3. She will star in another show.
4. She will forget about a show business career because she doesn't like to sing or act.

Pablita Velarde is a successful artist. As you read the selection, think about what might happen to her in her later years. What outcomes might you predict?

Meet a famous American artist, a woman honored by her tribe and others around the world. Meet . . .

"The Herd Dance."

PABLITA VELARDE
Artist of the Pueblos
by Marion E. Gridley

Pablita Velarde was born in the fall of 1918 in the pueblo (or village) of Santa Clara, New Mexico. She was given the name Tse Tsan, meaning "golden dawn," because she was born at daybreak. She was later called Pablita.

The Velarde family lived at the edge of the pueblo. When the great ceremonial dances were held, Pablita absorbed every detail of all the dances. Her mind photographed them as if it were a camera.

Pablita learned many customs and skills from her grandmother. She was a good pottery maker and she taught Pablita this art also. Pablita liked the feel of the clay. She liked the shaping of it, smoothing out the bends and rough spots and forming a smooth vessel.

On the Santa Clara reservation there are famous ruins called Puye [poo·yā′], or Pueblo of the Clouds, where the main cliff dwelling included two thousand rooms. Ancestors of the Santa Clara people had once lived there, and Pablita found the ruins a fascinating place to play. Here and there

Pablita painting the mural "The Herd Dance."

362

"The Basket Dance."

363

she discovered flat rocks with pictures on them. She stored those rock pictures in her memory.

In the summer months, when the work of the farm was done, Pablita's father told his children stories from the past. The images that the stories brought out remained in Pablita's mind. As she listened, the pictures would come as if they were painted before her eyes.

In 1932, Pablita went to the Santa Fe government school. Here she learned the basic facts of colors, how to handle brushes, and how to express action from memory. She experimented with old methods of grinding raw clays and rocks.

One of her first paintings was of a group of Santa Clara women molding clay into large jars. These jars were called *ollas* [ô'lyäs]. She began by making a sketch in charcoal and then filling it in with colored chalk. When she was happy with it, she made a final pencil sketch on watercolor paper and put in a soft color with almost no outlining. The painting was a simple one, but it was true to life.

The Santa Clara women were a favorite subject of Pablita. She painted women in many activities. All had the same honest strength. Then her mind filled with other ideas. She turned to the ceremonies of her people, remembering them with photographic detail.

One famous painting shows

"The Ant People."

the plaza at the pueblo while a ceremony is taking place. The painting shows people watching from the rooftops as dancers perform. The painting is alive with action.

When she had barely finished eighth grade, Pablita entered a number of her paintings of Santa Clara women in a school show. They caught the attention of Olive Rush. She was preparing a series of murals, or wall paintings, in Chicago. Rush chose one of Pablita's paintings for the show. Through Rush, Pablita found new avenues open to her. She was signed to do a wall painting in oils of Pueblo life in Santa Clara for a federal art project.

Then Pablita was asked to work on a wall painting for a store in Albuquerque. And in 1939, she was asked to do one for Bandelier National Monument Museum in Frijoles [frē·hō'les] Canyon. This was a cliff dwelling that was inhabited centuries ago.

This was one of Pablita's

happiest assignments. She painted the ways of life of the people who had lived in these cliffs. The work took nearly a year.

In time, Pablita became especially well known for her earth paintings. For these, she collected clays and stones, and she ground them by hand on a special grinding stone. The powder was sifted into jars and mixed with glue and water.

Remembering the stories that her father had told her when she was a child, Pablita spoke of writing and illustrating them. She kept pointing out that otherwise, there would be no one to carry on the tradition. The stories would be lost to the people forever.

Pablita made a painting of her father that is considered her finest work. It shows a man telling stories to a group of children sitting around him. Their faces are happy and their

"Old Father."

bodies bent close with attention. *Old Father* won the Grand Prize in the 1955 Intertribal Ceremonials exhibit at Gallup, New Mexico.

Pablita found a publisher for the collection of her father's stories. Each had been beautifully illustrated with her own fine drawings. The book, published in 1960, was said to be one of the best books of the year.

In 1968, Pablita received the Philbrook Special Trophy for outstanding contributions to Native American art. One of her paintings was presented by President Lyndon B. Johnson to the prime minister of Denmark.

Pablita Velarde is considered the principal painter of Pueblo life and one of our country's great artists.

But her success did not come without paying a high price—that of hard and endless work.

Understanding What You've Read

1. What did Pablita learn from her grandmother? From her father?
2. How did Pablita make her earth paintings?
3. What kinds of things does Pablita paint?

Applying the Skills Lesson

Which of the following outcomes might you predict for Pablita Velarde? (There is more than one.)

1. She will continue painting as long as she can, using a wide range of materials.
2. She will stop painting because she has received so many honors.
3. She will paint landscape pictures in Maine because she likes to travel.
4. She will paint pictures related mainly to her Pueblo tribe.

Predicting Outcomes

Sometimes textbook authors give you facts about something that is happening at the present time. Then they ask you to predict an outcome based on these facts. When you come to questions that ask you *What will happen?*, think about the facts that the author has given. Base your predictions on these facts.

As you read the following selection, refer to the sidenotes. They point out some things to consider when you try to predict an outcome.

Predicting Outcomes in Health

Getting Tired

Richard is finally going to clean up his room. As you can see, this will not be an easy job. Think about how hard his body will have to work. How will he probably feel by the time the job is done?

The author is asking you to predict an outcome. To do so, you need to study the first picture on page 368 and use your own experience.

When your body works hard for a long time, you usually end up feeling tired. Sometimes, it's the way you move that makes your body work hard. Sometimes, it's the way you don't move. Art and his family are taking a long trip. After Art sits like this for a while, how will he feel?

Your body can also make you tired when it hasn't had enough rest or sleep. How would you feel right now if you had stayed up too late last night?

Other things can make you tired, too. For homework tonight, Cathy has to work 37 division problems. How will she feel after that? Why?

If you have ever had a lot of homework, you can predict how Cathy will feel.

— Toward Your Future: Brown
Harcourt Brace Jovanovich

Building Skills

1. Read the second paragraph in the selection. What does the author ask you to predict?

2. Which of the following statements best predicts the outcomes for the people discussed above?

   a. Richard, Art, and Cathy will all feel full of energy.
   b. Richard, Art, and Cathy will all feel tired.
   c. Richard, Art, and Cathy will all get sick.

Predicting Outcomes in Science

There are no sidenotes for this selection. Read it and then answer the questions that follow.

Your emotions. Have you ever had a day when everything seemed to go right for you? If so, you probably were very happy. But how did you feel on a day when everything seemed to go wrong for you? Everyone experiences many different *emotions* or feelings. These emotions can affect your learning. For example, suppose some people are coming to visit your family for the evening. And suppose you really like these people. How might looking forward to this visit affect your learning at school that day? What are some other ways in which emotions might affect your learning and therefore your ability to adapt to your environment?

—*Exploring Science:* Red Book
Laidlaw Brothers

How might the emotions of these people affect their ability to adapt to their environment?

Building Skills

Which would be likely outcomes to this question from the selection: "How might looking forward to this visit affect your learning at school that day?" There is more than one answer.

You might:
1. study extra hard to make the day pass quickly
2. find it hard to concentrate in school
3. learn just as much as on any other day
4. be too angry to open your books

371

Books About Seeing It Through

Staying Power: Performing Artists Talk About Their Lives by Peter Barton. Dial Press, 1980. Actors, dancers, and musicians discuss the factors that inspired them to perform and the hard work involved in developing their talent.

Modern Women Superstars by Bill Gutman. Dodd, 1977. Seven sports stars, including Chris Evert Lloyd and Dorothy Hamill, are highlighted in this book.

Reggie Jackson's Scrapbook by Reggie Jackson. Windmill Bks., 1978. This baseball star tells how he developed his skills as a batter and a right fielder, and about his career in big league baseball.

The Cancer Lady: Maud Slye and Her Heredity Studies by J. J. McCoy. Nelson, 1977. You'll learn about a scientist and the importance of her discoveries in cancer research.

How I Came to Be a Writer by Phyllis Reynolds Naylor. Atheneum, 1978. This writer for young people tells how she developed an interest in writing and how she works at her craft.

Gordon Parks by Midge Turk. T. Y. Crowell, 1971. Here is the story of a well-known photographer. You'll find out how he became interested in photography and how he works as a photographer, film maker, and writer.

Patrick Des Jarlait: The Story of an American Indian Artist by Neva Williams. Lerner Pubns., 1975. In collaboration with the author, an American Indian artist tells about his childhood and how he became a painter.

Part 6

The Storyteller's Answer: Myths

UNDERSTANDING AND APPRECIATING LITERATURE

Myth

Understanding Myths

Read the cartoon above. The girl who is explaining why it thunders is remembering a myth. Most **myths** are stories that were first told many thousands of years ago. People in different parts of the world made up their own myths about events that were important to them. What is the myth in the cartoon? The myth is that the sound of thunder is caused by a band in the clouds playing drums and other noisy instruments. This myth tells why thunder happens. A story that

tells why an event in nature happens is a "why" story, or **"why" myth.**

Read the following myth.

The Sun and the Moon

At first, Sun and Moon lived on the Earth with Water. The three were good friends, but Water never visited the home of Sun and Moon. Water did not want to enter their house because it was too small.

Sun and Moon built a very large house and then invited Water to visit. But the new house was still too small. When Water poured in, it overflowed. Sun and Moon were pushed into the sky. And there they have remained to this day.

What event in nature does this myth explain? It explains why the sun and the moon are in the sky. The myth explains that the water on the Earth went to visit the sun and the moon in their house. What happened next? The water poured into the house and pushed the sun and the moon up into the sky.

Another Kind of Myth

Some myths tell about women and men who showed special qualities that people valued. What qualities do you think were valued? How were these qualities used in myths? People who valued tests of strength might have made up a tale about a person who showed the qualities of cleverness, strength, or swiftness. Such tales are called hero tales, or **hero myths.**

Read the following myth.

Perseus and the Medusa

Perseus was a young man who lived long ago. In his country was a terrible monster called Medusa. Medusa's hair was a mass of squirming snakes.

Anyone who looked upon the monster's face was turned instantly to stone.

Perseus wanted to save his people from Medusa. He had a plan that would let him battle Medusa without being turned to stone. First, he polished his silver shield until it shone like a mirror. Then, he went to the mountains and found Medusa. He was careful not to look at Medusa's face, but to watch only the monster's reflection in his shield.

The battle was long, but Perseus finally killed Medusa. At last his people were free.

Who is the hero in this myth? What special qualities did he have? Perseus is the hero: He was brave, strong, and willing to do battle with a terrible monster. He was also clever to use his shield as a mirror.

How is the myth about Perseus different from the myth about the sun and the moon? The myth about Perseus is about a hero, while the myth about the sun and the moon explains why something in nature happens.

What can you learn from myths? You can learn about the qualities that people living long ago admired. You can learn about the things that were important enough for people to wonder why these things came to be. Myths can tell why and describe heroes. And myths are for you to enjoy.

Try This

Read the following myth. Then answer the questions.

Atalanta and the Race

A king had a beautiful daughter named Atalanta. She was admired by the people of the kingdom, for she was a swift runner. Although Atalanta's friends had all married, Atalanta remained single. She said that she would marry the man who could defeat her in a race.

Many men raced with Atalanta and lost. One day, a young man named Hippomenes came to visit in the kingdom. When he met Atalanta, he liked her so much that he wished to marry her. So Hippomenes decided to enter a race with her.

The day of the race came. At the start, Atalanta was in the lead. An idea came to Hippomenes. In his pocket were three shiny apples. He threw one in Atalanta's path. Atalanta stopped to pick up the apple. A few moments later, Hippomenes threw another apple. Again, Atalanta stopped. As they neared the finish line, Hippomenes threw the third apple. As Atalanta stopped a third time, Hippomenes passed her and won the race.

1. Is this myth about a hero? Why or why not?
2. What special qualities does Atalanta have? Why might these qualities be important to her people?
3. How are Atalanta and Perseus alike? How are they different?

Writing

1. Write two or three sentences that describe a hero you have read about. What is the hero's name? What special qualities does this hero have?
2. Write a realistic or mythical sentence or paragraph to explain why one of the following events occurs.

   a. Leaves change color in the fall.
   b. Fish live in water.
   c. The moon comes out at night.
   d. Snow melts when it is warm.

As you read "The Storyteller's Answer: Myths," look for myths that tell "why," and for myths that tell of brave heroes.

The Royal Palm

by PURA BELPRÉ

Among the Taino Indians on the island of Boriquen there was once a man named Milomaki. He was tall, brave, and handsome, and he had a wonderful singing voice, a voice possessed of strange power. If you were sick, his singing made you well. If you were sad, it made you happy. His fame spread all over the island, and people came from far away to see and hear him. But his popularity and his power over the people soon angered the Indian gods. They became jealous and plotted against him.

One afternoon, as the Indians were returning with their catch of fresh fish from the river, they came upon Milomaki.

"Sing for us," they said, "for we have been working since dawn and we are tired."

Milomaki began to sing songs that had the coolness of a soft breeze, and the Indians forgot their weariness and were refreshed. Then Milomaki sang heroic songs, and the Indians felt like fishermen no longer but like Indian chiefs performing mighty deeds in war. As they listened, caught by the spell of the music, the hot sun shone down on them and on the fish they had caught.

After a while the songs ended. The Indians thanked Milomaki, picked up their fish, and went home.

When they arrived, their wives prepared the fish and they all sat down to enjoy the delicious meal. But after dinner a terrible thing happened. Everyone who had eaten the fish became ill.

"It is Milomaki's fault!" said the fishermen. "He made us forget the fish while he sang, and the hot sun spoiled them."

All their happiness turned to anger. Only the Indian gods were happy. They had been waiting for just such an incident to occur. Now they stirred up the men against Milomaki, filling their hearts with evil thoughts. The Indians decided that Milomaki must die.

"Burn him at the stake!" they shouted. Their anger made them forget their illness, and off they went in search of Milomaki. They searched all night. It was not until dawn that they caught up with him. They pounced on him and bound him, and he gave in without a struggle. He felt no anger toward them, only wonder and surprise. Were these the same men who only the day before had quietly listened to his singing?

The Indians tied him to a heavy log. Then they gathered firewood and built a great fire. Milomaki understood what they were going to do and he became very sad. When everything was ready they lifted him up to stand above the fire.

Suddenly he began to sing. His song was more beautiful than any they had ever heard. He sang and sang. He was still singing when a soft rain began to fall. It clung to the leaves of the trees, moistened the grass and moss underfoot, and touched with coolness the face of Milomaki as he sang.

His voice rose and fell under the spell of its own music. The Indians listened in awe and the spell of the music swept away their evil thoughts. Suddenly they were horrified at what they were about to do. Gone was their anger. A feeling of remorse surged through their bodies.

"Milomaki, Milomaki!" they cried, and they rushed to untie him. But they were too late. Right before their eyes Milomaki's form began to disappear. Where he had been standing there was now a tall, regal-looking palm tree, its crown of leafy fronds spread out toward the sky. A gust of wind blew through its branches, and they stirred with a soft rustling sound. The Indians had never seen such a tree before. Because it had a royal look and stood so tall and straight, they called it Royal Palm. Whenever they heard the wind blowing through its branches, they imagined it was Milomaki singing to them, and they would stop to listen with delight and wonder.

They told their children and their children's children the tale of Milomaki, and when more palm trees grew on the island, as straight and tall and beautiful as the first Royal Palm, the voice of the great singer could be heard in all of them.

Understanding What You've Read

1. What special power did Milomaki have?
2. Name three ways in which Milomaki helped the people.
3. What kind of person was Milomaki? Find examples in the story that support your answer.
4. What does this myth explain?

Writing

1. Write one or more sentences in which you tell why the story "The Royal Palm" *is* or *is not* a good explanation of where the palm tree came from and why the tree rustles when the wind blows through its branches.
2. Famous people who have been important in the history of a country are often considered heroes. Heroes often possess qualities that people admire. Make a list of Milomaki's special qualities. Then write a paragraph in which you tell why Milomaki might be considered a hero. Your first sentence might read: "Milomaki possessed many qualities admired by his people."

Three Maidens

by MIRRA GINSBURG

It is said there was a time, long, long ago, when seven suns rose every day over our mountains. The suns' rays, like milk, fed everything that lived. Grasses and trees grew taller and stronger every year. And the people who lived at the foot of the mountains grew happier and richer and more beautiful from generation to generation. For seven suns shone over the country. Our peasants reaped seven harvests every year, and the piles of grain rose higher than the mountain peaks. For seven suns shone over our country. Animals bore their young seven times every year; cows and sheep wandered over the mountains and meadows, and they were more numerous than the green branches on the pine trees growing on the mountains. For seven suns shone over our country.

The music of shepherd pipes was carried everywhere by the light breeze. The fields resounded with constant laughter and songs. People sang praises to the god of the suns and to time, which was as sweet as honey.

When the clouds of evening floated over the mountain range and the last sunrays disappeared, the Kazakh peasants and cattle breeders gathered around old trees, in the fields, and on the river banks to sing the evening prayer:

> Let the seven suns in the sky
> Sink calmly to rest,
> And rise again to greet us in the morning!

Years passed, and the seven suns continued to brighten the sky, and the Kazakhs lived happy lives.

383

But one day an evil spirit, a shaitan, appeared in an old mountain canyon. He saw the joy of all who lived around him in the country, and he swore:

"I shall not rest until I knock all seven suns out of the sky!"

The shaitan was the son of a hundred-year-old owl, and from his very birth he loved darkness and was afraid of light. He began to think of how to kill the suns and bring eternal darkness to the earth. And he devised a cunning plan.

By magic, he turned himself into a hundred winged men with eagle beaks. They spread their wings and flew to the highest mountain top. And every day they sent their steel arrows at the suns.

384

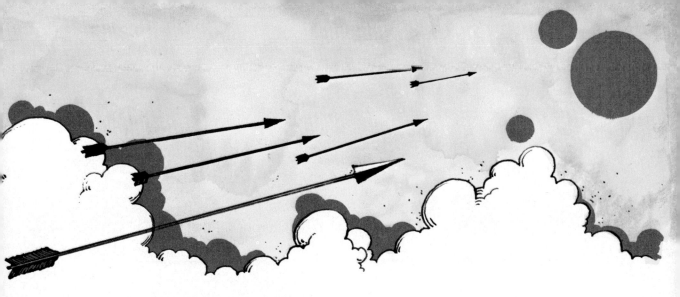

They shot down one sun, then another, then the third, the fourth, the fifth, the sixth. . . .

The Kazakhs stood by helplessly, watching the disappearance of their suns. All day they prayed and wept, but there was nothing they could do.

And then the last, the seventh, sun was shot down by a keen steel arrow. Eternal darkness descended on the mountains. In the valleys the trees and grasses lost the sap of life. The grain dried out in the fields. The cows and sheep died in the mountains and meadows. The illimitable orchards turned into dead wood, suitable only for making fires. Death-dealing clouds hung low over the Kazakhs. They faced famine and cold. They prayed, but hope went out of their hearts.

Then one day three brave maidens came before the people. They bowed first to the old men, then to the rest, and proudly said to them:

"Grandfathers, mothers, brothers, and sisters! Permit us to go forth to seek the suns and bring them back. We shall either find them, or perish in strange lands. Farewell!"

And the three maidens set out on their perilous journey. They felt their way in darkness. No one knows how many steep mountains they climbed, how many high

ridges they crossed, how many wide rivers they swam
across, and how many narrow streams they forded. And
who knows how much they suffered from parching heat
and bitter cold! Their garments tore and hung in shreds;
their feet were sore and weary; their hair had grown so
long that it trailed after them upon the ground like
mountain mist. But while their hearts were beating they
steadfastly went on and on. Where were the suns? They
did not know. Would they ever succeed in finding them?
They did not know. But, never despairing, they went ever
forward, step after step.

And one day there was thunder in the sky, and lightning flashed around them. In the blaze they saw an old,
old man with long white hair. His eyes gleamed with a
golden light, and he spoke gently to the maidens:

386

"Brave maidens, your resolution is stronger than the mountain peaks! Your hearts are purer than the snow on the highest mountains! You need no longer wander in search of the lost suns—stand here and wait! A fiery rider will gallop past you on a chestnut horse with flaming mane and tail, and every time you see him, one of the suns will come back to the skies. It will take many ages before all seven return to the Kazakh steppes, but if your patience equals your courage, they will come! Remember my words!"

The thunder ceased. The lightning vanished. The old man was gone. And all that could be heard now in the silence was the triumphant laughter of the three brave maidens.

In the morning, the fiery rider galloped past them on the chestnut horse with flaming mane and tail, and after him the sun rose bright and gay and lighted up the mountains and meadows. The Kazakhs went back to tending their fields and orchards, their cows and sheep. But they never forgot the three brave maidens.

Many years and many centuries have gone. The maidens kept their promise to the people. They died a long, long time ago, but on the spot where they had stood, amid the endless steppe, three mighty peaks rise high into the sky. Every morning, they are the first to see the sun. They will wait, as they have promised, for the fiery rider to gallop past again and again, until all seven suns are back over our land. The mountains are called the Three Maidens.

Understanding What You've Read

1. Why did the evil spirit kill the seven suns?
2. Why did the evil spirit, or shaitan, love darkness? Why was the evil spirit afraid of light? Of what importance were the seven suns to the Kazakh people?
3. What special qualities did the three maidens share? How important were these qualities to the people who heard or read this story?
4. Who was the fiery rider on the chestnut horse with the flaming mane and tail?
5. Why did the three maidens continue to wait for the other six suns after the first sun rose again?
6. Did the other suns ever return? How do you know?
7. Why are the mountains in the land of the Kazakhs called the "Three Maidens"?

Writing

1. Write a sentence that explains the real reason for the darkness in the story "Three Maidens."
2. Compare "Three Maidens" with other hero myths or stories that you have read. How are the stories similar? How are they different? What similarities can you find between the three maidens and other heroes? Write a sentence or paragraph that tells at least one similarity or difference between "Three Maidens" and another story or myth.

Why the Sea Is Salt

by VIRGINIA HAVILAND

Once upon a time — and it was a long, long time ago — there were two brothers. One of them was rich and one was poor.

The poor man had not so much as a crumb in his house, either of meat or of bread. So he went to his brother to ask him for something. It was not the first time he had called upon his rich brother for help.

The rich brother said, "If you will go away and never come back, I'll give you a whole side of bacon."

The poor brother, full of thanks, agreed to this.

"Well, here is the bacon," said the rich brother. "Now go straight away to the Land of Hunger."

The poor brother took the bacon and set off. He walked the whole day. At dusk he came to a place where he saw a very bright light.

"Maybe this is the place," said he and turned aside. The first person he saw was an old, old man with a long white beard, who was chopping wood.

"Good evening," said the man with the bacon.

"The same to you. Where are you going so late in the day?" asked the man.

"Oh, I'm going to the Land of Hunger, if only I can find the right way."

"Well, you are not far wrong, for this is that land," said the old man. "When you go inside, everyone there will want to buy your bacon, for meat is scarce here. But mind you don't sell it unless you get for it the hand mill which stands behind the door. When you come out again, I'll teach you how to handle the mill. You will be able to make it grind almost anything."

The man with the bacon thanked the other for his good advice. Then he gave a great knock at the door.

When he had entered, everything happened just as the old man had said it would. Everyone came swarming up to him like ants around an anthill. Each one tried to outbid the other for the bacon.

"Well," said the man, "by rights it is my wife and I who should have this bacon. However, since you have all set your hearts on it, I suppose I must let you have it. But if I do sell it, I must have in exchange that mill behind the door."

At first the people wouldn't hear of such a bargain. They chaffered and they haggled with the man. But he stuck to his bargain, and at last they had to part with the mill.

The man now carried the mill out into the yard and asked the old woodcutter how to handle it. As soon as the old man had shown him how to make it grind, he thanked him, and hurried off home as fast as he could.

"Wherever in the world have you been?" complained his wife. "Here I have sat hour after hour waiting and watching, without so much as two sticks to lay together under the broth."

"Well," said the man, "I couldn't get back earlier because I had to go a long way—first for one thing, and then for another. But now you shall see what you shall see!"

Carefully he set the mill on the table. First of all, he ordered it to grind lights. Next he asked for a tablecloth, then for meat, and so on. He had only to speak and the mill would grind out anything he asked for.

It wasn't long before he set up a farmhouse far finer than the one in which his brother lived. With the mill he ground so much gold that he covered the house with it.

Since the farm lay by the seaside, the golden house gleamed and glistened far away to ships at sea. All who sailed by put to shore to see the rich man in his golden house and to see the wonderful mill. Its fame spread far and wide, till there was nobody who hadn't heard tell of it.

One day a skipper sailed in to see the mill. The first thing he asked was whether it could grind salt.

"Grind salt!" said the owner. "I should think it could. It can grind anything."

When the skipper heard that, he said he must have the mill, cost what it would. If only he had it, he thought, he would no longer have to take long voyages across stormy seas for a cargo of salt.

At first the man wouldn't hear of parting with his mill. But the skipper begged so hard that at last he let him have it. However, the skipper had to pay a great deal of money for it.

When the skipper had the mill on his back, he went off with it at once. He was afraid the man would change his mind, so he took no time to ask how to handle the mill. He got on board his ship as fast as he could, and set sail.

When the skipper had sailed a good way off, he brought the mill up on deck and said:

"Grind salt, and grind both good and fast."

Well, the mill began to grind salt so that it poured out like water.

When the skipper had filled the ship, he wished to stop the mill. But whichever way he turned it, and however much he tried, it was no good. The mill kept grinding on, and the heap of salt grew higher and higher. At last it sank the ship. Now the mill lies at the bottom of the sea. It grinds away to this very day, and that is why the sea is salt.

Understanding What You've Read

1. How were the two brothers in the story alike? How were they different?
2. Why did the storyteller not give the two brothers names?
3. This story contains an element that many myths and stories have—a device that does the bidding of its master. How was the mill started? How do you imagine it was stopped?
4. Who was at fault in the outcome of the story—the man who sold the mill to the skipper, or the skipper himself?

Writing

1. Write a sentence in which you explain one of the following, not in a scientific way, but in the way people long ago might have explained it:

   a. why the sky is blue
   b. why there are stars in the sky
   c. why the sun rises in the east and sets in the west

2. Write a paragraph in which you tell what happens to the man and wife from the story in the days after they sold the mill to the skipper.

On the Island of Crete lived the terrible Minotaur, a monster that was half man and half bull. This monster was kept in the Labyrinth, a prison of mazes from which neither the Minotaur nor anyone else could escape. When the city of Athens lost a war against Crete, the Athenians received a terrible punishment. Every nine years, seven young Athenian men and seven young Athenian women had to be sent to Crete and be fed to the Minotaur.

Theseus: A Hero of Ancient Greece

by DORIS GATES

Nine years had elapsed since the last seven youths and seven maids had sailed away from their dear city to find death as the victims of the Minotaur in the Labyrinth. The time had come for the third offer of tribute to King Minos of Crete. Loud was the sorrowing of parents as they faced the possibility of having their children torn from them to die a hideous death. The king of Athens and his nobles gathered together where the lots to choose the victims were to be drawn. The voices of the noble families rose against the king, who was responsible for this threat to their sons and daughters.

When Theseus heard the cries against his father, a brave plan formed in his mind. Hesitating only a moment, he sprang to his feet and faced the assembly.

"Choose only six youths," he cried. "I offer myself as the seventh. It is not fair that the king's son be spared. I will go to Crete with your sons and daughters, and there I shall subdue the Minotaur or die in the attempt."

It was in vain that King Aegeus pleaded with Theseus to withdraw his offer. In vain he tried to persuade his son that the country would need his leadership, that it was folly to sacrifice himself, so favored by the gods, when any other youth would do as well.

"Dear Father," Theseus replied, "early in my life I took Heracles for my model. No more than Heracles will I turn away from danger. And the gods do favor me; I have proved that. Therefore it is my duty to face the Minotaur and perhaps put an end to this cruel tribute."

So they took ship, Theseus and his thirteen companions. Because of the sad nature of their journey, the ship was fitted with a black sail. But Aegeus had ordered a white sail to be put aboard. Then he made Theseus promise that if his mission were successful, he would sail into the port of Athens with the white sail in place. Thus would the king know that his son lived, and all the citizens of Athens would learn on sight that the tribute was ended. Theseus promised, and the ship started out, its black sail a somber shadow upon the bright waters.

The crossing to Crete was uneventful. But as the black-sailed ship approached the stone jetty where its prisoners would be unloaded, Theseus saw a crowd. Beyond it, though a considerable distance from the shore, the palace of King Minos rose impressively, terrace upon terrace. The victims were soon marching toward it. As they came slowly up the long slope of the processional way, Theseus was awed by the vastness of the palace. Arriving at the top, the Athenians were led across a wide, open area and into a huge court enclosed with massive wooden columns, brilliantly colored. They crossed it to enter a narrow corridor and then were in a large room

from which a wide stairway rose to the floor above. The
walls were alive with paintings so vivid and real their figures seemed to move. Theseus was dazzled by the splen-
dor. He vowed that if the gods should spare his life, he
would build palaces and temples the equal of this in
Athens when he became king.

The young people started up the stairway to the
hall where King Minos awaited them. Theseus saw that
there were openings in the walls above the stairs through
which the ladies of the court looked down upon the captives. One face in that crowd made him stop. He mar-
veled that a mere human could possess such beauty. Was
this then a goddess? Under his gaze the face blushed,
thus proclaiming it to be human. It was a young woman,
quite as struck by Theseus's beauty as he was by hers.

Neither gestured toward the other. Yet something as definite and final as an avowal passed between them. Thus
did the daughter of King Minos, Ariadne, and the hero
Theseus silently declare their instant love.

Ariadne was among those who thronged the throne
room where the young captives were brought and presented to the king. She thought of the awful fate that
awaited them. And she knew she would have to try to
save Theseus and his companions, even though this be-
trayal of her father might cost her life.

That evening, Ariadne sought the inventor Daedalus
where he strolled alone upon one of the high roof terraces
of the palace. The princess was accompanied by a trusted
serving woman.

Daedalus watched admiringly as Araidne approached
him across the paving under a sky full of stars.

"I have come, Daedalus, seeking your advice," she
said. "It concerns the hero Theseus. I want to save him."

Daedalus smiled. "I saw your gaze upon him today in the great hall. Your visit is not altogether unexpected."

Ariadne was grateful that the starlight was not bright enough to betray the blush his words called into her cheeks.

"How can he be saved?" she whispered.

"He has come here vowing to kill the Minotaur. Only the gods can aid him in that combat."

"He has achieved many great feats," said Ariadne. "I believe that he will kill the Minotaur. But suppose he does? How will he then escape the Labyrinth? This is what I need to know, Daedalus."

"And when you have learned the secret, then what?" asked the inventor.

"I will take the word to him somehow," Ariadne replied.

Daedalus studied her gentle face in the light of the

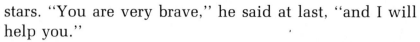

stars. "You are very brave," he said at last, "and I will help you."

She stepped closer to him. "Tell me quickly," she breathed.

"I have an idea," began Daedalus. "Like many good ideas, it is quite simple. One has only to think of it." His tone was slightly mocking. He thought of the several palace nobles who took a dim view of his accomplishments. They held that anyone might have done the same. One only had to have the idea first! "You must give Theseus a large spool of thread—silk would be best. Let him fasten the end of it to the doorpost at the entrance to the Labyrinth, unwinding it as he proceeds into those regions. When he has met with the Minotaur, and if he manages to kill him, he can wind up the string again, following it as he winds, until it brings him back to the entrance. Let his companions remain huddled there when he first goes in. When he comes again to the door, you must be the one to open it for him. Then be prepared to flee with Theseus and the others. Speed to his boat. But before setting sail, make sure he has scuttled the king's boats that lie in the harbor. That way, you will escape pursuit. For never doubt that Minos will want Theseus's blood—and yours."

Ariadne shuddered slightly. She drew her scarf closer around her shoulders. "The risks are very great, I know. Yet I love him enough to risk anything for his sake." She looked up earnestly at the inventor. "Thank you, Daedalus. And if I never see you again, may the gods smile upon you and keep you safe."

With that she turned and quickly crossed the terrace. The serving woman stepped out of the shadows where she had been waiting and, walking just a step behind the princess, disappeared with her into the palace.

Later that same evening, the single guardsman posted outside the cell of the young Athenians was surprised to

see a woman approaching along the dark corridor. Her head and features were hidden in a ragged scarf, and the rest of her attire was equally worn and poor. Obviously a beggar woman of the streets, thought the soldier, who had never beheld the face of his princess, Ariadne.

"I have come from the harbor," she said, "with a message for your prisoner Theseus. It is a last greeting from the pilot of the ship that brought him here."

"I have no orders to let anyone speak with Theseus." said the guard.

"The pilot told me to give you this." The woman held out a handful of coins.

The man, poor as he was ignorant, struggled with his conscience as he eyed the coins. This beggar plainly was harmless. And Theseus with all his comrades would soon be safely locked inside the Labyrinth with the fearsome Minotaur, where no one could be in contact with him again. Arriving at this thought, the guard hesitated no longer, but grinning cruelly, reached for the coins.

"Make it quick," he ordered as he shot the bolt to the cell door and rudely shoved the beggar inside.

The Athenians had leaped to their feet at the sound of the bolt. They were surprised to discover the young woman. They had expected the armed guard that would escort them to the Labyrinth.

"I wish to speak to Theseus," whispered Ariadne into the darkness.

"Here is Theseus," said a voice close beside her.

She turned and clutched his tunic. "I am the Princess Ariadne," she said, her words spoken swiftly. "We have only an instant, so listen carefully."

Clearly and quickly she explained what Daedalus had told her. Then, reaching into her ragged garment, she drew forth a spool of silk. "Here," she said, fumbling for his hand in the dark. "Hide it well, and may the gods be with you."

Theseus had just taken the spool into his hand when again there came the sound of the drawn bolt. The door swung open, and a shaft of light fell across the cell. In that light, a wisp in rags, as silent and secret as a wraith, slipped through the door and along the corridor and out of sight.

Some time later, those within the cell heard the measured thud of marching feet and the clang of weapons. The guard had arrived to escort them to the Labyrinth.

Flanked by the soldiery, the fourteen Athenian youths and maidens trudged along dim corridors to dark and narrow staircases, which led them always down, down to the bottommost recesses of this vast palace. At last, the captain of the guard called a halt. In the dim light of a single torch, Theseus, who stood at the head of the captive group, beheld a heavy door which seemed to close the side of a hill. They had reached the entrance to the Labyrinth!

The captain unbolted the door and pulled it slowly forward into the corridor. It came grudgingly, for it was heavy, and with it came a dreadful smell of sour earth and dampness. But overriding this, and striking a chill into every heart beating there, came the stink of beast and blood.

The captain motioned, and Theseus led the Athenians into the dark unknown. The door creaked shut behind them. Theseus put an ear tight against it. He heard the bolt shoot home and the measured sound of retreating footsteps. Had a guard been left behind? Had Ariadne succeeded in hiding herself nearby? Would her strength be equal to the heavy bolt and door? These questions whirled through his mind as he tried to look about him, his eyes gradually becoming accustomed to the darkness.

In the long years since the Labyrinth had been constructed, Crete had suffered many earthquakes. Thus slight cracks had opened between the palace structure and this subterranean earthwork. What had once been totally dark now offered in places a grim, gray twilight, the difference between black and charcoal. During the day, a rare trace of sunlight filtered through a narrow crack. At night, as now, the faint glimmer from the torches lighting the palace feebly pierced the gloom. Staring, Theseus

could barely discern just such a dubious light down the dark corridor.

He tied the thread to the doorpost while the others crowded around him.

"Feel this thread," he commanded them, "and remember where I have tied it. Let no one touch it, for if it breaks, I will never return to you, whether or not I conquer the Minotaur."

They stepped back from him obediently, but their whispers reached him from out of the dark.

"Take us with you, Theseus!"

"You are great, Theseus, but fourteen are better than one, even if that one is a hero!"

Theseus silenced them. "How could fourteen follow this frail thread? In the darkness and in the confusion of the struggle it would surely be broken. Then what would become of us? Better sudden death than slow starvation. Do as I have commanded you, pray to the gods for me, and all may yet be well."

And so he took leave of them and, holding to the thread, unwound it carefully as he advanced cautiously toward that lighter dark in the surrounding darkness.

He continued blindly and bravely on, stopping now and then to listen, ever mindful of his slender lifeline. Once his heart leaped as a sound reached him. He crouched in the darkness, waiting. Was this the Minotaur? There it was again. His breathing tightened. Should he set the spool down, hoping to find it when the fight was over — if he lived? For the third time the sound came, and now he could define it. It was nothing more than a bit of dirt rolling down the steep side of the passageway. But it gave him an idea. When again he came to a slightly lightened area, he stopped to consider the sloping wall above him. Yes, he thought it might be managed. Hurriedly, he slipped off his sandals and tucked them inside his belted tunic. He would need the grip of bare toes here.

Twice he leaped at the wall, only to slide back. But on the third try his toes held, and, clinging flat, he worked a toehold, and another and another. Inch by breathless inch, he wriggled upward until he came to a narrow ledge. It was a precarious perch, but he would make use of it until some better strategy came to mind. For Theseus had decided to fall upon the monster if he should come this way. Surprise has won many a battle, and Theseus was counting on the unexpectedness of his attack to give him the split-second advantage over the Minotaur that could make the difference between death and victory. So now he waited, his muscles tense, his ears straining for the first warning of the monster's approach.

He had not long to wait. His first awareness of the brute's approach was a sudden unexplainable, but utterly certain, knowledge of immediate danger. Nothing had moved in the shadows below him; no sound had reached his ears. Yet he *knew* the moment was now, and his every sense sharpened to meet it.

All at once he heard a quick and gentle *slap, slap, slap*, like someone running barefoot. Out of the wall of blackness into the region of shadow, the Minotaur trotted. Theseus had an instant's sight of a bull's head and horns and mighty shoulders slimming down into a man's waist and legs and feet. Quickly he hurled himself down on the monster's broad back.

The Minotaur met the attack with a bellow that shook the passageway, echoing and reechoing throughout the Labyrinth as if a dozen bulls were trumpeting their rage. If heard above ground, it might have sounded like the muffled rumblings that announce an earthquake's dreaded approach. The monster raised its bull's forelegs above its head in an effort to seize the enemy, but its cloven hooves were powerless to pluck this menace off his back.

That one bellow was the only one Theseus allowed him. The Minotaur staggered and slowly sank to his knees. Now Theseus rushed in recklessly and with blow after mighty blow, ended the torment. Then, with all his strength, Theseus drove a powerful blow against the monster's throat. In the dim and shadowy passage, the Minotaur lay dead.

The hero waited only a moment. Then, tugging the silken thread gently, he rolled the spool off the ledge and began his slow, cautious return, winding the thread as he went.

No time was spent in celebration of Theseus's return to his comrades. Even as they gasped out their first joy at what his return meant to all of them, Theseus was giving the signal that would cause Ariadne to open the door. If she was there. Theseus pressed his ear against the door to hear the welcome sound of the bolt being slowly drawn. Theseus put his shoulder against the door and it swung wide to reveal the startled Ariadne, alone in the corridor.

Quickly they sped away, Ariadne and Theseus running beside each other as she led them along the secret
windings of the underground regions. At this hour before
the dawn, the torches had almost burned out. The guards
were sleepy and careless. No one saw the jubilant refu-
gees as they slipped out of the palace and sped toward
the harbor. Working swiftly, they scuttled as many ships
as they could reach, then made for their own. Their pilot
was awake and watching, marveling at the Cretan boats
sinking out of sight one by one.

"Quick," said Theseus. "Run up the sail while we
take to the oars."

The pilot leaped to carry out his orders, and soon the
sail was in place, but hanging limp. With Ariadne safely
aboard, the Athenians bent to the oars, and the boat shot

away from the stone jetty. Stroke after stroke, and still all seemed quiet on the island of Crete. Now a puff of wind moved the sail, and a breeze filled it.

"Where to, master?" called the pilot, as he settled in the stern, the rudder in his hand.

"Naxos," answered Theseus, shipping his oars. King Minos, if he gave pursuit, would hardly look for them there, since it was off course for Athens.

The island proved to be verdant and well stocked with game. Before long, the pilot had set snares. He soon had the game he caught roasting over a fire kindled from the charcoal brazier aboard the boat.

That night, well fed and lulled by the gentle slap of waves against the shore, they all slept. Exhausted and drained by the anxiety they had suffered for so long, they slept the sleep of old dogs in the sun or kittens cuddled against their dam's safe side. Only Theseus moaned and tossed, struggling with the god of sleep, who had sent a dreadful dream to vex his slumbers.

The god Dionysus appeared before him in this dream. "Do not take Ariadne to Athens with you," he warned. "She is fated to become my bride and thus win immortality. I love her well, and she will be honored above all mortal women, as she deserves to be."

"She is deserving of such honor, I agree," Theseus replied in his dream, "but we have vowed our love for each other, and I cannot give her up, even for a god."

"Yet you must," replied Dionysus. "No mortal can deny the gods with safety. Thus far the gods have favored you, Theseus. But if you deny me Ariadne, it will go hard with you forevermore."

"You are one god among many," said Theseus, "and Ariadne is one woman out of all the earth. And she is mine."

At these defiant words, the god's bright face darkened in anger, but he kept his voice reasonable as he answered.

"Then consider this. Ariadne is the daughter of King Minos. At his command, twenty-eight of the choicest youths and maidens among Athens's citizenry have met hideous deaths. Will their fathers and mothers welcome that king's daughter as their future queen? Is your love so selfish you would take her into danger? Think again, Theseus."

The god vanished. The young prince tossed and moaned and at last awoke. He glanced quickly to where Ariadne lay in the leafy bower he had prepared to protect her against the night mists. He could faintly see the outline of her slender figure in the light of the approaching dawn. Then a spasm of pain crossed his face.

Dreams, he well knew, were portents. And his had been very real. The god's voice still sounded in his ears, its warning clear. Once again he saw the angry faces in that assembly where he had declared himself, and fear for Ariadne suddenly smothered every other emotion in him. Dionysus was right, as the gods always were. Minos's daughter must not go to Athens. Now he loved

her enough to leave her. And the god had promised to be kind.

Quickly, Theseus rose and wakened his companions. They were aghast at what he proposed. Yet they, too, saw at once that Ariadne could go to Athens only in peril of her life. Silently they stole aboard the boat while Theseus took a last farewell of his sleeping love. She lay with one arm crooked under her head, her cheek resting against the elbow. A small smile curved her sweet mouth and her lashes shadowed her cheek. Tears rushed into his eyes and such an ache came into his throat that he groaned. She stirred. Theseus turned and sped toward the waiting boat. In sorrow and silence, they ran up the sail and drew away from the island of Naxos, where lay, all unsuspecting, the sleeping Ariadne.

Now each day since Theseus and his companions had sailed for Crete, old King Aegeus had taken his place on a high cliff commanding a far view of the waters. Day after day he sat there, offering prayers for the return of his son and the thirteen with him. Sometimes other sorrowing parents joined him. So he was not alone on this particular day when a sail was sighted approaching Athens. All saw it and dread seized their hearts. But still no one spoke, for the boat was yet too far distant to identify it. They watched its approach with anxious eyes.

Suddenly there came a cry, so full of despair and suffering that no one there could ever again quite rid his ears of it. The old king had risen from his seat. His knotted fists were raised above his head as if to pummel the sky. "My son, my son!" he shrieked. Then, taking a step toward the cliff's edge, he shook a gnarled fist at the black sail that came into his view, crying, "My life ends with yours."

Before anyone could stop him, Aegeus hurled himself over the cliff's edge, plunging a thousand feet into the sea below.

Theseus and his companions, numb with sorrow at the loss of Ariadne, had forgotten to substitute the white sail for the black one. Their grief for the abandoned princess had quite wiped out of their minds their promise to King Aegeus.

When at last they came into port and made their way into the city, they were unprepared for the sad faces they met along their way. When the news of this fresh loss was borne to him, Theseus felt as if his heart could not endure its pain. He ordered a funeral prepared such as befitted an honored king. Then he took over the reins of government himself.

Theseus was a wise ruler. He consolidated his kingdom, fortified the city, and subdued all enemies who moved against it. He kept the vow made in Crete, erecting temples and palaces so that Athens became famed for beauty as well as good government. He lives in memory as the true founder of Athens and one of the great heroes of all time.

Understanding What You've Read

1. Why did Theseus volunteer to be sent to the island of Crete and fed to the Minotaur?
2. What special qualities did Theseus have that made him a hero?
3. Heroes in myths are faced with important or difficult problems to solve. With what problem or problems was Theseus faced? How did he solve them?
4. What danger did Theseus face? Could an ordinary person do what Theseus did? Why or why not?
5. As brave as Theseus was, could he have succeeded without the help of Ariadne? How did she aid him?
6. Why do you think hero tales were important to the people of ancient Greece?

Writing

1. Write a sentence in which you describe Theseus and the special qualities that made him a hero.
2. The following sentences are steps in the sequence of events that occurred when Theseus killed the Minotaur. Put the steps in the correct order. Then write a paragraph in which you tell about the downfall of the Minotaur. Give your paragraph a title.

   a. Theseus hurls himself on the Minotaur's back.
   b. Ariadne gives Theseus a spool of thread.
   c. With blow after blow, Theseus kills the Minotaur.
   d. Theseus hears a gentle *slap, slap, slap,* like someone running barefoot.
   e. Theseus hides on a narrow ledge.

More Myths to Read

A Companion to World Mythology by Richard Barber. Illustrated by Pauline Baynes. Delacorte Press, 1980. This reference book identifies the heroes, gods, and goddesses of the major world myths.

Once in Puerto Rico by Pura Belpré. Warne, 1973. This book includes legends about several of the heroes who were important in the history of Puerto Rico.

The Children's Homer by Padraic Colum. Illustrated by Willy Pogány. Macmillan, 1962. This is a retelling of the adventures in *The Iliad* and *The Odyssey*.

Olode the Hunter and Other Tales from Nigeria by Harold Courlander with Ezekiel A. Eshugbayi. Illustrated by Enrico Arno. Harcourt Brace Jovanovich, 1968. This collection of folklores and myths include comic as well as serious explanations of African traditions.

Beginnings: Creation Myths of the World compiled and edited by Penelope Farmer. Woodcuts by Antonio Frasconi. A Margaret K. McElderry Book. Atheneum, 1978. This is a collection of myths from Babylonia, New Guinea, Russia, and Australia.

White Serpent Castle by Lensey Namioka. McKay, 1979. This mystery story, set in sixteenth-century Japan, involves a ghost and two samurai heroes.

Stories of King Arthur and His Knights by Barbara Leonie Picard. Walck, 1955. Here are adventures of knights and deeds of chivalry in the early days of England.

Part 7

Nature's Ways

SKILLS LESSON

Recognizing Fact and Opinion

The poodle clearly doesn't agree with the judges' opinion. What do you think the poodle's opinion is?

Read the sentences below. Which sentences are statements of *fact*? Which is a statement of *opinion*?

1. A poodle won the Best-in-Show award at the Westminster Kennel Club in 1973.
2. Poodles are beautiful dogs.
3. The word *poodle* comes from a German word meaning "to splash in a puddle."

Did you say that sentences 1 and 3 are statements of fact? They're facts because they can be proved. Can sentence 2 be proved? No. Some people may share the opinion stated in sentence 2. But other people may have a different opinion. What's your opinion?

Opinions Based on Facts

Very often, authors mix statements of fact and opinion in the same selection. It is your job, as a careful reader, to recognize which statements are facts and which are opinions.

Read the following paragraph. Which sentences state facts? Which sentences state opinions? (Remember, a fact can be proved.)

The rope-bridge of San Luis Rey in Peru was one of the greatest engineering feats in history. The bridge was originally built by Incas in 1350. Almost forty meters high, it stretched fifty meters across the raging Apurímac River. The bridge was made only of hand-twisted plant fibers. It was repaired frequently and used until 1890, when it collapsed. Even modern bridges can't rival the ingenuity and beauty of the bridge of San Luis Rey.

Notice that the first and last sentences are opinions. These statements cannot be proved. The other statements are facts. Historical records could be found as proof that these statements are true. The author has used these facts to support the two opinions in the paragraph.

Judging the Author's Opinion

Must you always agree with an author's opinion? Of course not. You may feel that the author has not presented *enough* facts to convince you. You may feel that the facts given are *not strong enough* to convince you. Or you may recognize that the author has given "only one side of the story."

Before you read the following paragraph, decide what opinions you have about liver. (Do you like it? Is it good for you?)

Liver is a wonderful food. It's one of the best sources of iron. It's generally cheaper than most other meats that provide similar nutrition. To prepare liver, you just fry it for a few minutes in a pan with a dab of butter or margarine. Many people serve liver covered with onions.

The author has presented several facts about liver. These facts are used to support the opinion stated in the first sentence: *Liver is a wonderful food.* Did you like liver before you read the paragraph? If so, the facts the author gives might have reinforced your opinion. Before you read the paragraph, did you dislike liver? Has the author changed your opinion?

Leading You to an Opinion

Sometimes an author will not specifically state an opinion in a selection. Instead, the author may present a set of facts in such a way that you can figure out the author's opinion and what opinion he or she would like the reader to have, too.

Read the following paragraph. Notice the kinds of facts the author states about New York City.

Within New York City's limits there are over fifty museums, and many of them are free. Also, you can visit the Statue of Liberty, the Empire State Building, Grant's Tomb, the UN, and many other places of interest. Do you like to sample foods from different countries? In New York you can find restaurants that serve Cuban, Korean, Czechoslovakian, Greek, and many other kinds of foods. Do you enjoy music and the theater? Lincoln Center, the Metropolitan Opera, Carnegie Hall, and the open-air Shakespeare theater in Central Park are only a few of the places that house the arts in New York City.

Empire State Building.

Metropolitan Museum of Art.

Lincoln Center.

A New York subway.

The author has given you many facts about New York City. Each statement the author has made can be proved to be true. Notice that the author has *not* stated an opinion. Yet you can tell, from the kinds of facts that are given, that the author is trying to lead you to an opinion. Which sentence below states the opinion the author is trying to lead you to?

1. There is little to amuse a visitor to New York City.
2. There are many interesting things to do in New York.

The author is trying to lead you to the opinion stated in sentence 2. All the facts in the paragraph support that opinion.

Try This

1. Read the following sentences. Which state facts? Which state opinions?

   a. Louis Braille invented a system of raised dots that stand for letters of the alphabet.
   b. Lizards make wonderful pets.
   c. Sundews are the most interesting of all the insect-eating plants.
   d. Maria Mitchell received many honors for discovering a comet.

2. Read the following paragraph in which the sentences are numbered. Which sentences state facts? Which state opinions? Which sentence contains both a fact and an opinion?

   (1) Augusta Rogers was a very clever person. (2) Within a period of four years she had taken out a number of patents for her inventions. (3) She invented the first car heater that didn't use fire. (4) She also invented a folding chair and many other useful things. (5) It's a shame that Ms. Rogers never achieved great fame for her inventions.

VOCABULARY STUDY

Multiple Meanings

Word Play

See if you can use at least two meanings of *spine* in the same sentence. Do the same for *form* and *scale*.

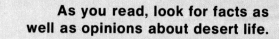

As you read, look for facts as well as opinions about desert life.

What did one person who liked lizards do for the summer? He went on an . . .

Adventure in the Desert

by Barbara Brenner

Gila Monster

My name is Alan Pippin (Pip for short). I spent a summer in the Arizona desert, watching lizards.

Actually, I watched a lot more than that. I got to know plants and animals I'd never even heard of before. I learned how they survive in that strange environment. And I learned a little about human survival, too.

Still, it was the lizards that got me out there. So it's lizards that stand out most clearly in my mind.

Why Lizards?

The trip wouldn't have happened at all if it hadn't been for my sister Jan. Jan is a botanist, and she was working at a research station in Arizona. I wrote and asked her to let me come and visit. I pleaded my interest in lizards and promised all sorts of cooperation and good behavior, which we both knew I couldn't possibly deliver. But Jan invited me to come stay with her for the summer anyway.

My parents were agreeable, so I spent a month preparing. I read a dozen books on the desert. I bought myself some high boots and a canteen. My father helped me make a noose for catching lizards. And my mother gave me a pocket thermometer for keeping records of desert temperatures.

I arrived at the Phoenix airport on a hot day in the middle of June. Jan was waiting for me in her ancient army jeep. We collected all my luggage—tent, backpack, suitcases, and the empty fish tanks I'd brought for housing live specimens—and we drove out to Jan's place. She was staying in a house on the outskirts of the city.

Jan and I spent our first evening catching up on family gossip. It was after dinner that the lizard question came up.

"Why lizards?" she asked me.

What she meant was that of all the members of the animal world, why had I focused on the *saurians* [sôr′ē·ənz], a suborder of the reptiles?

I laid out my reasons.

First of all, there's the fact that they're so ancient. Every time you look at a lizard, you're looking at a little piece of prehistory. Some lizards date back to the time of the dinosaurs. The dinosaurs became extinct, but their relatives, the lizards, have prospered; they're found in almost every part of the world. When I look at a lizard, it's great to know that somewhere, three million years ago, a creature very much like it was running around.

Leopard Lizard

I'm not alone in my attraction to lizards. Stories about them go back to the most ancient writings. Drawings and paintings of lizards can be seen among the oldest artifacts in the world.

Yet even if they didn't have such a long and impressive history, they'd still be a fascinating form of animal life. There are over three thousand different species of lizards. They are tiny, large, fat,

skinny, speckled, checkered, striped, spotted, smooth, lumpy, warty, blotchy, spiny, shiny, iridescent, bright, drab, or able to change color!

Some lizards are legless. Some have a third or *parietal* [pə·rī′ə·təl] "eye," which may aid the lizard in controlling its body temperature. Some Indonesian lizards have "wings" with which they can glide for distances up to eighty feet. The basilisk lizard of the American tropics can run across the surface of the water. And most gecko species have toe pads that allow them to walk up a wall or upside down on a ceiling.

Many species of lizards can grow a new tail to replace a broken or lost one, and all lizards can replace teeth as many times as is necessary.

There are a hundred other interesting ways of lizards. Some of those ways are unique to the saurians. Other ways are shared with all members of the class *Reptilia.* In any case, the lives of lizards have endless variety and color.

So, as I said to Jan, why *not* lizards?

The Place

It was Saturday. Jan wasn't working. We were going into the desert on our first full-scale lizard expedition.

"Are we taking all this for a one-day trip?" I asked as I helped load the car.

Banded Gecko

That was when my sister gave me my first lecture on desert travel. You don't just go cruising out into the desert, I was informed. Those who do, live to regret it—if they live. She was serious.

I watched her as she checked out her car. "This buggy is our only way out," she told me. "Not many people go where we're going, so you can't expect help from a friendly passer-by. And there are no gas stations."

She put an extra can of gas and a huge container of water in the back of the car. Then we filled our canteens with water. It seemed to me that with that amount of water we could have made our own river and floated to where we were going.

Next I was subjected to inspection. Jan approved my long pants and high boots, nixed my short-sleeved shirt and bare head. She said, "The more areas of your body you cover, the cooler you are in the desert." I changed to a long-sleeved shirt, and she gave me a broad-brimmed hat. At last we were ready to go.

In less than an hour we were deep in the desert. It was unreal—like a foreign country, or another planet. Nothing was familiar. Back home, my eye was used to seeing tree-lined streets and shady woods. Here in the desert were flat sunbaked roads and sand. There were almost no trees, and even the few we saw didn't look anything like our Connecticut maples and oaks and birches. We bounced along in the car, kicking up dust and watching

mirages develop and disappear on the road in front of us.

We talked about deserts. Jan told me what defines them—water. A desert, she said, is a place where the rainfall doesn't exceed ten inches a year.

Water is the key to the desert. It even shapes it. It cuts out the canyons, rubs the stones smooth, cracks the mud, and makes the oases [ō·ā′sēz]. Water even shapes the plants and animals.

"You take desert plants," said Jan. "Out here the most important thing is for every organism to conserve water. Desert plants, like other plants, carry water in their stems and leaves. If they had big leaves, they'd lose a lot of water through evaporation. So they've developed small leaves, or no leaves, like the cactus. They have long roots that reach down and get water from deep underground, or spread for long distances and soak up whatever rainwater falls onto the surface of the desert." Jan told me that some desert plants have roots that run for thirty or forty feet just below ground.

Teddy Bear Cholla Cactus

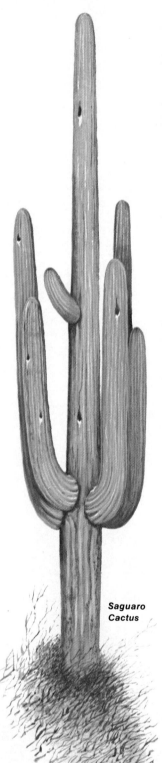
Saguaro
Cactus

We'd been driving around most of the morning, looking for a good spot to watch wildlife. We'd been circling, doubling back, trying little dirt roads, when suddenly we came on it. Before our eyes was a stretch of purely beautiful desert. Full of color and rimmed by mountains, the desert looked really pretty under a June sun.

We decided to stop. The spot we had picked was divided into two parts. On one side was a gentle slope called a bajada [bä·hä′də]. It was covered with low-growing plants and tall saguaro cacti.

At the base of the bajada was a sandy flatland. Here the ground was hot and dry. Everything was beige and tan and brown. Jan called off the names of the plants for me. Bursage [bûr′sāj′]. Creosote [krē′ə·sōt′]. Mesquite [mes·kēt′]. Cholla [choi′yə]. They were all pale desert colors. Even the cacti were pale green under that brutal sun. The only dark spots on the landscape were an occasional outcropping of lava rock and some areas where the ground was covered with flat stones made smooth by water. It was what the geologists called a desert "pavement."

There was a dry stream bed which separated the bajada from the flatland—an arroyo [ə·roi′ō]. It was about two feet deep and was cut into the earth in a clear path from the mountains.

There were trees along the banks of the arroyo—unfamiliar desert trees. Paloverde [pal′ō·vûr′dē]. Acacia [ə·kā′shə]. Ironwood. Jan knew all of them. She said they were there to catch the water that sometimes ran down from the mountains and through the arroyo. Right now they drooped like hungry beggars. The arroyo was dry as a bone.

I began to have a vague feeling that something was missing. I finally realized what it was.

"There's nothing here," I remember blurting out.

430

Jan didn't get my point at all. For her, there was plenty there—all kinds of low-growing plants and grasses, cacti, and bushes. She could have spent a year and still not investigated all the species of vegetation in that desert.

"I mean there are no living things," I amended.

She was annoyed. "What do you think plants are?"

"I mean where is everything? Where are all the animals? There aren't even any birds."

Jan tried to ease my disappointment. "It's getting to the hottest part of the day. This is when the birds go higher in the sky to catch the cooler currents of air. And you know the lizards go underground to cool off." I agreed that that was where they must be.

I guessed the rodents and insects were underground, too. We certainly did see holes. There were holes of every size and description. They could have been ant holes, beetle holes, badger and skunk holes, or holes of the ground squirrel. But there

Arizona Alligator

431

didn't seem to be a single living creature on top of the ground.

"Patience isn't your long suit, Pip," Jan told me. "You'll have to learn to be patient in the desert or you won't see anything. Why don't we have some lunch and then come back?"

While we ate and drank in the shade of the car, Jan explained to me that the desert requires a different kind of looking. "You have to learn to look under and inside and overhead," she said. "Your eye has to become attuned to tiny movements and to small differences in the contour of the ground. Try to separate colors to notice camouflage," she suggested. "Then you'll begin to see things."

After lunch we tried again. The first things we began to see were birds' nests. Soon we began to see birds. The cactus wrens hung out in the cholla, and gila woodpeckers popped in and out of holes in the saguaro. An occasional hawk flew high over our heads, looking for mice, ground squirrels, and lizards.

The hawk and I were having about the same luck with the lizards. By two o'clock I was sure there wasn't a single lizard in the whole Sonoran Desert. The living desert my foot, I thought.

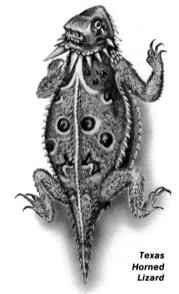

Texas
Horned
Lizard

Then I saw it out of the corner of my eye. A small movement near where Jan was standing. It had been scrambling up out of the arroyo when Jan moved and frightened it. It streaked past us and made for a bush, but not so fast that I didn't see its long tail and pointed snout, its tiny body and the stripes.

"It's too bad, Pip," Jan said sympathetically as we walked back to the car. "You didn't catch anything. We'll have to get up earlier, I can see that."

But somehow I didn't feel disappointed. At least I

had seen a lizard. And where there was one, there were bound to be more. After all, weren't lizards supposed to be the most plentiful desert animals?

I held my field guide happily and read aloud about the western whiptail—I had just seen my first lizard!

Western Whiptail

Understanding What You've Read

1. Name two reasons Pip gave for his interest in lizards.
2. What are some of the things that different species of lizards can do?
3. What is a desert? Why is water the "key" to the desert?
4. How did Jan explain the "different kind of looking" that a desert required?
5. Why wasn't Pip disappointed that he hadn't caught a lizard on his first expedition?

Applying the Skills Lesson

Read the following sentences from the selection. Which state facts? Which state opinions?

1. Drawings and paintings of lizards can be seen among the oldest artifacts in the world.
2. Yet even if they didn't have such a long and impressive history, they'd still be a fascinating form of animal life.
3. There are a hundred other interesting ways of lizards.
4. A desert . . . is a place where the rainfall doesn't exceed ten inches a year.
5. Desert plants, like other plants, carry water in their stems and leaves.

As you read, look for facts that scientists have proved about volcanoes. Look for the opinions that people long ago had about many volcanoes.

The eruption of a volcano is a fascinating, frightening event. Learn about where these mountains of fire come from in . . .

THE RESTLESS EARTH

by Barbara B. Simons

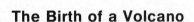

The Birth of a Volcano

From outer space the Earth looks like a beautiful blue-green ball with small brown continents scattered over it. It looks cool and peaceful, floating in space surrounded by white clouds. However, we know that the Earth is really not as cool and calm as it looks.

The part of the Earth we see and know and live on is just the top layer—the crust. Even the deepest mines go only a short way into the crust. Yet we have a good idea of what the inside of the Earth is like.

The crust is thin. It is only about three miles thick in some places, about fourteen miles thick at the thickest part. Although it seems heavy and solid to us, it is the lightest layer.

Below the crust is a large layer called the *mantle.* It is a much heavier layer. The part of the mantle just below the crust is a strange place. Pressure there is very great, and the temperatures are very high.

Sometimes the mantle rock melts. The molten rock, called *magma,* makes its way slowly toward the surface of the Earth. It can cool and harden just beneath the surface.

Sometimes, though, the rising magma finds a crack or weak spot in the Earth's crust. The heat and pressure from below push the mass of hot rock against the opening. Suddenly the surface gives way—and the molten rock explodes out of the opening as lava. This is how a volcano is born.

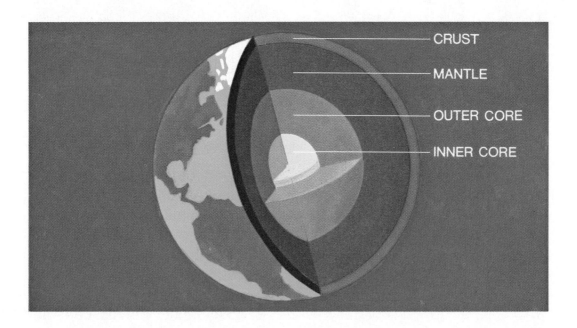

CRUST

MANTLE

OUTER CORE

INNER CORE

The Restless Earth

A few years ago, scientists carefully mapped all the places where the Earth is "restless." They looked at the sea floors and the deep ocean trenches. They examined the rocks in old and new mountains.

Gradually, the scientists built a new picture of the Earth. The crust is not one solid piece of rock. It is broken like a cracked eggshell. Pieces of this shell are sliding slowly around the Earth, bumping into each other, pulling apart, but always on the move.

Geologists now think that the Earth's crust today is divided up into about six huge pieces, or *plates,* and some smaller pieces. The plates are mainly under the ocean, with the continents riding on their backs. Wherever plates

meet, the Earth is restless. At the plate edges, volcanoes erupt, mountains are built, and earthquakes shake the land.

Volcano Myths

Before scientists began to study the way the Earth is made, people made up stories to explain volcanoes and earthquakes. These "mountains" that roared and smoked must be the homes of gods and goddesses, they said. And if the mountains could destroy the land, clearly the god must be very powerful — and very bad-tempered.

In Hawaii, a chain of islands built by undersea volcanoes, the myths are of the fire goddess Pele and her magic shovel. The islands of Hawaii were, in fact, built up one at a time — though not by Pele's magic shovel. The Pacific plate on which they ride has moved slowly to the north, over a spot where magma constantly breaks through.

The Mediterranean Sea is another restless part of the Earth. Many volcano myths were created by the ancient Greeks and Romans, who lived in the surrounding areas.

The Greek god Zeus, in one

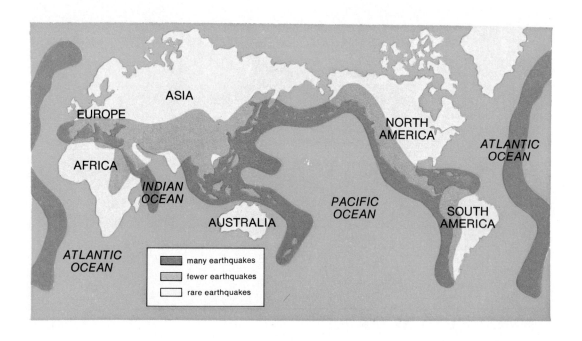

story, put the island of Sicily on top of a giant to keep the giant prisoner. The giant was so angry that he spouted flames and ashes out through the crater of Mount Etna. And he rolled around under the island, causing terrible earthquakes in Sicily.

Several Italian volcanoes were supposed to be the giant forge, or furnace, of the Roman god Vulcan. He worked with metal, making thunderbolts. The name of one of Vulcan's mountains—*Vulcano*—is the source of the word *volcano*.

Both Greeks and Romans thought that certain volcanoes and the eerie landscape around them were gates to the underworld, Hades, a land of fire and smoke. In a way, this belief was understandable. Volcanoes *do* come from the underworld—from the great masses of molten rock beneath the Earth's crust.

Understanding What You've Read

1. How is a volcano born?
2. How do geologists explain why the Earth is restless?
3. Why did people once make up stories to explain volcanoes and earthquakes?
4. Which myth is the source of the word *volcano*?

Applying the Skills Lesson

Read the following sentences from the selection. Which sentences state facts? Which state opinions?

1. It [the Earth] looks cool and peaceful, floating in space surrounded by white clouds.
2. The part of the Earth we see and know and live on is just the top layer—the crust.
3. The part of the mantle just below the crust is a strange place.
4. Before scientists began to study the way the Earth is made, people made up stories to explain volcanoes and earthquakes.

Recognizing Fact and Opinion

In textbooks, authors usually state facts. However, authors sometimes will state their own opinions or will explain another person's or group's opinion. Look for such phrases as "They believed," "She felt," "In their opinion." Such phrases signal an opinion. The sidenotes for the first selection will also help you notice opinions.

Recognizing Fact and Opinion in Social Studies

Australia: A Case Study

Some Europeans had already seen western and northern Australia. They did not give good reports of this land. One of these Europeans was William Dampier. Dampier had once been a pirate. This is part of his account: "The land is of dry sandy soil, destitute of (without) water." Dampier saw only a few of the people who lived there. He made up his mind quickly. He wrote that he thought these people must be "the miserablest people in the world."

What words in this sentence show that the phrase in quotes is an opinion?

Cook had read Dampier's account. He expected to find a dry, empty, barren land. He was surprised at what he saw on the southeastern coast. Cook wrote about it in his journal. He wrote that the country appeared "green and woody." At first he was not sure that there were people in the land. He saw

Might someone else have had a different opinion about what the smoke meant? (Hint: Lightning can set things on fire. Volcanoes give off smoke.)

no sign of anyone. But on the afternoon of the second day, the men on the *Endeavour* saw smoke rising far away. Cook felt sure the smoke meant there were people on this coast. Two days later, Cook caught sight of a few figures on the beach. Australia's eastern shore was not untouched by people after all.

—People and Change
Silver Burdett

Building Skills

1. What was Dampier's opinion of Australia? On what facts did he base his opinion?
2. What was Cook's opinion of Australia? On what facts did he base his opinion?
3. Why did the two men have different opinions?

An artist's drawing of Cook's ship, Endeavour, under sail.

Recognizing Fact and Opinion in Science

There are no sidenotes for this selection. Read it and then answer the questions that follow.

A New View of Change

People once thought that everything in the Universe remained pretty much the same. Now we know that things are not always what they seem. We do not feel that the Earth is moving, for example. Yet we know that the Earth is moving. It is rotating. It is also revolving around the Sun.

The Moon revolves around the Earth. The Earth revolves around our star, the Sun. And the Sun itself is moving. All the billions of stars in our galaxy are moving. And all the millions of galaxies in the Universe are moving, too.

The Universe is vast, and there is much in it that we do not yet understand. But we do understand that all things in the Universe are in motion. And we do understand that all things change.

—*Concepts in Science:* Brown
Harcourt Brace Jovanovich

Building Skills

1. Read the first sentence of the selection again. What opinion did people once have about the Universe?
2. Find four facts given in the selection to prove that the Universe is always changing.

443

Recognizing Slanted Writing

When an author uses **slanted writing,** it doesn't literally mean that the writing is crooked. What is slanted writing? Read the newspaper articles on page 445. The one on the left does *not* give all the facts. It also contains words that are meant to slant the reader's opinion on the topic. It's an example of **slanted writing.** The one on the right is an example of **objective writing.** It presents *all* the important facts.

Smedley Loses in Tough Race

by GLORIA SWOONSOON

Last night was a sad night for Hardy Oaks. In a tough race, our well-loved, hard-working mayor was beaten by Ms. Millicent Murbly.

In his home last night, Mayor Smedley offered the winner his best wishes. He said that voter apathy was a major reason for his defeat. Otherwise, he said, the job would not have gone to "this unqualified young woman."

Murbly Elected Mayor

by RACHEL BACKSTER

Last night, Mr. John Smedley lost his bid for reelection as Mayor of Hardy Oaks to Ms. Millicent Murbly. Ms. Murbly is a lawyer and has been president of the Town Council for the past six years.

The turnout was a record high for the town, with 90% of the eligible voters casting 692 votes for Ms. Murbly. Mayor Smedley received only 82 votes.

One likely reason for Mayor Smedley's defeat was his having lived in France for ten months last year.

Notice that Gloria Swoonsoon does not state these facts in her article:

The vote was 692 to 82.
Ninety percent of those eligible voted.
Mayor Smedley lived in France for ten months last year.

Swoonsoon's article also uses **loaded words** and phrases to slant the reader's feelings in favor of Mayor Smedley. Some of these loaded words and phrases are:

> well-loved   hard-working
> a sad night for Hardy Oaks   voter apathy
> tough race   unqualified

Suppose you had read only Swoonsoon's article. You would not be getting a true picture of the election. How does the second article help you to see how Swoonsoon has slanted the facts in favor of Mayor Smedley?

Slanted Writing and the Author's Purpose

Why do authors use slanted writing? Sometimes the authors themselves are not completely aware that they are slanting the facts. They may be so caught up in their own feelings about something that they fail to consider all the facts. In other words, they fail to be *objective.* Other times, of course, an author may know all the facts. But he or she may deliberately omit important information or use loaded words in order to persuade you to think or do something.

Read the following advertisement. Because it's an ad, you know that the author's purpose is to get the reader to buy something. What facts might the author be leaving out? What examples of loaded words can you find in the ad?

How would *you* like to have your pick of the best music ever? At prices that will amaze you? You can get a terrific selection of the all-time greats, no matter what your musical tastes. Do you like rock? We'll send it to you. Jazz? Show tunes? Classical? Folk? Country and Western? You name it. You can have it—by joining the *Record-of-the-Week Club.*

How do you become a member of this fabulous club? Just fill out the handy order form below. Send no money. We'll bill you later. And if you act now, as a bonus we'll send you any four of the records shown in the picture for the unbelievable price of only $1.35.

What does the author mean by "the best music ever"? Is it possible that the author's choice of "all-time greats" would not match your tastes in music? Notice some of the other loaded words the author uses to make you think favorably of the Record-of-the-Week Club: *terrific, fabulous, handy, bonus, unbelievable.*

When you read an ad, such as the one on page 446, remember to pay attention to what is *not* said. Does the ad tell you clearly how much *each* record will cost? No. Are the musicians and singers well known or unknown? You can't tell from the ad. What is the minimum number of records you must buy if you join the Record-of-the-Week Club? Again, the ad doesn't give you this information.

When reading an ad—or an article or a book—try to be aware of whether or not the author is giving you all the facts objectively. Try to understand the author's purpose, and be on the lookout for loaded words. Don't get caught by slanted writing!

Try This

1. Read the following pairs of sentences. Which sentence in each pair presents the information objectively?

   a. Marcia won by a landslide.
      Marcia received 55 percent of the votes.
   b. Ellen's play closed after four weeks.
      Ellen's play was a flop.
   c. Your cake will be as light as a feather.
      Your cake will weigh 500 grams.
   d. The Hawks shut out the Beavers, 8–0.
      The game was an embarrassing defeat for the Beavers.

2. Read the ad below and study the picture. What facts have been left out of the ad?

FOR SALE Used car. Only 3 years old. Driven for only 12,000 miles. Dark green. Needs a few repairs. $500. Call 520-3520.

VOCABULARY STUDY

Compound Words

"Words!" yelled the sorcerer. "I ordered a box of little warts! But somebody sent little words!"

"I've got an idea, Sir," said the sorcerer's apprentice. "Let's put some of the words together. We can use them in a potion to turn rattlesnakes into suitcases."

"OK. Here's the word *lion*. Stick it with the word *fish* and make a fish that looks like a lion."

"All right. I put the lionfish in the potion pot."

"Here's some salt. Perhaps we can make some saltwater."

"Sure. We can use rainwater from the rooftop. What's next?"

"There're lots of *fish* in the box. Stick them on other words. Make a jewelfish, an angelfish, a rudderfish. Say, is there jelly in the refrigerator?"

"No sooner said than done! A jellyfish! Should I taste it now, Sir?"

"No. I will. Earthquakes and Thunderbolts! This doesn't taste like a potion. It tastes like seaweed stew! Even a Venus's flytrap wouldn't eat this!"

"Why not, Sir?"

"We forgot to add an eggplant."

Word Play

Compound words are two or more words put together to make one word. Find the compound words in the story. (Hint: There are sixteen.) Then separate each compound word into its base words.

449

As you read this selection, watch for "loaded" words that show the author's opinion of insect-eating plants.

You know that there are many insects that eat plants. Did you know that there are also plants that trap and eat insects? You'll learn more about the Venus's flytrap, the sundew, and others in . . .

INSECT EATERS OF THE PLANT WORLD

by Ross E. Hutchins

It is supposed to be news when a person bites a dog. So it is probably news when a plant bites an insect. Oddly enough, this happens more often than you might think. There are a number of plants that live on a partial diet of animal life such as insects, snails, and spiders. To understand why some plants have developed this strange habit, it will help to consider the food needs of plants that are found in any garden.

Plants have roots reaching down into the soil to get water and several chemical elements they need in order to grow. One of the most important of these elements is nitrogen. The soil in most swampy areas seems to be lacking in nitrogen, an element found in the bodies of all animals, including insects. So some swamp plants catch and eat animals to get the nitrogen they need. But plants are attached to the ground by roots. How, then,

451

do they catch animals? As you shall see, they set traps and wait for the game to come to them.

Venus's Flytrap

One of the most interesting of the insect-eating plants is the Venus's flytrap. This plant lives in only one small area of the world —the coastal marshes of North and South Carolina. The Venus's flytrap doesn't look unusual. Its habits, however, make it truly a plant wonder.

The plant is small. There are a dozen or so leaves arranged in the form of a rosette, or circle. These leaves lie flat and slightly raised above the ground. During the blooming season, the plant sends up a thin stem bearing a number of small white blossoms. But it is the leaves themselves that are especially interesting.

Their outer ends are hinged in the center and bear long, sharp spines along their edges. When they are open in the "set" position, these leaf-traps have reddish centers that help attract insects. These colored surfaces have many tiny glands which secrete a sweet-smelling liquid that helps to lure insects to their doom. The lobes of the leaves are hinged so that they can close and trap small creatures. But, you might ask, how does the leaf-trap know when to snap shut?

Botanists have found that on the inner surfaces of the leaf-traps there are several trigger hairs. Through these hairs the plant senses the presence of prey. Remarkably, if you touch one of these trigger hairs with a straw or your finger, the trap will not close. In order to spring the trap, you must touch at least two of the trigger hairs or you must touch one twice!

Why has nature made the plant in this way? If only one touch were needed to spring the leaf-traps, they would be snapping shut each time a drop of rain fell into them or whenever a blade of grass brushed against them. Because of this clever arrangement, it is hard to fool the Venus's flytrap, and it usually snaps shut only when an insect crawls across it. When the plant does make a mistake, it is usually several hours before the leaf will reset itself.

It has been found that the leaf-traps take about one or two seconds to close, but this seems fast enough to catch most insects. Actually, an insect like a fly could easily escape before the trap shuts, but usually the insects do not seem to realize what is happening until it is too late. The more the caught insect struggles to free itself, the tighter the plant holds it. In the meantime, minute glands on the leaf-trap surface begin secreting a fluid that slowly dissolves the edible parts of the unfortunate captive. After a few days the trap will open again, ready to catch the next insect foolish enough to walk into it.

The flower of the Venus's flytrap.

453

Pitcher Plants

Another family of insect-eating plants is found in many parts of the United States. They are called pitcher plants. These plant trappers have leaves that are hollow and shaped like thin pitchers or horns. They usually grow best in damp bogs or marshes—the same sort of places where other kinds of insect-eating plants are found.

How these pitcher plants lure insects to their doom has been studied by many botanists, but there is still much to learn about them. The leaf, of course, is the trap, as in the Venus's flytrap. But it works in an entirely different way.

If you cut open some of these leaves, you will always find them partly full of insects and insect remains. The insects have been trapped by a trick that the plant plays on them. Near the top of the leaf-pitcher, on the inside, there are cells which secrete a sweet material with a fruity or honeylike fragrance. This odor attracts any insects crawling or flying around the plant. When they enter the open top of the pitcher, they are delighted with the sweets which the plant has prepared for them. But the inside walls of the leaf-tube are slippery. The insects soon find it hard to hang on, so they try to fly out. In so doing, they usually bump into the canopy that curves over the top. They then drop to the pit at the bottom. Some kinds of pitcher plants even have "see-through" windows near the top of the leaf-tubes, and insects often try to escape through these false openings. The insects bang into them and then drop into the deep well from which there is little chance of escape.

Each of the pitcher plant's leaves is partly filled with a watery fluid. When an insect or even a small tree frog falls in, it soon stops its struggles. Why? Because this amazing plant secretes a drug which soon causes the trapped creature to lose conciousness. Besides this drug, the fluid in the leaf also contains juices similar to those found in our stomachs. These juices slowly dissolve the insect bodies.

Sundews

Sundews are another kind of insect-eating plant often found growing in damp places. They are small, not much larger than buttons, but in the sun they sparkle like jewels against their green background of moss. The sundews, too, catch insects. But their method is unlike that of either the Venus's flytrap or the pitcher plant.

One kind of sundew plant has a number of small, reddish leaves around a central stem. These leaves are shaped somewhat like tiny soup spoons with the handles at the center. The outer, larger ends of the leaves are covered, especially on their upper surfaces, with many

small, short hairs. These hairs make each leaf look like a tiny pincushion. Upon each of the hairs there sparkles a small, gem-like drop of thick, clear liquid. These droplets make the little plant sparkle in the sun, and they give it the name "sundew."

These little drops that shine so brightly in the sun are not "dew" at all. Each one is a trap. The little drops are actually a natural flypaper. Any small insect coming into contact with the sticky, clear fluid at once finds itself helplessly trapped. The

more it struggles, the more firmly the gluelike fluid holds it.

The tiny sundew plant has yet another trick to prevent the escape of the doomed insect. Within a couple of hours, the hairs begin to bend slowly toward the insect until it is at last tightly pinned and slowly digested.

It is strange and interesting that the leaves of the sundew also have a sense of smell. They can somehow tell when an insect is nearby.

The Venus's flytrap, the pitcher plant, and the sundew are just a few of the many insect-eating plants. Of all the world's strange plant life, they are probably the most fascinating.

Understanding What You've Read

1. Why do some plants eat insects?
2. What causes the leaves of the Venus's flytrap to snap shut?
3. What "trick" does the pitcher plant play on insects?
4. How did the sundew get its name?

Applying the Skills Lesson

Each sentence below contains a word or words that express the author's opinions. Find such "loaded" words in each sentence. Are the author's feelings favorable or unfavorable toward the plants?

1. Because of this clever arrangement, it is hard to fool the Venus's flytrap, and it usually snaps shut only when an insect crawls across it.
2. After a few days the trap will open again, ready to catch the next insect foolish enough to walk into it.
3. They [the sundews] are small, not much larger than buttons, but in the sun they sparkle like jewels against their green background of moss.
4. Of all the world's strange plant life, they [the insect eaters] are probably the most fascinating.

As you read the selection, decide whether or not the author is presenting both sides of the story about crows. See if you can figure out the
author's opinions about these birds.

*Are crows really fooled by scarecrows? It's hard to
believe that such a simple trick could fool a . . .*

Genius with Feathers

by Josephine C. Walker

"If people wore feathers and wings, very few of them would be clever enough to be crows." So someone once said.

That person was right. The black-feathered and quick-witted crows are unique in the bird world for their amazing intelligence. True, sometimes this intelligence leads them into stealing and mischief-making. But, as one farmer said, "If it is not your corn that has been stolen, you cannot help but admire their skill and daring."

Tough, resourceful, and sly, crows above all other birds seem to have mastered the problem of survival against heavy odds. One major reason is their amazing communications system.

They seem to have built-in radar for detecting danger. They also communicate with one another through a relay system. People cannot understand it, but apparently it is very clear to crows. For example, a crow will make two or more noises at evenly spaced intervals. Far back in the forest, another crow repeats the message with exactly the same note, with the same pitch, at the same intervals. Depending on the tone, they appear to be passing the message along —"Here's food!" "Lie low. . . . Quiet!" "All clear."

A farmer, putting out poisoned corn for crows, learns that in a matter of minutes all crows in the area know to stay clear.

In addition to this relay system, crows have a strong sense of caution. While on the hunt for food, they appoint a crow to stand guard. High up in a tree, the guard can spot a gun a half-mile away, never mistaking it for a pole or stick. When anyone with a gun comes near, on a signal from the guard the flock makes a quick, quiet retreat. They fly at a speed of perhaps forty-five miles an hour.

Crows work in teams and suc-

ceed by the theory: "United we stand; divided we fall." For example: A dog is enjoying a small bit of meat. Three crows decide they want it. One flies down to the left of the dog, catching the dog's attention with caw-caws and much flapping of its wings. A second crow flies down, repeating this from the other side. When the dog's attention is away from the meat, the third crow cleverly darts down and grabs the meat. All three crows fly triumphantly away.

Crows like to stay in groups as they nest, too. Sometimes there are fifty or sixty nests within a small area. Often they play sly tricks among themselves. A crow thinks nothing of stealing a neighbor's nesting material while that neighbor is off searching for food.

Crows have another gift. They are great mimics. They can learn to talk and imitate animal sounds. Some have been known to learn 100 words, and even whole

phrases. They can imitate the squawk of a chicken, the whine of a dog, or the meow of a cat.

Games have a certain fascination to crows. In a game of hide-and-seek, a crow hides in the hollow of a tree and then sounds a distress caw. The others rush to the spot, look around, then flap away. This may be done over and over, after which the young crow pops out of its hiding place and caws gleefully. Far from being annoyed at this, the flock bursts into loud cawing themselves. They seem to like the trick that has been played on them.

Food is not much of a problem for crows. They eat almost anything—fruits, vegetables, nuts, wasps, toads, even poison ivy! Their way of getting food is so clever that they never seem to

have trouble satisfying their needs. If everything else fails, they have scavenger instincts and fly up and down highways looking for trash that might have been thrown from cars.

Attacking is sometimes part of a crow's life, too. Its greatest enemy is the owl. In wanting to attack its enemy, the crow forgets its usual caution and makes loud and furious sounds.

Crows are like people in a most interesting way. They try their own criminals in a court of law. They hold trials and, amazingly, dish out justice.

One naturalist told of a strange experience. By accident he became an observer of an odd trial. About 100 crows were arranged in a semicircle around two other crows. On the topmost branch of a nearby tree sat two guards. It seemed these guards were so concerned with the trial that they did not notice the approach of the man. He quietly hid himself beneath some vines.

The crows cawed back and forth to one another, deciding the fate of the two crows in the center. Suddenly one of them saw the man. With a scream of alarm, the whole court flew toward the two guards in the treetop. In a very few minutes, these untrustworthy guards were killed. This was the punishment for not letting the crow-court know of the danger. Soon the crows flew away, probably to go on with the trial somewhere else with more trustworthy guards.

Crows are also cautious when they gather in autumn to migrate. They meet where no bushes block their vision. They chatter noisily for a time and then send a few scouts out to be sure no enemy is around. Finally, in small companies, they quietly slip away. Sometimes as many as 3,000 crows gather in one place in this manner. Then they fly to their winter roosts, sometimes as far as 1,500 miles.

One scientist at Johns Hopkins University figures that there are 320,000 crows each year at one winter roost near Baltimore, Maryland. Another roost near Arlington National Cemetery has held 130,000 crows.

For centuries there has been an argument among bird lovers about crows—whether they do more harm than good. However, one fact causes no argument: Everyone agrees that the crow is one of the smartest, most quick-witted birds living. Someone has predicted, and it may well be true, that when people are gone, there will still be crows!

Understanding What You've Read

1. How do crows communicate with each other?
2. What are some ways that crows help each other?
3. In what ways are crows like people?
4. What facts about crows did you find most interesting?

Applying the Skills Lesson

Which of the following sentences present the crow favorably? Which presents the crow unfavorably?

1. The black-feathered and quick-witted crows are unique in the bird world for their amazing intelligence.
2. A crow thinks nothing of stealing a neighbor's nesting material while that neighbor is off searching for food.
3. Everyone agrees that the crow is one of the smartest, most quick-witted birds living.

Distinguishing Between Objective Writing and Slanted Writing

Textbook authors generally write objectively. That is, they present mostly facts and very few opinions. They usually give "both sides of the story." Occasionally, however, a textbook author may not give "both sides" or all the facts. If you think the author may not be presenting both sides, ask yourself, "What's the other side of this story?"

The sidenotes for the following selections point out facts and opinions. Refer to them as you read. Think about whether the facts and opinions are favorable or unfavorable.

Distinguishing Between Objective Writing and Slanted Writing in Social Studies

Stories of Early Government

The author is careful to point out that the details may not be factual. Notice the words *The stories say . . .* and *He was supposed to. . . .*

This sentence is the author's opinion. The word *seem* is a clue. (A legend is a story that has come down from earlier times and is often thought by many people to be partly true.)

Some of the old Chinese stories tell of Yao and Shun. Yao and Shun ruled long after the time of the Holy Emperors. The stories say that Yao lived for 116 years. He was supposed to have ruled for 100 years. Such details seem to tell us that these stories, too, are legends.

It is said that Yao lived simply. His main food was soup. He ate it with a wooden spoon from a rough bowl. His "palace" was a simple, plain house. Yao cared nothing about making a show of wealth and power. He lived as simply as the poorest of his people.

A peaceful time. The stories say that Yao ruled the land fairly and well. The country was peaceful. No person attacked others or stole their goods. When people had quarrels, they took them to Yao to settle. He was fair to all the people. A bell and a tablet hung outside Yao's door. Anyone needing the ruler's help could sound the bell at any time. Any person having a complaint could write it on the tablet. The emperor would be sure to read it. The stories say that the land enjoyed real peace in Yao's day. People did not even lock their doors at night.

All the details in this legend may lead you to an opinion about Yao.

—People and Change
Silver Burdett

Building Skills

1. List five favorable things that the author of this selection says about Yao.
2. Does the author mention anything to make you believe that Yao was not a good leader?
3. Which of the following statements best shows the opinion of Yao the author is presenting?

   a. Yao was a grand and mighty ruler.
   b. According to legend, Yao was a fair and humble ruler.
   c. It is certain that Yao was a fair and humble ruler.

Distinguishing Between Objective Writing and Slanted Writing in Language Arts

A Book to Read

TITLE: *Sunrise Island*
AUTHOR: Carella Alden
PUBLISHER: Parents Magazine Press

Book reviews often use slanted writing since the author's purpose is to tell you his or her opinion. What facts are given in this review? What is the author's opinion of the book?

Between the Pacific Ocean and the Sea of Japan lies Sunrise Island. Actually, there are four main islands and many smaller ones that form Sunrise Island, or the country we know as Japan. One way to discover how a country has developed and grown is to take a look at its art. In this book, history is the story, and art is the teller of the tale.

Sunrise Island begins with the "birth" of Japan and moves into its early history with the use of bronze and clay for sculpture. Shōtoku, who was responsible for bringing Buddhism to Japan, is honored in many works of art. Scrolls, delicately lettered with Japanese ideographs, are shown along with many lovely lacquered pieces. Bold art depicts the members of the samurai, the hereditary warrior class in feudal society. The ancient tea ceremony and the Imperial Palace, home of the Emperor, show other forms of Japanese art. The gardens give us a glimpse into a fascinating aspect of Japanese culture.

Sunrise Island traces the progress of one of the world's great cultures by showing us its art.

— *Language for Daily Use:* Brown
Harcourt Brace Jovanovich

Building Skills

Read each of the following sentences. What words in each sentence suggest that the author has a favorable opinion of the book?

1. Scrolls, delicately lettered with Japanese ideographs, are shown along with many lovely lacquered pieces.
2. The gardens give us a glimpse into a fascinating aspect of Japanese culture.
3. *Sunrise Island* traces the progress of one of the world's great cultures by showing us its art.

Inferring from Pictures

How many times have you laughed at a cartoon or a picture even when it had no caption? Your laughter means, of course, that you "got the joke." Even without words, you were able to figure out the point the artist or photographer was trying to make. By studying the details and using your own experiences, you discovered an idea that was not directly shown. In other words, you made an **inference.**

From pictures, you can learn a number of things by paying attention to the details. Look at the chair the cat is sitting on in the picture above. What do you notice about it? There is a worn patch on the side. Two details help you figure out what caused the damage. First, the spot is low on the *outside* of the chair. Second, the fabric has been torn as if something sharp had been drawn across it. The area is low enough for the cat to reach with its front paws, and you know that a cat's claws are sharp enough to tear fabric. Even though the picture doesn't *show* the cat clawing the fabric, you can infer that the damage was done by the cat.

There are many different kinds of details in pictures that you can use to make inferences. Look at the photograph below and answer the questions.

1. What is the weather like?
2. Where was the photograph taken?
3. During what time period was the photograph taken?
4. Why have the people gathered in a group?

What kind of clothing are the people in the photograph wearing? Notice that the young boy has shorts on and that almost everyone's blouse or shirt is short-sleeved. Notice, too, that the sun is bright and that the trees in the background are in full bloom. By observing these details, you can infer that the weather is warm, perhaps even hot. It is probably spring or summer.

Where do you think the photograph was taken? The tall buildings suggest a city or other metropolitan area.

You may not know the exact date the photograph was taken, but you can infer that it was within the last thirty years.

Why? Look at the hairstyles and clothing. Would these be different if the photograph had been taken in 1890? In 1920?

Finally, *why* have the people gathered? What details in the picture tell you they probably are waiting for something? Nearly everyone is looking in the same direction.

Pictures can accompany almost every kind of reading selection. Sometimes they illustrate an exciting scene from a short story, the topic of a chapter, or an important point an author is trying to make. Very often, the inference you draw from a picture can help you to understand and enjoy the reading selection.

Try This

1. Study the picture below. Then answer the questions that follow it.

   a. Where was the picture taken?
   b. What happened shortly before the picture was taken?

2. Which of the lettered statements can you infer from the picture below?

   a. The picture was taken in the spring.
   b. The web was made by a spider.
   c. Spiders sometimes make webs on branches.
   d. You'll always find a spider web in a cherry tree.

VOCABULARY STUDY

Prefixes

"I was watching a movie down at the bottom of the ocean," said Thaddeus the blue whale. "I have to submerge now."

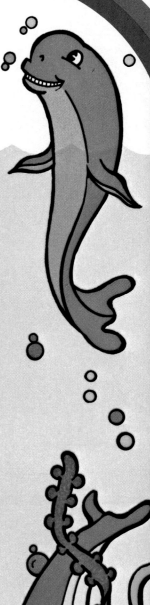

"Wait! Don't go under!" cried the reporter for *Marine Semi-monthly Magazine.* "I need only one more fact for my story about the order, or group, of large fishlike mammals. I've already talked to a dolphin and a porpoise. I just need a few comments from someone in the **suborder** of whales."

"The prefix *sub-* means 'under.' So a suborder is a division under an order of living things."

"Yes," agreed the reporter. "Please come back. Just swim in a **semicircle** back to me so we can talk."

"The prefix *semi-* means 'half.' So you don't want me to swim all the way around your ship—just halfway around?"

"Yes, Thaddeus. Now here's my question. How long have whales been on the Earth?"

"Since **prehistory**," answered Thaddeus. "The prefix *pre-* means 'before.' We've been around since *before* humans first wrote histories thousands of years ago. Now I really must get back to my movie. I left just at the part where Moby Dick meets Son of Flipper."

Word Play

Match each word on the left with its meaning on the right. Then use each word in a sentence.

1. semimonthly
2. suborder
3. prefix
4. semicircle
5. submerge
6. prehistory

a. half a circle
b. go under the water
c. before history was written
d. happening every half month
e. a division under an order (group) of living things
f. a word part added before a root word.

As you read, study the pictures. You should be able to draw conclusions about Cappy Anson and underwater hunting from them.

Cappy Anson explores the underwater world with scuba gear and a hand net in order to . . .

BRING 'EM BACK ALIVE

by John J. Floherty
and Mike McGrady

We awakened two hours before sunrise and unhitched our power boat from its offshore moorings. There was no breeze, and the Florida seas were calm. No clear line separated the sky and the ocean. Ahead we could see only night.

"It'll be a fine day," Cappy Anson predicted, "a fine day for the hunt."

The twenty-three-year-old hunter headed toward the Florida Keys. Unlike other skin-diving hunters, Cappy Anson used no spear gun in his search for rare and unusual fish. He aimed to "bring 'em back alive."

As we rounded the tip of the Florida peninsula, Cappy changed direction, heading west toward the Gulf of Mexico. The skies behind us lightened, and the May sun quickly scattered the mist hanging over the water.

"Where are we heading, Cappy?" we questioned.

"To my favorite hunting spot," he answered. "To the coral reefs."

Although Cappy had been there before, this was our first visit to the reefs—ledges of living coral that follow the Florida shoreline from south of Miami to Tortuga Island. Made of millions of almost microscopically tiny animals, the reefs at some places rest ten fathoms beneath the surface and at other places jut up to form small islands.

"What fish are you hunting today?" we then asked.

"The lionfish," he said. "These are fairly rare. Each one should net us about a hundred dollars."

"A hundred dollars!" we exclaimed. "That seems like a lot of money to spend on just one fish."

"Well, there is one little catch," Cappy explained. "The lionfish belongs to the family of scorpion fish. Its sharp fins can slice through your hand as though it were butter. But that's not the worst of it. Those spines are hollow and filled with poison. Just one drop of that poison is enough to kill a person."

We thought about what Cappy had just told us as we tested our gear. Then we climbed down the ladder and entered the warm water. Our only protection against the poisonous lionfish was a small net, similar to the type used by butterfly hunters. The summer sun bounced against the white sand and lit the entire undersea world. Objects over 100 feet away could be seen with ease.

The Coral Reef — An Underwater Wonderland

As we neared the reef itself, we admired its different colors. It seemed painted with pale shades of red and yellow and violet.

Cappy interrupted our study of the reef by signaling us to move on with the hunt. We turned our attention to the tropical fish. We then understood why these fish were sought and prized by aquariums and private collectors everywhere.

Never before had we seen such colors as these. There were brilliant stripes and polka dots. It was as though the fish had been hand-painted by an artist with an odd sense of color and strange sense of humor. Shining like jewels, these fish made the inhabitants of other seas seem dull in comparison. Our eyes searched among the fish, but we saw no sign of the lionfish.

Checking our air supply after what seemed like only

minutes, we discovered that we had been below for nearly half an hour. Turning regretfully away from the reef, we paddled back toward the boat, rising slowly toward the surface as we went. After climbing aboard, we rested for a few moments.

"There were so many fish down there," we said. "How do you know which one is a lionfish?"

"There's no mistaking a lionfish," Cappy answered. "Just look for an underwater nightmare."

"An underwater nightmare?"

"You'll understand when—and if—we find one," he said. "Meanwhile, we'll look for some other varieties. While we're resting, we might as well move to some new territory."

Cappy started the powerful motors and lifted the anchor. Moving at the slowest possible speed, we followed the reef and studied the sea terrain through a plate-glass window built into the boat's bottom. The window gave us a clear view below, acting much the same as the diver's face mask.

A Second Dive

Our second dive turned up no creature that came close to looking like an "underwater nightmare." Most of the fish seemed carved from dreams of a definitely pleasant nature. Pointing to one group of strange fish, Cappy held up his underwater slate and wrote the word "angel." These fish—the queen angelfish—were about two feet in length. Of blue and yellow shades, they had fins flowing from them like trails of liquid gold.

Following Cappy's lead, we moved toward them cautiously, slowly. After he had netted one, we each followed suit. Returning to the boat with our prizes, we were quite proud of the ease with which we had landed them. But Cappy quickly rejected our offerings and returned them to the sea. As he placed his fish in one of the boat's saltwater tanks, he explained why.

The queen angelfish.

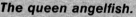

"Don't feel bad," he said. "The queen angelfish looks peaceful enough, but two of them kept in the same tank would turn on each other."

On later trips below we did much better. On one trip we brought in several jewelfish, valued at almost thirty dollars each. On the next trip, we caught our first sight of the Portuguese man-of-war, one of the most deadly kinds of jellyfish.

Seen from the surface, the man-of-war appears quite harmless. It floats along like a half-inflated balloon topped by a small saillike structure. However, seen from the skin diver's point of view, it takes on a different appearance. Long stingers, shining red and green, may hang a full ten feet beneath the creature's floating cap. These stingers have caused great pain to skin divers and fish.

Knowing this, we were surprised to discover several small fish swimming safely through the stingers. Apparently these fish were not bothered by the man-of-war's poison. The tiny silver-and-blue rudderfish seemed to grow well in these dangerous surroundings. Cappy motioned us back. He signaled that he was going to try to trap some of the rudderfish.

The dangerous Portuguese man-of-war.

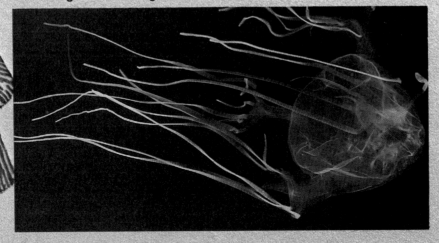

An Unfortunate Incident

Cappy circled the giant jellyfish, keeping just out of reach of the poisonous arms. Then, in a single quick motion, he threw his net into the center of the mass.

At first it looked as though he had succeeded. Moving away from the Portuguese man-of-war, he held two of the small fish in his net. Then, when he appeared to be free and clear, he suddenly dropped his catch and grabbed his right arm.

We rushed to Cappy's side and eased him back toward the boat. However, before rising to the surface, Cappy picked up a handful of white sand from the bottom. Once aboard the boat, he began furiously to rub his right arm with the sand.

"I'll be all right," he said. "This isn't a bad sting."

It may not have been a bad sting, but the pain showed in Cappy Anson's face. After scraping off any of the stingers that might still be holding fast to his arm, he splashed some gasoline over it. Gasoline or alcohol will help kill the tiny stinging cells that remain in the flesh.

"You can't see them," Cappy said, "but you sure can feel them."

Moments later the pain had stopped. Only a narrow

strip of pink skin remained to remind us of Cappy's painful meeting with the Portuguese man-of-war. During the rest of the day we looked for less harmful fish. Our enthusiasm mounted with each trip, and we soon forgot about our original prey—the rare and very dangerous lionfish.

An Underwater Nightmare

As our long day of hunting neared its end, we discovered a most unusual rock among the seaweed. It seemed to carry many unusual colors—bright markings set against a background of pink. Cappy, swimming ahead of us, did not notice the stone. However, we lowered ourselves for a closer look.

As we studied it, the strange rock suddenly moved. The seaweed also moved. Then we realized that the "seaweed" was attached to the fish.

Cappy, turning back, also saw our find and immediately placed his hand across his throat. This was the skin diver's signal for danger. It was then that we realized that we had finally discovered the dreaded lionfish. And at the same time, the lionfish discovered us.

The dreaded lionfish with spikelike poisonous fins.

As the fish rose to greet us, we remembered Cappy's warning to treat it with all the respect we would show a rattlesnake. We froze. The absence of air bubbles showed that we were both holding our breath.

Cappy's description of the "underwater nightmare" had been quite true. The fish looked like a pint-sized left-over from the days of the dinosaur. Yellows, browns, and pinks formed a frightening pattern over the ugly fish's spotted skin.

Our eyes never left the dorsal fins—the poison-carrying spikes sticking out of its back. The fish showed neither fear nor anger. It studied us with its lidless eyes.

Cappy, moving toward us all too slowly, waited no longer. With one quick sweep of his hand net, he ended the hunt on a happy note. The lionfish twisted and turned, but could not escape from the trap. Then, as though it realized the uselessness of a fight, it gave up.

Only then did the bubbles flow again from our aqualungs. Only then did we breathe with ease.

The End of the Hunt

As we headed back with our catch, we found that the work of the "live hunter" does not end with the hunt. Great care has to be taken to avoid rough water. Strangely enough, the fish will get seasick if there's too much motion.

Once we were ashore, we had to package the fish to ship them. They were placed in a plastic bag filled with ocean water that had been collected from the incoming tide. To keep the water "fresh" twenty-four hours, we then put in a tube leading to a tank of compressed oxygen and inflated the bag. This was then placed in a second bag made of the same heavy plastic. Then it was placed in a box labeled "Live Fish." The boxes were rushed to a nearby airport so that they could be flown to aquariums as far away as Iowa.

Cappy Anson is just one of many skin divers who enjoys the excitement of underwater hunting without killing their prey. Indeed, these people bring 'em back alive!

Understanding What You've Read

1. Why does Cappy Anson hunt fish and bring them back alive?
2. Why do you think the coral reefs were Cappy's favorite hunting spot?
3. How did the men breathe underwater?
4. Why is the lionfish called an "underwater nightmare"?
5. What work must the "live hunter" do after the hunt?
6. Look back at page 472. List some details about the rare lionfish.

Applying the Skills Lesson

1. Which of the following can you infer from the picture of the coral reef on page 470?

   a. The water in the Florida area is very clear.
   b. Coral can be different colors and shapes.
   c. The fish that live there don't live in any other part of the world.

2. Which of the following can you infer about underwater hunting in the Florida area from the other pictures in the selection?

   a. Underwater hunting can mean facing danger from poisonous fish.
   b. Underwater hunters always use a spear gun.
   c. The water into which the hunters dive is warm.
   d. There are many varieties of fish in the Florida waters.

Inferring from Pictures

Do most or all of your textbooks have pictures? You probably already know how important they are. They help explain the text or give you more information. When you read your textbooks, study the pictures. You can learn a lot from them.

The sidenotes in the following selections point out text references to pictures. As you read the selections and study the pictures, think about the kinds of information that pictures can give you.

Inferring from Pictures in Social Studies

A

B

C

D

F

G

E

H

Identify the Pictures

Take a sheet of paper and jot down a few words describing what you think is happening in each picture. Look, for example, at the pictures marked A and E. What is shown in each one? Is it something you have experienced yourself?

This sentence asks you to make an inference about each picture.

Now look over all the pictures. Not all of them show single dramatic events in a person's life. Instead, some of them represent stages or periods of life. Are most people in this country likely to go through these stages and events? How about most people in the world?

These sentences ask you to compare the pictures to what you already know.

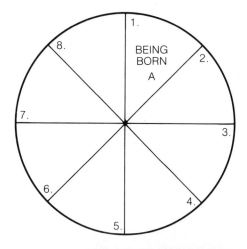

This paragraph asks you to write about the inferences you have made.

Figure Out the Order

The pictures are not in the right order. Figure out in what order they would probably take place in most people's lives. Write down on your paper the letters of the pictures in the order that you work out.

On another piece of paper draw a circle much larger than the one shown. Divide the circle into eight sections. Give each section a number.

In each section of the circle that you've drawn, print a short description of one of the pictures. Be sure to follow the order that you worked out for the pictures. Also print the letter of the picture you choose for each section of the circle. To help you get started, the first section of the circle shown here has been filled in.

— *The Way People Live*
Houghton Mifflin

Building Skills

Read each group of words below. Then tell which group of words best describes the stage of life shown in each picture.

- being born
- getting married
- graduating from school
- starting in school

- dying
- growing older
- becoming parents
- being a teen-ager

Inferring from Pictures in Science

An Apprentice Investigation into a Lever

NEEDED: Some books, a ruler, a chair, string, tape, and a spring scale

Lift a book with the spring scale. How much force does it take? Here is what happened in one trial.

The symbol is a "key" to the first picture.

Now try lifting the same book using a lever. Tie the book to one end of the ruler. (You may want to tape the string to the ruler so that the string can't slip.) Tie the spring scale to the

Notice that the scale shows that the book weighs 650 grams.

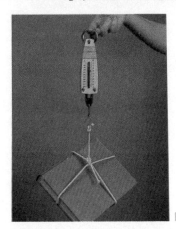

483

The picture should help you understand *fulcrum.* Check the glossary to make sure you understand it.

The picture next to the ▲ shows you what to do.

The scale in the picture says 375 grams when the lever (the ruler) is used.

other end of the ruler *by the ring,* so that you can pull down on the hook of the scale.

Use the back of a chair for a ful-crum. Have the fulcrum much closer to the book than to the scale.▲ Lift the book by pulling down on the spring scale.

How much force does it take to lift the book with this lever? Here is the result of one trial.◆

How does this force compare with the force needed to lift the book without the lever? Do you have any evidence that this lever multiplies force?

—Concepts in Science: Brown
Harcourt Brace Jovanovich

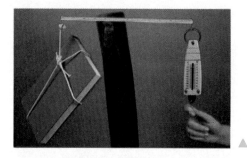 ▲

 ◆

Building Skills

Which of the following can you infer from the pictures?

1. More force is needed to lift the book when the lever is used.
2. Less force is needed to lift the book when the lever is used.
3. It takes the same amount of force to lift the book whether or not the lever is used.

SKILLS LESSON

Reading Newspapers

There's something for everyone in a newspaper.

What's in a newspaper? There are news stories and book and movie reviews. There are movie and TV listings, sports pages, and puzzles. There are sections that predict the weather and sections that predict how your day will turn out. There are advertisements and comics.

If someone asked, "What's in a newspaper?" could you answer in just four words? Yes—if you answered this way: "*News stories* and *features*."

News stories are articles or reports about important events in the world, in the nation, or in your neighborhood or town. Generally, you'll find the most important news stories—about world, national, or local events—near the front of the paper. In the later pages, you'll find the features.

What are the features? They are items that usually appear in a paper every day. Some newspapers have an *index* to features. It usually appears on the first or second page of the paper. The one below will give you an idea of the kinds of features you'll find in a newspaper. Notice that a newspaper's index to features does *not* list news stories.

This is a section of ads put in by people for cars or houses for sale, jobs, and so on.

In this section, you might find book and movie reviews.

This is a list of people who died recently.

Most likely you know what many of these features are. You can probably figure out that you'll find recipes and articles about food on page 23. But what kind of articles might you find under the *Family/Living* heading on page 22? You might find a story about how a family built its own telescope. You might find a story about how the neighborhood is fixing up a local park. You might even read about some young people who put on puppet shows in hospitals.

Facts and Opinions in Newspapers

The main purpose of a newspaper is to report news. Reporters and editors have to work very fast in order to report things as soon as they happen. They also try to make sure that a news story is made up only of facts. (Of course, every newspaper makes a mistake now and then.)

The story below is a local news article. As you read it, use the sidenotes to help you understand more about reading a news story.

Girl Saves Police Officer's Life

by MARCIE MULLIGAN

Last night at about 9:00 P.M., thirteen-year-old Sylvie Thurgood was walking her dog on East 25th Street near Stanton Road when she heard someone yelling for help. At about 8:45 P.M., Sergeant Peter Wein had been walking by the building site in that area. He had thought he heard some strange noises coming from an open pit and had gone to investigate. At that moment, a beam from the partly built building fell and knocked Sergeant Wein into the pit.

The title is called a *headline.*

Why do you think this is called a *by-line?*

Is each sentence in this story a fact?

Sergeant Wein said, "I was trapped at the bottom of the pit. There was no way to climb out, nothing I could get a grip on. I'd been yelling for help for about 15 minutes. Then Sylvie called down to me. I called up telling her who I was."

Sylvie found some strong wiring and *(continued on page 12)*

Major news stories start near the front of the paper. You have to turn to a later page to finish the story. Hold the last sentence in your mind as you turn to the rest of the story.

On page 12, the headline is repeated—but in a short form—to help you find your place quickly.

The three dots are called *ellipsis* marks. They mean some words were omitted.

Girl Saves Police Officer

(continued from page 1) tied her dog's leash to it to make it long enough to reach the bottom of the pit. She then tied the dog's leash around a telephone pole. Sergeant Wein was able to pull himself up to street level just moments before—as he put it—". . . there was a terrific landslide. It's a good thing that Sylvie came along when she did and that she thought so fast. If she hadn't, I'd have been trapped under tons of earth."

488

Each of the statements you just read is a fact. Newspaper writers and editors generally try to present the facts by answering the W–H questions. These questions are *Who? What? When? Where? Why?* and *How?* Notice that Marcie Mulligan, the writer of the article above, gave facts as answers to these questions:

Who? Sylvie Thurgood.

What? Saved Sergeant Peter Wein.

When? Last night at about 9:00 P.M.

Where? At a building site on East 25th Street near Stanton Road.

Why? Because he had fallen into a pit and she heard him calling for help.

How? By tying her dog's chain leash and a heavy wire around a telephone pole so that he could pull himself up to safety.

Newspapers give opinions, too—but generally not in a news story. You can find opinions in movie or book reviews, advice columns, letters to the editor, editorials, and some feature articles. On page 490 is an editorial. It is written by an editor of the paper. It expresses the newspaper's opinion.

Down with the Ajax Building Company

For the past year, this paper has been giving its opinion on the Ajax Building Company. Last night's events point out, once again, that great problem Ajax is causing. If it weren't for the quick-thinking actions of Sylvie Thurgood, a police officer might have been hurt or killed.

It is time that our town passed better safety laws that building companies must obey. It is time that you, the readers, write to the Town Council and attend town meetings to make your voices heard on this important issue.

Let's all be glad that Sergeant Wein was not hurt. But let's not wait until someone *is* hurt. A fast-thinking and brave citizen like Sylvie Thurgood may not be around to help the next time one of Ajax's sites caves in.

Notice that an editorial states opinions based on facts. What is the editor's opinion of the Ajax Building Company? What is the editor's opinion about Sylvie Thurgood? What is the editor's opinion about what the Town Council should do?

Letters that readers send to the editor also state opinions. What opinion is being expressed in the letter below?

To the Editor:

I am angry about your attacks on the Ajax Building Company. My house was built by the Ajax Company, and it's beautiful, well made, and comfortable. No one got hurt when it was being built. My father says it's the best building company in town.

Dotty Ajax

Whose opinion is expressed in this sentence?

490

Try This

1. Below are the first parts of three newspaper articles. Which one is probably an editorial? Which is probably a news story? Which is probably a feature story?

a.
Centreville Ice Cream Factory Explodes
by MARY REYNOLD

Late last night, the Chilly Cone Ice Cream factory on East Harbinger Lane in Centreville exploded. . . .

b.
Why East Harbinger Lane Needs a Stoplight

In the past six months, there have been several bad traffic accidents on the corner of Third Street and East Harbinger Lane. Nevertheless, our overpaid and underworked City Council has ignored the community's pleas for a traffic light at that corner. . . .

c.
I Scream, You Scream, We All Scream for Ice Cream
by JACK FROST

What could be more cooling on an August afternoon than a dish of homemade ice cream? It's easy to make. If you have a large family or lots of friends to make it for, you can save money by making your own. Here are the ways several people I interviewed make their own ice cream. . . .

2. What are the headlines in the articles above?
3. What are the by-lines in the articles above?

Etymologies

Panel 1:

TAKE YOUR TIME LOOKING AT THE HOUSE. BUT PLEASE DON'T TOUCH ANYTHING.

WHAT A PRETTY LITTLE VASE. IT MUST BE VERY OLD.

CAREFUL! THE OWNER GETS ANGRY IF ANYONE TOUCHES HER THINGS. YES, THE VASE WAS MADE IN GREECE **CENTURIES** AGO.

Panel 2:

WHY, THAT'S NOT GREEK. CENTUM IS LATIN FOR A "HUNDRED." IT WAS MADE HUNDREDS OF YEARS AGO IN ROME.

MY, MY. YOU DO KNOW A LOT ABOUT OLD THINGS. I **PREDICT** YOU'RE GOING TO LIKE THIS HOUSE. LET ME SHOW YOU THE LIBRARY.

Panel 3:

PREDICT. THAT'S LATIN, TOO. PRE- MEANS "BEFORE." AND DICTIO IS LATIN FOR "SAY." YOU'RE SAYING I'M GOING TO LIKE THIS HOUSE EVEN BEFORE I'VE SEEN IT!... WHAT A STRANGE LIBRARY. THE ONLY BOOKS ARE GREEK AND LATIN DICTIONARIES. OH, WHAT AN INTERESTING PAINTING. WHO ARE THE THREE WOMEN?

Word Play

1. Tell the meaning of each word in boldface. Where does each word come from?
2. An etymology is the history of a word. Find one word in the story that comes from *Furies* and one from the Latin words *dictio* and *centum*. Use each in a sentence.

As you read the following newspaper article, look for the facts that answer the W–H questions. Notice that the few opinions reported begin with the words such as "It is thought . . ." or "If, as most authorities believe, . . ."

Monarch butterflies make news in the New York Times, *August 1, 1976. Read all about it!*

BUTTERFLY HUNT REVEALS SECRET
Millions of Monarchs Spend Winter in Mexico Woods

by Boyce Rensberger

Scientists have just learned where monarch butterflies go every winter. Millions of them migrate from all over the eastern United States and southern Canada to a tiny, wooded 20-acre region in the mountains just north of Mexico City.

The butterflies swarm over the pine trees so thickly that their weight can snap branches three inches in diameter.

In the spring, the orange and black monarchs head north, mating on the way. It is thought that most, if not all, of the adults die shortly afterward, leaving their offspring to complete the return trip.

The discovery was announced in the August issue of *National Geographic* magazine by Dr. Fred A. Urquhart, a Canadian zoologist who has been searching for the

(continued on the following page)

wintering grounds of the monarch since 1937.

It had been known that the relatively small number of monarchs from the western states overwinter on California's Monterey peninsula, turning orange the trees in the town of Pacific Grove. And it had been known that a few eastern monarchs go to Central America for the winter. But no one knew where the bulk of the huge population of eastern monarchs went.

Monarchs Tagged

In recent years, Dr. Urquhart and volunteers from the Insect Migration Association had tagged several thousand monarchs using waterproof gummed labels on the wings. Printed on the labels were the words, "Send to Zoology University Toronto Canada," referring to Dr. Urquhart's academic affiliation.

Using the locations from which tagged butterflies were sent to him in the mail, Dr. Urquhart drew up migration maps. The dots fell into lines pointing to Mexico, but there the lines faded out without converging.

Advertisements in Mexican newspapers for volunteers to become butterfly spotters brought a response from Kenneth C. Brugger of Mexico City. In January 1975, he telephoned Dr. Urquhart to report that he had found millions of monarchs roosting on trees north of the city.

Last January, Dr. Urquhart flew to Mexico City and, with Mr. Brugger, went into the mountains to confirm the finding. The site is at an altitude of 9,000 feet where it never freezes but where the air is chilly enough to virtually inactivate the butterflies. Thus millions of the insects can remain in one spot without having to eat.

The two men found one butterfly that had been tagged in Minnesota.

Ten thousand of the Mexico City monarchs were tagged in an effort to see how far north they would make it on the return trip. Results of the tagging are not known yet. If, as most authorities believe, the adults do not make it all the way north, scientists will be left with another mystery: How does the new generation of butterflies know where to go for the summer and how to find that little piney woods north of Mexico City in the fall?

Understanding What You've Read

1. Where do most monarch butterflies spend the winter?
2. How did Dr. Urquhart and other scientists discover the monarch butterflies' wintering place?
3. Why can so many monarch butterflies stay in one place during the winter without having to eat?
4. Why do you think it was important to Dr. Urquhart to find out where monarch butterflies spend the winter?

Applying the Skills Lesson

1. What is this article's headline? What is its by-line?
2. How is this newspaper story different from a letter to the editor or an editorial?
3. Name the facts that Boyce Rensberger gives to the W–H questions—Who? What? When? Where? Why? How?

Lucinda Gates was written about in newspapers several times when she was alive. As you read, think about what facts might have been included in an article about her.

You might not be having ketchup on your hamburger or tomatoes in your salad if it weren't for the work of . . .

Lucinda Gates:
Plant Breeder, Plant Hunter

by Charles Morrow Wilson

Lucinda Gates was the only child of James Gates, a market gardener from Salem, Massachusetts. Her mother died when she was only three, and Lucinda (Lucy) Gates grew up working with her father.

In 1804, the year of Lucy's birth, an almanac called *The American Gardener* gave directions for growing what it called the "love apple." The book said the love apple was a healthy and beautiful golden garden fruit. Nevertheless, many Americans continued to believe it was a pretty fruit and not edible. They thought that love apples were poisonous.

The love apple was really a golden tomato. The name "tomato" comes from the Inca word *tomatl*. Many centuries before the time of Columbus, the Incas had found and developed the tomatl as a food crop. This yellow fruit was also grown in the Caribbean Islands and upper South America.

The New World natives often used the tomatl as a medicine. They believed it could cure or prevent several illnesses. Early explorers, particularly the Spanish and Portuguese, borrowed this early American remedy. They carried the unusual plants back to their homelands. The Spanish called the fruit *tomate*. The English translated it as *tomato*.

The name "love apples" for tomatoes came from another source. It seems that the French called tomatoes *pommes d'amour*—"apples of love." So the English got the name "love apples" by translating the French term. That name also "took" in the United States.

By 1812, markets in New Orleans and Philadelphia were selling love apples. During that year, an artist and gardener named Michel Felix Corne moved from New Orleans to Salem, Massachusetts. He brought along a boxful of seeds of various vegetables and fruits, including love apples.

Michel Corne befriended Lucy Gates and her father, bought their vegetables, and shared his seed collection with them. In his spare time, he used whatever glass he could get in order to build what he called a "warming house," that is, a greenhouse. It was the first greenhouse to be built in the Salem area.

Next Corne experimented with growing a number of different plants in the greenhouse. Lucy was fascinated. She brought in wild-growing plants to add to his underglass collection, and she learned how a greenhouse works. She found the idea of year-round—or almost year-round—gardening under glass very exciting.

Early in 1815, toward the middle of a long, cold New England winter, Lucy and her father helped Corne with his underglass garden. Because of the cold weather, most of the vegetable seeds did not grow. However, some of the plants, including the love apples, thrived.

When Corne's poor health forced him to move to South Carolina, Lucy and her father took over the care of the greenhouse. Although the other plants grew poorly, the love apples grew in abundance from early June through August. Lucy, who often helped her father sell vegetables from door to door, worked to convince the customers that the love apples were not poisonous. The Gateses pulled through the extremely cold season, and Lucy became known as the "Love Apple Girl."

Weather forecasts for the next year, 1816, seemed to agree that it would be the worst year ever. The Gateses planned ahead. They knew that practically anything edible would surely be sold. So they placed new soil and planting trays in the greenhouse. They used every available foot of greenhouse space for the love apples.

The hard-to-believe year, 1816, was known as the American "year without a summer." Some people even called it "Eighteen-Hundred-and-Froze-to-Death." They had their reasons. All along the East Coast in 1816, there were heavy frosts and killing freezes during every month of the year. During the second week of June, an almost unbelievable snowstorm whitened fourteen of the then nineteen states. Crops throughout the country were destroyed. Many forests changed from green to black, and many fruit trees failed to bloom. Harvests were very small.

About three-fourths of all Americans then lived by farming. With the crops ruined, many people turned to hunting and fishing. Still more people ate edible wild plants for part or most of their diet. A great many edible plants, such as wild sweet potatoes, wild onions, and numerous wild fruits and berries, survived the bad weather much better than the planted crops.

Lucy and her father fared a little better than most other Americans during that terrible year. Their careful planning ahead and successful growing of the golden love apples in the greenhouse brought them eager buyers. Lucy and her father survived the year without a summer because of the love apples.

The year without a summer was followed by "the year of love apples." Well-known people encouraged everyone to eat the yellow fruit. Several popular magazines joined what amounted to a love-apple crusade.

Back in Salem, Massachusetts, Lucy continued growing her love apples. At the age of fifteen, she scored her first success as a plant breeder. By carefully choosing superior parent plants, she grew a dependable, strong yellow variety of love apples, called the "Gates."

When she was seventeen, Lucy turned to plant hunting. She had been deeply impressed by the beauty and usefulness of wild-growing plants. She began to

"strengthen" some of these plants by crossing their pollen with tastier plants. In time, she developed a good-tasting parsnip and a few other edible vegetables.

In 1822, when Lucy was eighteen, she married Abra Holloway, a gardener. He suggested a new location, near Boston, for their market garden. The family moved their business and grew and sold many varieties of vegetables, including, of course, the golden tomatoes.

Lucy, her father, and her husband continued to do well. During the late 1830's they pioneered in growing and selling the first widely used variety of red tomato.

To the surprise of many, including the Gates-Holloway family, the changeover from yellow to red greatly strengthened the popularity of the tomato. So Lucy spent more time seeking garden crops of brighter and more appealing color. At the time, no one knew very much about how to change the color of plants.

A traveler-friend sent Lucy a packet of tomato seeds that had been given to him by a farmer in Mexico. When the seedlings grew, they produced large, good-tasting tomatoes. But their color was a deep turquoise blue! Lucy thought even more about the importance of color when it turned out that nobody wanted to buy blue tomatoes.

By the 1840's, Boston and most other American cities were growing and prospering. Market gardening became an important business as town and city people broadened their usual bread, meat, and cheese diet with more vegetables.

During the Mexican-American War of 1846, Lucy's husband was killed. Her father also died at the same time. Lucy sought to ease her double sorrow with work. She took charge of all the Gates-Holloway Market Gardens.

By 1850, the Gates-Holloway Market Gardens had become the biggest market gardens in the United States. *The Daily Advertiser,* then a leading Boston newspaper, reported that the one-time Love Apple Girl from Salem had gardened her way to impressive wealth.

In 1866, Lucy celebrated her sixty-second birthday with a grand adventure she had dreamed of since her childhood. She set out for a plant-hunting and garden-viewing tour of the European countries.

In Italy, Lucy grew very interested in an ancient vegetable that was important to the Old World but almost unknown in the United States. She viewed with wonder its big grayish-green leaves and the large fruit or seedpods that changed from shiny green to a dark blue-purple. When she asked the name of the fruit, someone who spoke English said, "Eggplant."

"It is too beautiful to eat," Lucy thought. "I would gladly think of it as a thing of beauty alone."

Later, back home in Boston after she had planted and grown her first collection of eggplant seeds, Lucy's neighbors and several of her customers took the same view of the beautiful vegetable. The people wanted to buy entire plants to be placed in their flower beds or gardens rather than in their vegetable gardens.

504

In 1878, even though her failing health made it hard for her "to go it alone at open gardening," Lucy opened a fresh produce shop, or "green grocery," in downtown Boston. In this enterprise her most successful trade was once more in "True, Vine-Ripened New England Tomatoes."

Understanding What You've Read

1. How did Lucy Gates become interested in plant hunting and growing plants in a greenhouse?
2. What things happened during 1816–1817 that changed people's minds about eating love apples?
3. What did Lucy, her husband, and her father discover about the color of the tomato?
4. Why did market gardening become such an important business by the 1840's?
5. Why did Lucy go to Europe?

Applying the Skills Lesson

1. What facts might be included in a news story about Lucinda Gates? Name the facts that give answers to the W-H questions: Who? What? When? Where? Why? How?
2. Read the headlines below. Which headline might be used for a news story about Lucinda Gates? Which might be used for an editorial? Which might be used for a feature article?

   a. Lucinda Gates Gardens Her Way to Impressive Wealth
   b. Growing Tomatoes in a Greenhouse Can Be Fun— and Profitable
   c. This City Needs More Market Gardens Like the Gates-Holloway Market Gardens

TEXTBOOK STUDY

Comparing Newspaper Reading to Textbook Reading

Reading newspapers calls for some of the same skills you use in reading textbooks. Textbooks, like newspapers, present mostly facts. In a textbook selection, as in a newspaper article, the author often answers the W–H questions: Who? What? When? Where? Why? How? The sidenotes in the following selection point out some comparisons.

Comparing Newspaper Reading to Reading in Mathematics

Using Decimals: The 1972 Summer Olympics

Does the information in this sentence and the tables below it answer the W–H questions?

If this were a newspaper story, the numerals in this chart would replace letters A–F in the paragraphs on page 507.

Use the tables to complete the news story about the 1972 Summer Olympics in Munich.

Weight Lifting: Middle Heavyweight

Medal	Athlete	Country	Pounds lifted
Gold	Nikolov	Bulgaria	1157.41
Silver	Chopov	Bulgaria	1140.88
Bronze	Bettembourg	Sweden	1129.85

Men's 100-Meter Backstroke

Medal	Athlete	Country	Time in seconds
Gold	Matthes	East Germany	56.58
Silver	Stamm	United States	57.70
Bronze	Murphy	United States	58.35

Women's Springboard Diving

Medal	Athlete	Country	Points
Gold	King	United States	450.03
Silver	Knape	Sweden	434.19
Bronze	Janicke	East Germany	430.92

In the Women's Springboard Diving, Micki King of the United States won the Gold Medal, beating second-place Ulrika Knape by (A) points. Bronze Medal winner Marina Janicke was (B) points behind King and (C) points behind Knape.

Notice that this article gives facts about two events. Are any opinions given in the article?

In the swimming competition, Roland Matthes of East Germany won the 100-Meter Backstroke, beating the previous Olympic record of 58.15 seconds by (D) seconds. Mike Stamm of the United States missed the Gold Medal by (E) seconds. John Murphy, the Bronze Medal winner, was (F) seconds behind Stamm.

— Mathematics Around Us
Scott, Foresman

Building Skills

Which of the following "headlines" best states the main idea of the selection?

1. Murphy Finishes Less Than a Second After Stamm
2. United States Wins Three Medals at Olympics
3. Marina Janicke Wins a Bronze Medal in Diving

Comparing Newspaper Reading to Reading in Health

There are no sidenotes for this selection. Read it and then answer the questions that follow.

What Do I Want?

In 1845 Elizabeth Blackwell had to make a choice about her future. A man she loved wanted to marry her. She wanted to become a doctor, the first woman doctor in the United States.

Many people advised her to marry. They said she would be happier as a wife and mother. But Elizabeth Blackwell knew what she wanted. She chose to study medicine. First she worked to earn money for her education. But she couldn't find a medical school to admit her because she was a woman. Finally, she was admitted to a medical school. She had five years of hard study.

When she became a doctor, no hospital would hire her because she was a woman. After many years of struggle, she opened her own hospital. It was the first hospital in the world that was run by women and for women.

—Toward Your Future: Brown
Harcourt Brace Jovanovich

Building Skills

Find the answers to the following W–H questions in the selection on page 508.

1. *Whom* is the selection about?
2. *What* did Elizabeth Blackwell do?
3. *Where* (in what country) did she live?
4. *When* did she make a choice about her future?
5. *Why* was it hard for her to get into medical school?
6. *How* did she overcome the problem of not being able to find a hospital that would hire her?

Books About Nature's Ways

Wild Animals, Gentle Women by Margery Facklam. Harcourt Brace Jovanovich, 1978. The author tells about eleven scientists who work with animals in the wild and what they have learned about animals.

Why Does a Turtle Live Longer Than a Dog? A Report on Animal Longevity by Barbara Ford. Morrow, 1980. This book describes research on animal aging and suggests that people may be able to lengthen their lives.

Small Worlds Close Up by Lisa Grillone and Joseph Gennaro. Crown, 1978. These authors use an electron microscope to show you the beauty found in the structure of everyday things.

Animals of the Deserts by Sylvia Johnson. Lerner Pubns., 1978. Here you'll meet many desert animals and learn about their homes, their food, and much more.

The View from the Oak by Herbert Kohl and Judith Kohl. Sierra Club Books—Scribners, 1977. Here you will see how life appears to the many different kinds of animals that live in an oak tree.

Beyond the Arctic Circle by George Laycock. Four Winds, Schol. Bk. Serv., 1978. Take a tour of the Arctic Circle and meet the people, animals, and plants that live there.

Volcanoes: Nature's Fireworks by Hershell H. Nixon and Joan Lowery Nixon. Dodd, 1978. Many interesting facts about volcanoes are found in this book.

Part **8**

Poets and Their Poetry: Impressions

UNDERSTANDING AND APPRECIATING LITERATURE

Elements of Poetry

The sun was shining on the sea,
  Shining with all his might:
He did his very best to make
  The billows smooth and bright—
And this was odd, because it was
  The middle of the night.

by LEWIS CARROLL

Poets use many different elements to make their poems special. You know that rhyme, stanzas, and different kinds of comparisons are some of the elements that poets use. Poets may also use **alliteration, onomatopoeia,** and **repetition.**

Understanding Elements of Poetry

Alliteration is the occurrence of the same sound, often the beginning sound, in two or more words in a line, stanza, or poem. Poets use alliteration to create certain effects in a poem. The first line of the poem in the cartoon contains alliteration. What words in this line are alliterative? The words *sun* and *sea* are alliterative. Now read the poem below and listen for alliteration.

Snowy Morning

by LILIAN MOORE

Wake
gently this morning
to a different day.
Listen.

There is no bray
of buses,
no brake growls,
no siren howls and
no horns
blow.
There is only
the silence
of a city
hushed
by snow.

Which words in the first stanza are an example of alliteration? The words *different* and *day* are alliterative. They begin with the sound of the letter *d*. What are some examples of alliteration in the second stanza? The words *bray, buses, brake,* and *blow* are alliterative, as are *silence, city,* and *snow*.

"Snowy Morning" also contains **onomatopoeia.** Onomatopoeia is the occurrence of words that sound like what they mean. The words *buzz* and *crack* are often used as onomatopoeia. What words in "Snowy Morning" are examples of onomatopoeia? The words *growls* and *howls* are examples of onomatopoeia.

"Snowy Morning" also contains **metaphor.** Buses, brakes, and sirens are compared to animals that bray, growl, and howl. In this poem, onomatopoeia and metaphor are combined. The words that sound like noises from an animal are used with objects like buses, brakes, and sirens. For example, brakes make a noise similar to a growl.

Another element that poets sometimes use is **repetition.** Poets sometimes repeat a word or phrase for emphasis or to create a special effect. Read the following poem.

> Go with the poem.
> Hang glide
> above new landscape
> into other weather.
>
> Sail the poem.
> Lift.
> Drift over treetops
> and towers.
>
> Loop with the poem.
> Swoop, dip.
> Land.
> Where?
> Trust the poem.

by LILIAN MOORE

What words or phrases are repeated in the poem? The words *with the poem* and *the poem* are repeated. By repeating the word *poem*, the poet emphasizes what the poem is about — enjoying a poem when you read it.

Poets use many elements to make their poetry special. Alliteration is the occurrence of two or more words that begin with the same sound. Onomatopoeia is the occurrence of words that sound like what they mean. Repetition is the repeating of words and phrases. Why do poets use these elements? Perhaps they simply want you to enjoy poetry.

Try This

Read the poem below and answer the questions.

Crickets

by DAVID McCORD

all busy punching tickets,
clicking their little punches.   2
The tickets come in bunches,
good for a brief excursion,   4
good for a cricket's version
of travel (before it snows) to   6
the places a cricket goes to.
Alas! the crickets sing alas   8
in the dry September grass.
Alas, alas, in every acre,   10
every one a ticket-taker.

1. Which line of the poem contains an example of onomato-poeia?
2. Which lines of the poem contain examples of repetition?
3. Which lines of the poem contain alliteration?

Writing

1. Finish each sentence below so that it contains a comparison, onomatopoeia, or alliteration.

   a. The strong wind . . .   c. The birds . . .
   b. The dragon kite . . .   d. The sky . . .

2. Use one or more of the sentences you completed above in your own poem. Before you begin, decide what elements of poetry you will use. You may wish to use repetition.

As you read "Poets and Their Poetry: Impressions," notice the elements the poets use to make each poem special.

In the poem below and in those on the pages ahead, look for comparisons; listen for alliteration and repetition.

Limericks

by DAVID McCORD

A limerick shapes to the eye
Like a small very squat butterfly,
    With its wings opened wide,
    Lots of nectar inside,
And a terrible urge to fly high.

The limerick's lively to write:
Five lines to it—all nice and tight.
    Two long ones, two trick
    Little short ones; then quick
As a flash here's the last one in sight.

Steam Shovel

by CHARLES MALAM

The dinosaurs are not all dead.
I saw one raise its iron head
To watch me walking down the road
Beyond our house today.
Its jaws were dripping with a load
Of earth and grass that it had cropped.
It must have heard me where I stopped,
Snorted white steam my way,
And stretched its long neck out to see,
And chewed, and grinned quite amiably.

Seal

by WILLIAM JAY SMITH

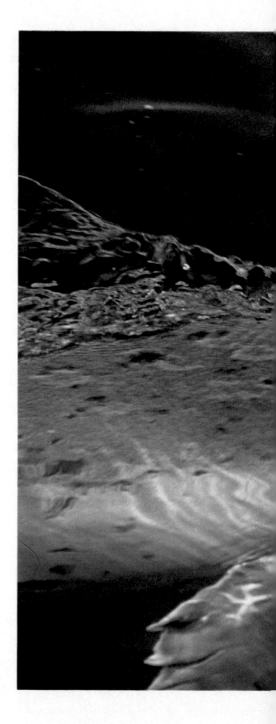

See how he dives
From the rocks with a zoom!
See how he darts
Through his watery room
Past crabs and eels
And green seaweed,
Past fluffs of sandy
Minnow feed!
See how he swims
With a swerve and a twist,
A flip of the flipper,
A flick of the wrist!
Quicksilver-quick,
Softer than spray,
Down he plunges
And sweeps away;
Before you can think,
Before you can utter
Words like "Dill pickle"
Or "Apple butter,"
Back up he swims
Past sting-ray and shark,
Out with a zoom,
A whoop, a bark;
Before you can say
Whatever you wish,
He plops at your side
With a mouthful of fish!

The Women's 400 Meters

by LILLIAN MORRISON

Skittish,
they flex knees, drum heels and
shiver at the starting line

waiting the gun
to pour them over the stretch
like a breaking wave.

Bang! they're off
careening down the lanes,
each chased by her own bright tiger.

The Base Stealer

by ROBERT FRANCIS

Poised between going on and back, pulled
Both ways taut like a tightrope-walker,
Fingertips pointing the opposites,
Now bouncing tiptoe like a dropped ball
Or a kid skipping rope, come on, come on,
Running a scattering of steps sidewise,
How he teeters, skitters, tingles, teases,
Taunts them, hovers like an ecstatic bird,
He's only flirting, crowd him, crowd him,
Delicate, delicate, delicate, delicate——now!

Narcissa

by GWENDOLYN BROOKS

Some of the girls are playing jacks.
Some are playing ball.
But small Narcissa is not playing
Anything at all.

Small Narcissa sits upon
A brick in her backyard
And looks at tiger-lilies,
And shakes her pigtails hard.

First she is an ancient queen
In pomp and purple veil.
Soon she is a singing wind.
And, next, a nightingale.

How fine to be Narcissa,
A-changing like all that!
While sitting still, as still, as still
As anyone ever sat!

Esmé on Her Brother's Bicycle

by RUSSELL HOBAN

One foot on, one foot pushing, Esmé starting off beside
Wheels too tall to mount astride,
Swings the off leg forward featly,
Clears the high bar nimbly, neatly,
With a concentrated frown
Bears the upper pedal down
As the lower rises, then
Brings her whole weight round again,
Leaning forward, gripping tight,
With her knuckles showing white,
Down the road goes, fast and small,
Never sitting down at all.

Knoxville, Tennessee

by NIKKI GIOVANNI

I always like summer
best
you can eat fresh corn
from daddy's garden
and okra
and greens
and cabbage
and lots of
barbecue
and buttermilk
and homemade ice-cream
at the church picnic
and listen to
gospel music
outside
at the church
homecoming
and go to the mountains with
your grandmother
and go barefooted
and be warm
all the time
not only when you go to bed
and sleep

The Runaway

by ROBERT FROST

Once when the snow of the year was beginning to fall,
We stopped by a mountain pasture to say, "Whose colt?"
A little Morgan had one forefoot on the wall,
The other curled at his breast. He dipped his head
And snorted at us. And then he had to bolt.
We heard the miniature thunder where he fled,
And we saw him, or thought we saw him, dim and gray,
Like a shadow against the curtain of falling flakes.
"I think the little fellow's afraid of the snow.
He isn't winter-broken. It isn't play
With the little fellow at all. He's running away.
I doubt if even his mother could tell him, 'Sakes,
It's only weather.' He'd think she didn't know!
Where is his mother? He can't be out alone."
And now he comes again with clatter of stone,
And mounts the wall again with whited eyes
And all his tail that isn't hair up straight.
He shudders his coat as if to throw off flies.
"Whoever it is that leaves him out so late,
When other creatures have gone to stall and bin,
Ought to be told to come and take him in."

Understanding What You've Read

1. To what does Charles Malam compare a steam shovel in his poem "Steam Shovel" (page 517)?
2. In "Seal" (page 518) by William Jay Smith, which words are alliterative?
3. Which words does Robert Francis repeat in "The Base Stealer" (page 522)? Does this repetition make the meaning clearer? Why or why not?
4. In "Esmé on Her Brother's Bicycle" (page 524) by Russell Hoban, where does the poet use alliteration?

Writing

1. In "Seal" (page 518), William Jay Smith uses alliteration in groups of words such as the following:

   a. "swims with a swerve"   c. "quicksilver-quick"
   b. "a flip of the flipper,   d. "past sting-ray and
      a flick of the wrist"   shark"

   Write your own word groups or sentences using alliteration. For example, you might say, "My dog walks with a waddle."
2. In "Knoxville, Tennessee" (page 527), Nikki Giovanni begins her poem with the sentence "I always like summer best." Then she lists the things she likes about summer. Choose the season you like best. Then list the things you like best about that season. Use your list to write a paragraph. You may also wish to arrange your list in the form of a poem.

On the following pages, Myra Cohn Livingston and Joseph Bruchac share some of their poetry with you and answer some of the questions people often ask poets.

Author Study

A Little About Me

by MYRA COHN LIVINGSTON

One of the most exciting things about being a poet is that the ideas and materials for writing poetry are everywhere, and very often appear when one least expects them. There can be as much material for a poem in a hockey game or a garbage can as there is in a beautiful spring day!

Myra Cohn Livingston at her desk

Myra Cohn Livingston playing the French horn

I write about events or things that arouse special feelings in me—shutting my closet door at night so the monsters won't creep out, growing angry at pollution, crunching on carrot sticks, or trying to catch grunion at the beach. From the time I was old enough to spell I discovered joy in writing and have always kept a journal of ideas that might possibly turn into stories or plays or poems. (Some have, and some haven't.) When I was in sixth grade I enjoyed camping and working on the school newspaper, and I began playing the French horn. By the time I was thirteen, I was a professional musician, played with orchestras, and even worked in the movies. But poetry won out over everything else. I wrote my first book, *Whispers and Other Poems,* when I was a freshman in college. Since then I have published almost thirty books.

People always ask me where I get the ideas for my poems. A great many come from my own childhood experiences and from watching my own three children as they grow up. When my daughter, Jennie, was in sixth grade she discovered the books of Ursula Le Guin. Every day she would rush home from school to read them, and watching her I remembered my own delight in the fantasies I had read. In the poem "Fantasy: For Jennie," on page 534, I pretended that I was Jennie, lost in the "worlds and words" of the unknown and of dreams—someone who recognizes that fantasy may not be so unbelievable after all.

The "silly dog" in the poem of the same name on page 535 could be any one of a number of dogs we've had in our family over the years. Each one has had his own personality, and each has done the same foolish thing—beg to go out in the rain and then come in dripping water all over the floor!

Many memories went into "Fantasy: For Jennie" and "Silly Dog," but "Power Lines," on page 536, was written in a different way. I was driving on the San Diego Freeway one day when I suddenly noticed a row of power lines. They seemed to have bodies and long arms and hands. I had driven on this freeway hundreds of times before. Yet, as often happens, something we have grown accustomed to seeing can suddenly seem new and different. It is only a ten-minute drive from these power lines to my home in the Santa Monica Mountains, but by the time I reached my front door I had the poem in my mind. (Most poems do not come so easily, however!)

For me the essential thing is to put my own ideas and my own feelings into a poem, using my unique sensitivities and my individual voice. What I see or hear or feel may not be what my family or friends see, hear, or feel. People who want to write poetry must find what is important to them, discover their special way of looking, and express this in their own words and rhythms.

Fantasy: For Jennie

by MYRA COHN LIVINGSTON

Worlds and words
Are calling me
In a book I know.

What I've never seen,
What I've never known
Comes true.

It is in my dream,
It is what I own,
It's new.

What I've never heard,
What may never be
Can be so.

Silly Dog

by MYRA COHN LIVINGSTON

There she is, out in the rain,
My silly old dog come back again

To whine and whimper and lick my hands,
Telling me that she understands

That it's better to stay where it's warm and dry,
Not to go fighting with a sky

Spilling over with cold and wet
But I know when it rains again, she'll forget,

And she'll bark and beg to go out again
To try and outsmart the pouring rain.

Power Lines

by MYRA COHN LIVINGSTON

Thin robots,
Spun of wire lace,
Plant their feet down
Each in one place.

Standing tall
In a measured row,
Watching over
Highways below.

Holding hands
With steel strand rope,
Gray, faceless.
No fear. No hope.

The Tape

by MYRA COHN LIVINGSTON

Poor song,
    going around in your cassette
    over and over again, repeating
    the same old tune,
    can you breathe in there?

Come, song,
    going around in your cassette
    over and over again, break out!
    Let me play you
    fresh on my guitar!

Walking in Balance

by JOSEPH BRUCHAC

I was born in Saratoga Springs, New York, in 1942, during the time of year the Iroquois people call the Moon of Falling Leaves — the month of October. I grew up in Greenfield Center, three miles from Saratoga Springs, living with my mother's parents in a house which I still live in with my wife and children today.

I think it must have been from my grandmother that I first learned to love books and poetry. And it was my grandfather who first showed me the things I would later write about. He would walk with me in the woods near our house, teaching me how to "fit the ground to plant," and telling me stories about his experiences in the woods as a lumberman or working for the county roads. My grandfather's background was American Indian and it showed in his closeness to nature and the way he treated people.

I remember my childhood as being rather lonely. There were few children of my age around and much

Joseph
Bruchac

of my time was spent in the woods and the fields, listening to nature.

My first memory of writing a poem is from the second grade. It was Valentine's Day and I hadn't brought a card for my teacher, although everyone else in the class had. I made a card at my desk and wrote a few verses on it. I kept on writing and before long people were telling me that they liked the poems I wrote.

I've tried to remember my own childhood and my American Indian heritage when dealing with my own two sons, James and Jesse, or when working with other children.

My first real experience of working with poetry with young people came just after I had finished college and graduate school. I spent three years as a teacher in Ghana, West Africa. My African students taught *me* a great deal. I came away from Ghana with an even deeper respect for traditional cultures and the knowledge that just about all people, no matter who they are, where they are from, or how old they are, can find meaning in poetry and enjoy writing poems.

Since returning to America, I worked with the Poetry in the Schools Programs in several states. I work with students from third grade on up through high school. I read them my own poems and work by other poets. And I help them write poems of their own.

My poems are usually about experiences in my own life. Sometimes, I try to write poems that will tell people things that I think are important or useful. "This Earth Is a Drum," on page 541, is a poem like that. If you've ever walked in the mountains and seen, as I have, names carved on trees and cans and bottles by the trails, you may have felt a kind of sorrow. I believe that if we do things to nature, we will suffer for it in the long run. I often repeat the words which were given to me by an American Indian friend: "Walk in balance." "This Earth Is a Drum" is about that balance.

Many centuries ago a Chinese poet named Tu Fu said, "The ideas of a poet should be noble and simple." "Camping near Trumansburg" (page 542) is a simple poem. In it I try, as the old Chinese writers did, to make pictures with words. I've described the things that happened on a camping trip by using comparisons which may help someone who reads the poem see those things as I saw them. The first stanza is a good example of that. Instead of just saying that I set the logs on the fire, I describe my match as a "key that unlocks the sun." Within the wood there is energy stored from the sun's rays which the fire of the match releases. That match really *is* a key.

"Homestead" (page 544) was written after coming across an old house deserted in the woods. In that house I could see the cycles of the seasons, the way things change and still remain the same. The board fence looked like arms trying to protect the house, and that old house seemed just then like a person, like you or me . . . or like our footsteps in the earth. The earth lasts longer than our footprints do. After the old house is gone, the earth will still be there. To me that is a comforting thought, perhaps because I have been reminded by my American Indian teachers that this earth is our mother. If we treat it well, it will treat us well in return.

I'm happy to have shared some of my life and some of my thoughts about poems with you.

Be well and walk in balance.

This Earth Is a Drum

by JOSEPH BRUCHAC

Near the mountains
Footsteps on the ground
sound hollow.

This is to remind you
this Earth is a drum.

We must watch our steps closely
to play the right tune.

Birdfoot's Grampa

by JOSEPH BRUCHAC

The Old Man
must have stopped our car
two dozen times to climb out
and gather into his hands
the small toads blinded
by our lights and leaping
like live drops of rain.

The rain was falling,
a mist around his white hair,
and I kept saying,
"You can't save them all,
accept it, get in,
we've got places to go."

But, leathery hands full
of wet brown life,
knee deep in the summer
roadside grass,
he just smiled and said,
"They have places to go, too."

Camping near Trumansburg

by JOSEPH BRUCHAC

Kneeling to light the pine logs,
my match is a key that unlocks the sun,
a golden fountain, lighter than air

One bird crosses the dark sky,
its call clear as the distance between hills

Deep in the valley, through a field
the headlight of a motorcycle bobs,
a drop of quicksilver
and the road, a bright string
stretched between the lakes,
vibrates under the wheels of spring

Coming back down from the hilltop,
my flashlight's beam taps the path
like a blindman's cane.

Homestead

by JOSEPH BRUCHAC

The walls of the old house
lean away like friends
getting ready to leave.

At the edge of the yard
twisted grass holds down
the grey board fence
that is trying to rise
and stand like a circle
of protecting arms.

Footprints lead
past crocuses and dahlias,
corn stalks and rustling leaves.

They belong to no one,
bits and pieces of you
left in them returning
to the land.

Understanding What You've Read

1. Find examples of alliteration in "Fantasy: For Jennie" (page 534) by Myra Cohn Livingston. Which words does the poet repeat? Why do you think she repeats these words?
2. Where does Myra Cohn Livingston use alliteration in "Silly Dog" (page 535)?
3. Poets see things differently. To what does Myra Cohn Livingston compare the power-line towers in "Power Lines" (page 536)? Where does the poet use repetition in the poem? Which word is repeated?
4. Where does Myra Cohn Livingston use repetition in "The Tape" (page 537)?
5. To what does Joseph Bruchac compare the Earth in "This Earth Is a Drum" (page 541)? What do you call this kind of comparison?
6. In which lines of "Birdfoot's Grampa" (page 542) does Joseph Bruchac use alliteration? Which words begin with the same sounds?
7. Find examples of alliteration in "Camping near Trumansburg" (page 543) by Joseph Bruchac. Find an example of onomatopoeia in the poem.
8. To what does Joseph Bruchac compare the walls of the old house in the first stanza of "Homestead" (page 544)? What other comparison can you find in the poem?

Writing

1. Write a sentence describing a pet or an animal. Use words beginning with the same sounds, or alliteration. For example: "My cat can't call a cab."
2. Choose a poem. Write a sentence or paragraph telling about at least one element of poetry the poet used.

The two poems that follow are narrative poems—they tell a story. Notice how alliteration and repetition add to your enjoyment of the poems.

Sweet Betsy

Did you ever hear tell of Sweet Betsy from Pike,
Who crossed the wide mountains with her husband Ike,
With two yoke of cattle and one spotted hog,
A tall Shanghai rooster and an old yellow dog.

CHORUS:
Hoodle dang fol-de di-do, hoodle dang fol-de day.

They swam the wide rivers and climbed the tall peaks
And camped on the prairies for weeks upon weeks,
Starvation and cholera, hard work and slaughter,
They reached California spite of heat and high water. (CHO.)

The wagon tipped over with a terrible crash
And out on the prairie rolled all sorts of trash,
Sweet Betsy got up with a great deal of pain
And declared she'd go back to Pike County again. (CHO.)

They passed the Sierras through mountains of snow,
Till old California was sighted below.
Sweet Betsy she hollered, and Ike gave a cheer,
Saying, 'Betsy, my darlin', I'm a made millioneer.' (CHO.)

"Sweet Betsy from Pike" (lyrics only) collected, adapted and arranged by John A. Lomax and Alan Lomax. © 1934 and renewed 1962 by Ludlow Music, Inc., New York. Used by permission of The Richmond Organization.

The Pedaling Man

by RUSSELL HOBAN

We put him on the roof and we painted him blue,
And the pedaling man knew what to do—
He just pedaled, yes he pedaled:
He rode through the night with the wind just right
And he rode clear into the morning,
Riding easy, riding breezy, riding
Slow in the sunrise and the wind out of the east.

A weathervane was what he was—
Cast-iron man with a sheet-iron propeller, riding a
Worm gear, holding a little steering wheel,
Iron legs pumping up and down—show him a
Wind and he'd go. Work all day and
All his pay was the weather. Nights, too,
We'd lie in bed and hear him
Creak up there in the dark as he
Swung into the wind and worked up speed,
Humming and thrumming so you could
Feel it all through the house—
The more wind, the faster he went, right through
Spring, summer, and fall.

He rode warm winds out of the south,
Wet winds out of the east, and the
Dry west winds, rode them all with a
Serious iron face. Hard-nosed, tight-mouthed
Yankee-looking kind of an iron man.
"Show me a wind and I'll go," he said.
"I'm a pedaling fool and I'm heading for weather."
The weather came and he kept on going, right into
Winter, and the wind out of the north and no letup—
We lived on a hill, and wind was what we got a lot of.

Then a night came along, and a blizzard was making,
Windows rattling and the whole house shaking,
But the iron man just hummed with the blast,
Said, "Come on, wind, and come on fast,
Show me your winter, make it nice and cool,
Show me your weather—I'm a pedaling fool!"
Gears all spinning, joints all shivering,
Sheet-iron clattering, cast-iron quivering till WHOMP!
The humming stopped, and we all sat up in bed with
Nothing to listen to but the wind right through
    into morning.

And there he was when we dug him out, propeller
   all bent,
One eye in the snow and one eye
Staring up at the sky, still looking for weather.
He never let on he was beat, not him.

Well, my father put him up on the roof again, this time
Without the propeller.
"Let him ride easy," he said. "A man can only take
Just so much north wind, even if he's iron."

Understanding What You've Read

1. Which stanzas of "Sweet Betsy" (page 547) contain alliteration? Which words are alliterative?
2. Which stanzas of "The Pedaling Man" (page 548) by Russell Hoban contain repetition? Does this add to your enjoyment of the poem? Why or why not?
3. Russell Hoban also uses onomatopoeia to describe the sound the weathervane made when the wind blew. Which words describe this sound? Which words describe the pedaling man's last ride?

Writing

1. "Sweet Betsy" is about an event in American history — the California gold rush. Think of an event, such as the Boston Tea Party or an astronaut team's voyage. Write a sentence using alliteration, repetition, or onomatopoeia to describe the event. Read the example:

   The shiny silver rocket lifted its load from the pad with a flaming ruby-red roar rushing, rushing from its trembling tail.

2. Write a sentence in which you compare one object to another. First, think of two objects that are alike in some way. Think how you might compare them. For example, how might you compare the moon to a balloon? You could write a sentence like the following:

   The moon was a shiny silver balloon in the evening sky.

More About Books of Poetry

Celebration: A New Anthology of Black American Poetry edited by Arnold Adoff. Follett, 1977. This book includes 240 poems by twentieth-century black American poets.

The Buffalo in the Syracuse Zoo and Other Poems by Joseph Bruchac. Greenfield Review Press, 1972. These poems describe the poet's feelings about the world around him.

The Yellow Canary Whose Eye Is So Black: Poems from Spanish-Speaking Latin America edited and translated by Cheli Duran. Macmillan, 1977. Here are poems from many different Latin American cultures, both ancient and modern.

Straight on Till Morning: Poems of the Imaginary World selected by Helen Hill, Agnes Perkins, and Althea Helag. T. Y. Crowell, 1977. This book includes poems of magic and mystery.

Bring Me All of Your Dreams selected by Nancy Larrick. M. Evans, 1980. Here are poems about dreams and dreamers, illustrated with photographs.

The Moment of Wonder: A Collection of Chinese and Japanese Poetry collected by Richard Lewis. Dial, 1964. Here is a book of beautiful, imaginative poems.

4-Way Stop and Other Poems by Myra Cohn Livingston. Atheneum, 1976. These poems are based on the poet's experiences and beliefs.

Glossary

This glossary is a little dictionary. It contains the difficult words found in this book. The pronunciation, which tells you how to say the word, is given next to each word. That is followed by a word's meaning or meanings. Sometimes, a different form of the word follows the definition. It appears in boldfaced type.

The special symbols used to show the pronunciation are explained in the key that follows.

PRONUNCIATION KEY*

a	add, map	m	move, seem	u	up, done
ā	ace, rate	n	nice, tin	û(r)	urn, term
â(r)	care, air	ng	ring, song	yōō	use, few
ä	palm, father	o	odd, hot	v	vain, eve
b	bat, rub	ō	open, so	w	win, away
ch	check, catch	ô	order, jaw	y	yet, yearn
d	dog, rod	oi	oil, boy	z	zest, muse
e	end, pet	ou	out, now	zh	vision, pleasure
ē	even, tree	ōō	pool, food	ə	the schwa,
f	fit, half	ŏŏ	took, full		an unstressed
g	go, log	p	pit, stop		vowel representing
h	hope, hate	r	run, poor		the sound spelled
i	it, give	s	see, pass		*a* in above
ī	ice, write	sh	sure, rush		*e* in sicken
j	joy, ledge	t	talk, sit		*i* in possible
k	cook, take	th	thin, both		*o* in melon
l	look, rule	t͟h	this, bathe		*u* in circus

Foreign: N is used following nasal sound: French *Jean* [zhäN].
˷ indicates the [ny] sound. Spanish *señor* [sā·nyôr′].

In the pronunciations an accent mark (′) is used to show which syllable of a word receives the most stress. The word *bandage* [ban′dij], for example, is stressed on the first syllable. Sometimes there is also a lighter accent mark (′) that shows where there is a lighter stress, as in the word *combination* [kom′bə·nā′shən].

The following abbreviations are used throughout the glossary: *n.*, noun; *v.*, verb; *adj.*, adjective; *adv.*, adverb; *pl.*, plural; *sing.*, singular.

*The Pronunciation Key and the short form of the key that appears on the following right-hand pages are reprinted from *The HBJ School Dictionary*, copyright © 1977, 1972, 1968 by Harcourt Brace Jovanovich, Inc.

A

ab·sorb [ab·sôrb′ *or* ab·zôrb′] *v.* **ab·sorbed** To take and hold: *absorb* information.

ab·stract [ab′strakt] *adj.* **1** Having a form or pattern rather than representing real objects. **2** Not dealing with anything specific; general.

a·bun·dance [ə·bun′dəns] *n.* A great amount; more than enough.

ac·a·dem·ic [ak′ə·dem′ik] *adj.* Of or having to do with school or studies.

ac·ti·vate [ak′tə·vāt] *v.* **ac·ti·vat·ed** To make active; put into action.

a·dapt [ə·dapt′] *v.* **1** To adjust to new conditions. **2** To change for a new use.

Ae·ge·us [i·jē′əs] In Greek myths, a king of Athens and the father of Theseus.

af·fil·i·a·tion [ə·fil′ē·ā′shən] *n.* A connection, as with a large group.

al·cove [al′kōv] *n.* A small section of a room opening out from the main section.

al·ter·a·tion [ôl′tə·rā′shən] *n.* **1** A change made. **2** The act of changing something.

am·bas·sa·dor [am·bas′ə·dər *or* am·bas′ə·dôr] *n.* A person who represents his or her government in another country.

am·bi·tion [am·bish′ən] *n.* A goal; an eager desire to succeed or achieve something.

a·mend [ə·mend′] *v.* **a·mend·ed** To correct; add.

a·mi·a·bly [ā′mē·ə·blē] *adv.* In a pleasing or friendly manner. — **a·mi·a·ble,** *adj.*

an·cients [ān′shənts] *n., pl.* People of long ago.

an·gle [ang′gəl] *n.* **1** A special approach for accomplishing something: What's your *angle*? **2** The figure that is formed by two lines that meet.

An·glo-Sax·on [ang′glō-sak′sən] **1** *n.* The language (Old English) of the Germanic people living in England, who were conquered by the Normans (French) in 1066. **2** *n.* A member of this Germanic people. **3** *adj.* Of or having to do with these people or their language: an *Anglo-Saxon* word.

an·thro·pol·o·gist [an′thrə·pol′ə·jist] *n.* A scientist who studies the social, physical, and cultural development of people. This science is called *anthropology.*

an·tiq·ui·ty [an·tik′wə·tē] *n.* **1** Ancient times. **2** The quality of being very old.

anx·i·e·ty [ang·zī′ə·tē] *n.* An uneasy, worried feeling; concern.

apt·ly [apt′lē] *adv.* **1** Fittingly. **2** Likely.

aq·ua·lung [ak′wə·lung′] *n.* A tank (or tanks) of compressed air used for breathing underwater. The tanks, worn on the diver's back, supply air through a mask.

aq·ue·duct [ak′wə·dukt] *n.* A pipeline or channel carrying water from a distance.

ar·chae·ol·o·gist [är′kē·ol′ə·jist] *n.* An expert in archaeology.

ar·chae·ol·o·gy [är′kē·ol′ə·jē] *n.* The study of past times and cultures, mainly carried on by digging up and examining remains, as of the cities or graves of ancient cultures.

ar·chi·tec·tur·al [är′kə·tek′chər·əl] *adj.* Of or having to do with architecture. This is the profession of designing and putting up buildings or other structures.

A·ri·ad·ne [a·rē·ad′nē] In Greek mythology, the daughter of King Minos who gave Theseus the silk thread by which he found his way out of the Labyrinth.

a·rouse [ə·rouz′] *v.* **a·roused** To stir up; awaken.

ar·ti·fact [är′tə·fakt] *n.* Anything made by human labor, or art.

as·phalt [as′fôlt] *n.* A brown or black substance like tar, found in natural beds.

as·pir·ing [ə·spīr′ing] *adj.* Having great hope or ambition: an *aspiring* actor.

a·stride [ə·strīd′] *adj., adv.* With one leg on each side.

at·tire [ə·tīr′] *n.* Dress; clothing.

at·tune [ə·t(y)o͞on′] *v.* **at·tuned** To become used to; familiar with.

554

au·di·tion [ô·dish′ən] **1** *n.* A trial hearing to test the skills and suitability of an actor, singer, etc., for a certain job or role. **2** *v.* To give someone such a trial hearing.

au·then·tic [ô·then′tik] *adj.* Real; genuine.

au·thor·i·ty [ə·thôr′ə·tē] *n.* **1** The right to command, act, make decisions, etc. **2** A person who governs and enforces laws.— **au·thor·i·ties**, *pl.*

av·er·age [av′rij] *adj.* Of or like the ordinary or usual type; medium.

a·vow·al [ə·vou′əl] *n.* An open declaration; frank admission.

B

---

bac·te·ri·a [bak·tir′ē·ə] *n., pl.* One-celled living things that can be seen only through a microscope. Some bacteria do helpful things, such as enrich the soil; other bacteria cause disease.

bar·ren [bar′ən] *adj.* Bare; empty.

bars [bärz] *n.* In gymnastics, a set of parallel rods on which athletes do balance exercises.

beam [bēm] *n.* **1** In gymnastics, a raised horizontal piece of wood four inches wide, on which athletes walk and do balance routines. **2** A long piece of wood, as in a building's frame.

ben·e·fi·cial [ben′ə·fish′əl] *adj.* Useful or helpful.

ben·e·fit [ben′ə·fit] **1** *n.* Something that is helpful or good. **2** *v.* To receive help; profit: to *benefit* from experience.

be·wil·der·ment [bi·wil′dər·mənt] *n.* A confused and puzzled state.

bi·son [bī′sən *or* bī′zən] *n.* A large wild animal having a big, shaggy head, short horns, and a humped back.

blade [blād] *n.* **1** The flat, sharp-edged part of a knife, saw, saber, etc. **2** A sword. **3** The leaf of grasses or grains: a *blade* of grass.

blaze [blāz] *v.* **blazed 1** To burn, as with great feeling or anger: His eyes did *blaze*. **2** To burn with a bright, glowing flame.

block·ade [blo·kād′] *n.* **1** Anything that obstructs or blocks passage. **2** The shutting off of a coast by ships or troops.

blurt [blûrt] *v.* **blurt·ing** To speak on impulse and without thought.

boar [bôr] *n.* **1** A wild hog. **2** A male pig or hog.

bob [bob] *v.* To move up and down with short, jerky motions.

bom·bard [bom·bärd′] *v.* **bom·bard·ed** To attack: Don't *bombard* me with questions.

borne [bôrn] *v.* To be supported or carried. Past participle of **bear**, *v.*

bot·an·ist [bot′ə·nist] *n.* A scientist who studies plants.

bow·er [bou′ər] *n.* A shelter or shady spot made of branches, flowers, or vines.

bra·vo [brä′vō] *n.* A shout meaning "well done," mostly heard at performances.

browse [brouz] *v.* **browsed** To look at books, reading a little here and there.

---

add, āce, câre, pälm;   end, ēqual;   it, īce;   odd, ōpen, ôrder;   tŏŏk, pōōl;   up, bûrn;
ə = a in *above*, e in *sicken*, i in *possible*, o in *melon*, u in *circus*;   yōō = u in *fuse;*   oil;   pout;
check;   ring;   thin;   this;   zh in *vision.*

c

cam·ou·flage [kam′ə·fläzh] *n.* **1** Any disguise that hides or protects. **2** The act or technique of using paint, leaves, etc., to change the appearance of, so as to hide.

can·di·date [kan′də·dāt] *n.* A person who seeks an honor, a degree, or an office: a Ph.D. *candidate.*

can·o·py [kan′ə·pē] *n.* Any covering overhead.

cap·tive [kap′tiv] *n.* A person or thing captured and held in confinement.

car·bo·hy·drate [kär′bō·hī′drāt] *n.* Any of a large group of compounds of carbon, hydrogen, and oxygen. Green plants make carbohydrates out of carbon dioxide and water. Sugars and starches are carbohydrates.

car·bon di·ox·ide [kär′bən dī·ok′sīd] *n.* An odorless, colorless, gaseous compound of carbon and oxygen. Animals breathe it out, and plants absorb it as food.

ca·reen [cə·rēn′] *v.* **ca·reen·ing** To lurch from side to side while moving, as if out of control.

cat·a·pult [kat′ə·pult] *v.* **cat·a·pult·ed** To throw or be thrown with great force.

catch [kach] **1** *n.* A hidden trick or difficulty. **2** *v.* To capture after a chase. **3** *v.* To ensnare.

cel·list [chel′ist] *n.* A person who plays the cello.

cel·lo [chel′ō] *n.* A large instrument with the shape of a violin, but bigger and with a deeper tone. It is held between the knees when played.

cen·tu·ry [sen′chə·rē] *n.* A period of 100 years. —**cen·tu·ries,** *pl.*

cer·e·mo·ni·al [ser′ə·mō′nē·əl] *adj.* **1** Very elaborate or formal. **2** Of, like, or used in a ceremony.

cer·tif·i·cate [sər·tif′ə·kit] *n.* A printed or written document stating officially that something is a fact: a marriage *certificate.*

chaf·fer [chaf′ər] *v.* **chaf·fered 1** To exchange small talk. **2** To bargain.

char·ac·ter [kar′ik·tər] *n.* **1** A person, animal, etc., in a play, novel, poem, etc. **2** All of the qualities, habits, etc., that make up the nature of a person. **3** A letter, figure, or mark, used in writing or printing.

char·i·ot [char′ē·ət] *n.* A two-wheeled vehicle pulled by horses, used in ancient times for travel, races, war, parades, etc.

cher·ish [cher′ish] *v.* To hold dear.

chif·fon [shi·fon′ *or* shif′on] *n.* A very thin cloth made of silk, nylon, or rayon, used for dresses, scarves, etc.

choir [kwīr] *n.* A group of singers, especially in a religious service.

chol·er·a [kol′ər·ə] *n.* An infectious bacterial disease that attacks the intestines, often causing death.

chor·tle [chôr′təl] *v.* **chor·tled** To chuckle or laugh loudly or joyfully.

chron·i·cle [kron′i·kəl] *n.* A written record of events as they happened in time.

cir·cuit [sûr′kit] *n.* A route or path that turns back to where it began.

cit·a·del [sit′ə·dəl] *n.* A fortress overlooking a town or city.

clo·ven [klō′vən] *adj.* Split or divided: a *cloven* hoof.

clutch [kluch] **1** *n.* A tightly held hand. **2** *n.* A nest of eggs. **3** *n.* Power or control. **4** *v.* To grasp and hold firmly.

coke [kōk] *n.* A solid fuel made from coal.

col·la·gen·ite [kə·la′jən·it] *n.* A material made of a chemical compound mostly obtained from protein.

com·bat zone [kom′bat zōn] *n.* The place where a battle is fought.

com·mer·cial [kə·mûr′shəl] **1** *adj.* Of or having to do with business or industry. **2** *n.* An advertisement on radio or television.

com·pressed [kəm·prest′] *adj.* Squeezed together.

con·duct [kən·dukt′] *v.* **1** To guide or lead, as an orchestra. **2** To act or behave: She did *conduct* herself well. —**con·duc·tor,** *n.*

con·firm [kən·fûrm′] *v.* To make certain of: Will you *confirm* the appointment?

con·i·cal [kon′i·kəl] *adj.* Cone-shaped.

con·scious·ness [kon′shəs·nis] *n.* A condition in which one is able to see, hear, feel, etc.; awareness.

con·serve [kən·sûrv′] *v.* To use carefully; to keep from being used up, lost, etc.: to *conserve* energy.

con·sid·er·a·ble [kən·sid′ər·ə·bəl] *adj.* **1** Rather large. **2** Worth noticing.

con·sol·i·date [kən·sol′ə·dāt] *v.* **con·sol·i·dat·ed** To combine; bring together or unite firmly.

con·sta·ble [kon′stə·bəl] *n.* A police officer.

con·tour [kon′tŏor] *n.* The outline of a figure or body.

con·tract [kən·trakt′] *v.* **con·tract·ed** To acquire or catch: He *contracted* a disease.

con·trite [kən·trīt′ *or* kon′trīt] *adj.* Deeply sorry for having done wrong.

con·verge [kən·vûrj′] *v.* **con·verg·ing** To move toward a point; come or draw together.

con·vic·tion [kən·vik′shən] *n.* A strong, firm belief.

core [kôr] *n.* **1** The central or innermost part of anything. **2** The hard central part of certain fruits, such as apples or pears.

cor·o·na·tion [kôr′ə·nā′shən] *n.* The crowning of a royal ruler.

cou·ri·er [kŏor′ē·ər *or* kûr′ē·ər] *n.* A messenger who must deliver a message quickly.

crick·et [krik′it] *n.* A game played on a large field, with bats, a ball, and wickets, by two teams, each with eleven players.

crit·ic [krit′ik] *n.* **1** A person whose job is to form and write judgments of the quality or value of books, art, music, plays, etc. **2** Any person who judges the quality of books, music, art, etc.

cru·sade [krōo·sād′] *n.* **1** A hard struggle in favor of a cause. **2** (*often written* **Crusade**) One of a series of wars fought during the Middle Ages over possession of the Holy Land.

crys·tal [kris′təl] *n.* **1** A body formed when something, such as water, becomes solid. Crystals have flat surfaces and angles in regular patterns: ice *crystals.* **2** A type of fine, clear glass.

cul·ture [kul′chər] *n.* The entire way of life of a particular people, including their customs, religions, ideas, inventions, etc. —**cul·tur·al,** *adj.*

---

add, āce, câre, pälm;   end, ēqual;   it, īce;   odd, ōpen, ôrder;   tŏok, pōol;   up, bûrn;
ə = a in *above*, e in *sicken*, i in *possible*, o in *melon*, u in *circus*;   yōo = u in *fuse*;   oil;   pout;
      check;   ring;   thin;   this;   zh in *vision*.

cu·pid [kyōō′pid] *n.* A picture or statue of a winged baby carrying a bow and arrow.

cus·tom [kus′təm] *n.* The usual way of doing something; something done as a matter of course among a people.

D

Daed·a·lus [ded′ə·ləs] In Greek mythology, the architect of the Labyrinth at Crete where the Minotaur was kept.

de·but [di·byōō′ *or* dā′byōō] *n.* A first public appearance: an actor's *debut*.

dec·o·ra·tion [dek′ə·rā′shən] *n.* Something used to make something else more fancy, pretty, or attractive; ornament.

de·gree [di·grē′] *n.* **1** A title awarded to a student who has completed a course of study or to a person as an honor. **2** A step in a series, or a stage in a process.

del·i·cate·ly [del′ə·kit·lē] *adv.* Finely made in structure, design, shape, etc.

de·pict [di·pikt′] *v.* To show by a picture; to describe in words.

de·rive [di·rīv′] *v.* **de·rived 1** To come from a particular source: The word *zoo* is *derived* from Greek. **2** To get or receive.

de·spair [di·spâr′] *n.* The heavy feeling that comes when all hope is lost or given up.

des·per·ate [des′pər·it] *adj.* Reckless because all hope or choice seems gone: a *desperate* effort to escape. — **des·per·a·tion,** *n.*

de·ter·mi·na·tion [di·tûr′mə·nā′shən] *n.* **1** Firmness of purpose; courage. **2** The act of deciding or settling finally.

de·vise [di·vīz′] *v.* **de·vised** To figure out; invent.

de·vote [di·vōt′] *v.* To give over (oneself, one's time, etc.) to a person or activity: She *devotes* hours to music. — **de·vot·ed,** *adj.* Feeling or showing love.

de·vo·tion [di·vō′shən] *n.* **1** Dedication: a lifelong *devotion* to the arts. **2** A strong, loyal affection.

di·ag·o·nal [dī·ag′ə·nəl] *n.* A line crossing in a slanting direction either from corner to corner or from side to side.

di·am·e·ter [dī·am′ə·tər] *n.* **1** The length of a line joining two points on a circle and passing through its center. **2** The line itself.

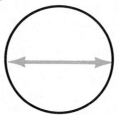

dig·ni·ty [dig′nə·tē] *n.* The quality of worth, character, or nobility that commands respect.

Di·o·ny·sus [dī′ə·nī′səs] In Greek mythology, the god of wine.

dis·dain·ful·ly [dis·dān′fə·lē] *adv.* In a manner showing that one looks down on or scorns a person, thing, or act; scornfully.

dis·joint·ed [dis·join′tid] *adj.* Not organized; disconnected.

dis·may [dis·mā′] *v.* **dis·mayed** To fill with worry and fear.

dis·re·gard [dis′ri·gard′] *v.* **dis·re·gard·ed** To ignore.

dis·solve [di·zolv′] *v.* To make or become liquid.

dis·tress [dis·tres′] *n.* Extreme pain or trouble requiring help.

Don [don] *n.* A Spanish title of respect used before a man's first name; Mr.; Sir.

doom [do͞om] **1** *n.* A terrible or tragic outcome or fortune. **2** *n.* A harsh judgment or punishment. — **doomed** *adj.* Headed for a tragic outcome: A *doomed* person.

drab [drab] *adj.* Dull in appearance or quality.

drone [drōn] *n.* A deep humming or buzzing sound.

drop·let [drop′lit] *n.* A tiny drop.

du·bi·ous [d(y)o͞o′bē·əs] *adj.* Not certain; not sure; doubtful.

E

---

eb·on·y [eb′ə·nē] *n.* A hard, heavy, dark wood, usually black.

e·con·o·my [i·kon′ə·mē] *n.* Careful use of something, such as money or food, to avoid waste.

ec·stat·ic [ek·stat′ik] *adj.* Full of or showing great happiness or delight.

ed·i·ble [ed′ə·bəl] *adj.* Suitable for food; fit to eat.

e·di·tion [i·dish′ən] *n.* **1** The copies of a publication printed and issued at any one time: Saturday's *edition* of the paper. **2** The form in which a work of literature is published: a three-volume *edition*.

ee·rie [ir′ē *or* ē′rē] *adj.* Strange; frightening.

ef·fect [i·fekt′] *n.* Something brought about by some action or cause; result.

ef·fi·cient [i·fish′ənt] *adj.* Producing results with the least effort or waste: an *efficient* motor.

el·e·gant [el′ə·gənt] *adj.* Beautiful and in good taste.

el·e·ment [el′ə·mənt] *n.* **1** Any of the limited number of substances of which all matter is made. **2** A necessary or basic part of anything: Hard work is an *element* of success.

em·blem [em′bləm] *n.* Something that stands for an idea, belief, club, nation, etc.: The lion was the club's *emblem*.

em·bry·o [em′brē·ō] *n.* A living thing in its earliest stages and not yet born, as a bird or reptile in its egg.

e·merge [i·mûrj′] *v.* **e·merged** To come out or become visible.

em·i·grate [em′ə·grāt] *v.* **em·i·grat·ed** To move from one country or section of a country to settle in another.

en·dur·ance [in·d(y)o͞or′əns] *n.* The ability to last or stick to something for a long time under continued hardship.

en·ter·prise [en′tər·prīz] *n.* A project requiring great effort, ability, or daring.

en·thu·si·asm [in·tho͞o′zē·az′əm] *n.* Great interest or liking.

en·tomb [in·to͞om′] *v.* **en·tombed** To bury in a tomb.

e·rup·tion [i·rup′shən] *n.* The act or process of erupting or casting forth, as a volcano spills lava, steam, etc.

es·cort [*v.* es·kôrt′, *n.* es′kôrt] **1** *v.* To accompany and protect someone on a journey. **2** *n.* One or more planes, ships, cars, etc., moving along with another so as to protect, guide, or honor. **3** *n.* A person who accompanies another on a trip, to a party, etc.: Joe acted as my *escort* at the wedding.

e·ter·nal [i·tûr′nəl] *adj.* Lasting forever; unchanging.

e·ven·tu·al·ly [i·ven′cho͞o·əl·ē] *adv.* In the course of time; in the end.

ev·i·dence [ev′ə·dəns] *n.* Something that proves or gives reason to believe that something is true or not true: The broken lock was *evidence* that someone had tried to break into the house.

ex·hib·it [ig·zib′it] **1** *n.* A public display, as of art. **2** *n.* A thing or things put on display. **3** *v.* To display or show publicly.

ex·hi·bi·tion [ek′sə·bish′ən] *n.* **1** An open showing; display. **2** A public display, as of art.

ex·pire [ik·spīr′] *v.* To run out; to end its term.

---

add, āce, câre, pälm;   end, ēqual;   it, īce;   odd, ōpen, ôrder;   to͝ok, po͞ol;   up, bûrn;
ə = a in *above*, e in *sicken*, i in *possible*, o in *melon*, u in *circus;*   yo͞o = u in *fuse;*   oil;   pout;
check;   **r**ing;   **th**in;   **th**is;   **zh** in *vision*.

ex·tinct [ik·stingkt′] *adj.* **1** No longer in existence: an *extinct* animal. **2** No longer active; extinguished: an *extinct* volcano.

F

fab·u·lous [fab′yə·ləs] *adj.* **1** Imaginary; known or told about in stories or fables. **2** Amazing.

fac·tu·al [fak′chōō·əl] *adj.* Made up of or relying on things known to be true.

fal·ter [fôl′tər] *v.* **fal·tered** To speak or move in an unsteady, stumbling way; hesitate.

fam·ine [fam′in] *n.* **1** Starvation. **2** Any serious shortage: a water *famine.*

fare [fâr] *v.* **fared** To get along; manage.

fath·om [fath′əm] *n.* A measure of length equal to six feet (about two meters), used mainly to measure the depth of water.

fed·er·al [fed′ər·əl] *adj.* Of, having, or belonging to the national government.

fee·bly [fē′blē] *adv.* Weakly.

fel·low·ship [fel′ō·ship] *n.* A grant or sum of money given to a student to pay for further study after graduation from college.

fe·roc·i·ty [fə·ros′ə·tē] *n.* Extreme fierceness; cruelty.

feu·dal [fyōōd′(ə)l] *adj.* Of or having to do with a kind of society in which people are ruled by powerful lords.

fi·ber [fī′bər] *n.* A thread or threadlike part, as from a fabric or plant.

fier·y [fī′rē *or* fī′ər·ē] *adj.* **1** Like fire. **2** Bright or hot as fire. **3** Intense.

fiord [fyôrd] *n.* A long, narrow inlet of the sea between high cliffs or banks.

fool·har·dy [fōōl′här′dē] *adj.* Daring in a foolish way.

ford [fôrd] **1** *v.* To cross a body of water by wading in a shallow place.—**ford·ed 2** *n.* A shallow place in a body of water.

form [fôrm] *n.* **1** A piece of paper with blanks to be filled in with information. **2** A shape or outline of something. **3** Condition of body or mind for performance: an athlete in top *form.*

for·mal [fôr′məl] *adj.* **1** Requiring elaborate dress or manners. **2** Strictly or stiffly following set rules or patterns.

for·tress [fôr′tris] *n.* A fort or series of forts; stronghold.

fos·sil [fos′əl] **1** *n.* The remains of a plant or animal of an earlier age, hardened and kept from rotting in earth or rock. **2** *adj.* Like or being a fossil: a *fossil* fern.

frag·ile [fraj′əl] *adj.* Easily broken; weak; delicate.

frond [frond] *n.* A large leaf or leaflike part, as of a palm tree or fern.

ful·crum [fōōl′krəm] *n.* A support on which a lever rests or turns when raising or moving a weight.

fu·ri·ous [fyōōr′ē·əs] *adj.* **1** Very angry. **2** Very strong or fierce: a *furious* wind.—**fu·ri·ous·ly,** *adv.:* The wind blew *furiously.*

G

gait [gāt] *n.* A way of walking, stepping, or running.

gal·ax·y [gal′ək·sē] *n.* A large, bright group of stars, planets, etc. Earth is part of the Milky Way Galaxy.—**gal·ax·ies,** *pl.*

gal·ler·y [gal′ər·ē] *n.* A long passageway or corridor, sometimes with one side open.

ga·to [gä′tō] *n. Spanish* Cat.

gear [gir] *n.* A toothed wheel that meshes with another such wheel and makes it turn.

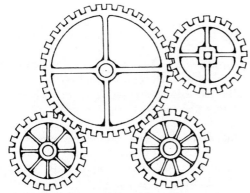

ge·ol·o·gist [jē·ol′ə·jist] *n.* A person who studies the history and structure of the Earth's crust, especially as recorded in rocks.

ges·ture [jes′chər] **1** *n.* A motion of the hands, head, or other part of the body that expresses or emphasizes some feeling or idea. **2** *v.* To make gestures.

GI [jē·ī] *n.* A soldier in the U.S. Army. GI is an acronym for *government issue.*

gla·cier [glā′shər] *n.* A large mass or field of ice that moves very slowly down a mountain valley or across land until it melts or breaks off in the sea to form icebergs.

gland [gland] *n.* **1** A part of a plant that performs some definite function, such as secretion. **2** Any of several organs of the body that have to do with the production, storage, or secretion of certain substances for certain purposes. The liver, pancreas, thyroid, and adrenals are glands.

glazed [glāzd] *adj.* Coated with a glass surface: *glazed* pottery. —**glaze,** *v., n.*

glint [glint] **1** *n.* A gleam; flash. **2** *v.* To gleam or flash; glitter.

glow·er [glou′ər] *v.* **glow·ered** To look or stare at in an angry way.

gorge [gôrj] *n.* A narrow, very deep canyon; ravine.

gos·pel [gos′pəl] *n. music* Religious songs based on a biblical or spiritual theme. American in origin, the melodies have elements of spirituals and jazz.

grad·u·al·ly [graj′ōō·əl·ē] *adv.* Happening slowly in small steps; little by little.

grad·u·ate stu·dent [graj′ōō·it st(y)ōōd′(ə)nt] *n.* A person who has finished college and is going on for additional study in a particular field, usually at a university.

gram·mar [gram′ər] *n.* **1** Language rules telling how to use words and form sentences. **2** The study of the forms and arrangements of words as used in language.

gran·ite [gran′it] *n.* A hard rock that is often used as a building material.

gri·to [grē′tō] *n. Spanish* A yell or scream, as made by cowhands.

grudg·ing·ly [gruj′ing·lē] *adv.* Not willingly.

gym·nas·tics [jim·nas′tiks] *n., pl.* Exercises and stunts that develop and use muscular strength and control.

H

hab·i·ta·tion [hab′ə·tā′shən] *n.* **1** A place where someone lives. **2** The act or state of living in: fit for human *habitation.*

hag·gle [hag′əl] *v.* **hag·gled** To bargain in a petty way.

han·ker·ing [hang′kər·ing] *n.* A wishing or longing for something. —**han·ker,** *v.*

---

add, āce, câre, pälm;   end, ēqual;   it, īce;   odd, ōpen, ôrder;   tŏŏk, pōōl;   up, bûrn;

ə = a in *above,* e in *sicken,* i in *possible,* o in *melon,* u in *circus;*   **yōō** = u in *fuse;*   oil;   pout;

check;   **r**ing;   **th**in;   **th**is;   **zh** in *vision.*

harp·si·chord [härp′sə·kôrd] *n.* An instrument like a piano but invented earlier. When the keys are pressed, the strings are plucked by points of leather or quill.

haw·thorn [hô′thôrn] *n.* A small, thorny tree of the rose family.

Her·a·cles [her′ə·klēz] In Greek mythology, a hero of great strength. Known as *Hercules* in Roman mythology.

he·red·i·tar·y [hə·red′ə·ter′ē] *adj.* 1 Left to one by an ancestor; inherited: a *hereditary* title. 2 Passed down from parents to children: a *hereditary* disease.

her·i·tage [her′ə·tij] *n.* A tradition, belief, attitude, etc., handed down from the past.

hi·ber·nate [hī′bər·nāt] *v.* To spend the winter sleeping or inactive, as bears and some other animals do.

hid·e·ous [hid′ē·əs] *adj.* Horrible; very ugly.

hinged [hinjd] *adj.* Having a hinge—a joint that allows a door, lid, leaf, etc., to turn or open.

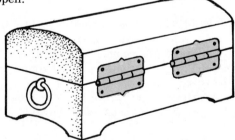

hoist [hoist] *v.* **hoist·ed** To raise or lift.

hos·pi·ta·ble [hos′pi·tə·bəl *or* hos·pit′ə·bəl] *adj.* Having a liking for guests; welcoming and being generous toward them.

hov·er [huv′ər *or* hov′ər] *v.* To remain in or near one place in the air, as birds, etc., do. 2 To linger or remain nearby.

I

---

i·de·o·graph [id′ē·ə·graf] *n.* A picture or symbol used to represent an idea.

il·lim·it·a·ble [i·lim′it·ə·bəl] *adj.* Endless; having no limits.

il·lu·mi·na·tion [i·lo͞o′mə·nā′shən] *n.* Light; brightness.

il·lus·tra·ted [il′ə·strā·tid] *adj.* Containing pictures that help explain a story.— **il·lus·trate,** *v.*

im·age [im′ij] *n.* 1 A mental picture. 2 A statue or other likeness of some person or thing.

im·ag·i·na·tive [i·maj′ə·nə·tiv *or* i·maj′ə·na′tiv] *adj.* Full of or showing the power to see things in new ways, form new ideas, or create new things from thought.

im·mov·able [i·mo͞o′və·bəl] *adj.* Fixed tightly; not able to change position or action.

im·pres·sive [im·pres′iv] *adj.* Producing a strong feeling of admiration or awe.

in·ac·ti·vate [in·ak′tiv·āt] *v.* To make idle, or to stop working.

in·ci·dent [in′sə·dənt] *n.* An event, often one of little importance.

in·cur·a·ble [in·kyo͞or′ə·bəl] *adj.* Not able to be gotten rid of or corrected by means of treatment, such as medicine or diet: an *incurable* disease.

in·hab·it [in·hab′it] *v.* **in·hab·it·ed** To live in.

in·hab·i·tant [in·hab′ə·tənt] *n.* A person or animal that lives in a particular place; resident.

in·spire [in·spīr′] *v.* **in·spired** 1 To direct or guide, as if by some divine influence. 2 To fill with a certain thought, feeling, or desire to do something: He does *inspire* us to work harder.

in·stance [in′stəns] *n.* An example or illustration: for *instance.*

in·sur·mount·a·ble [in′sər·moun′tə·bəl] *adj.* Incapable of being overcome.

in·tact [in·takt'] *adj.* Left whole, with no part taken away.

in·ter·tri·bal [in'tər·trī'bəl] *adj.* Between or among tribes. Tribes are groups of people who share the same customs and beliefs.

in·val·u·a·ble [in·val'y($\overline{oo}$·)ə·bəl] *adj.* Worth more than can be estimated; priceless.

ir·i·des·cent [ir'ə·des'ənt] *adj.* Showing the colors of the rainbow in changing patterns.

is·sue [ish'$\overline{oo}$] *n.* Something supplied, distributed, or sent out, as a magazine, a stamp, etc.

J

jave·lin [jav'(ə)lin] *n.* A light spear once used as a weapon but now thrown for distance in athletic contests.

jeal·ous [jel'əs] *adj.* **1** Fearful of losing someone's love to a rival. **2** Begrudging someone what he or she has; envious.

jet·ty [jet'ē] *n.* **1** A structure built out into a body of water to break a current or protect a harbor. **2** A pier.

jock·ey [jok'ē] *v.* **jock·eyed** To make planned moves in a skillful or tricky way.

jour·nal [jûr'nəl] *n.* A daily record or account, as of events, business transactions, thoughts, etc.

junk [jungk] *n.* **1** A large Chinese sailing ship. **2** Worthless or worn-out things.

jut [jut] *v.* To extend outward; project: The shelf will *jut* out too far.

K

Ka·zakh [kä·zäk'] *n.* A people of Central Asia. The word means "adventurer."

L

lab·y·rinth [lab'ə·rinth] *n.* An arrangement of winding passages or paths made to confuse anyone trying to find his or her way through; a maze.

lac·quered [lak'ərd] *adj.* Covered with a shiny, clear liquid that dries to form a hard surface.

land mass [land mas] *n.* A very large area of land, especially a continent.

learn·ed [lûr'nid] *adj.* Full of much learning or knowledge.

lease [lēs] **1** To rent or give use of property by means of a contract: The woman will *lease* the apartment. —**leased 2** *n.* A contract in which one person agrees to let another live in or use his or her property.

lec·tur·er [lek'chər·ər] *n.* A person who teaches at a college or university but who is not a regular faculty member.

let·up [let'up'] *n. informal* A pausing, relaxing, or brief stopping of some activity; a lessening of effort.

lib·er·ate [lib'ə·rāt] *v.* **lib·er·at·ed** To set free; release.

lime·stone [līm'stōn'] *n.* A type of rock like marble.

lit·er·a·ture [lit'ər·ə·chər] *n.* All written works on a special subject, considered to have permanent value.

---

add, āce, câre, pälm;   end, ēqual;   it, īce;   odd, ōpen, ôrder;   tŏŏk, pōōl;   up, bûrn;
ə = a in *above,* e in *sicken,* i in *possible,* o in *melon,* u in *circus;*   y$\overline{oo}$ = u in *fuse;*   oil;   pout;
check;   ring;   thin;   this;   zh in *vision.*

563

lla·ma [lä′mə] *n.* A South American animal, like a small camel but with no hump: A *llama* can carry goods on its back.

lobe [lōb] *n.* A curved or rounded part, as of a leaf or an organ of the body, that juts out.

lo·cal [lō′kəl] *adj.* Having to do with a neighborhood, region, or small area: the *local* people.

log [lôg *or* log] *n.* **1** The daily record of a ship's voyage. **2** Part of the trunk or a limb of a tree that has been cut down.

loot [lo͞ot] **1** *n.* A slang term for money. **2** *n.* Goods taken from an enemy at war. **3** *n.* Any prize or gain. **4** *v.* To steal goods or property.

lure [lo͞or] *v.* **lured** To attract, especially to danger.

M

---

maes·tro [mī′strō] *n.* A master in any art, especially an important conductor or performer of music.

mah·jong [mä′zhong′] *n.* A game of Chinese origin, usually played with tiles by four players.

ma·jor·i·ty [mə·jôr′ə·tē] *n.* More than half of a given number or group: the greater part.

mam·mal [mam′əl] *n.* Any of the group of animals that have a spinal column or backbone and whose females produce milk for their young. Humans beings, whales, cows, cats, and mice are examples of mammals.

mam·moth [mam′əth] *n.* A large, now extinct, animal related to the elephant. A mammoth had hairy skin and long tusks that curved upward.

man·tel·piece [man′təl·pēs′] *n.* The shelf above a fireplace. Also called *mantel.*

mar·ket gar·den [mär′kit gär′dən] *n.* A plot in which vegetables are raised for market. Also, a market that sells those vegetables.

mass [mas] *n.* **1** A body of matter with no definite shape or size: a *mass* of clay. **2** A great size; volume.

mas·sive [mas′iv] *adj.* Big and heavy or bulky.

mas·ter·piece [mas′tər·pēs′] *n.* **1** The greatest thing done by its creator. **2** Something of outstanding excellence; great achievement.

mas·ter's de·gree [mas′tərz di·grē′] *n.* A college or university degree above a bachelor's and below a doctor's.

mat [mat] *n.* **1** In gymnastics, a pad on which tumbling is performed. **2** A rough, flat piece of material made of straw, rope, etc., used to cover floors, to wipe the feet on, etc.

maze [māz] *n.* A complicated network of paths in which it is hard to find the way.

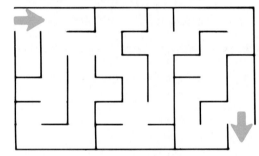

me·di·o·cre [mē′dē·ō′kər] *adj.* Neither good nor bad; just fair or ordinary.

meet [mēt] **1** *n.* A contest or sports event: a track *meet.* **2** *v.* To keep an appointment with: I'll *meet* you there. **3** *v.* To come upon; come face to face with: She happened to *meet* a friend. **4** *v.* To come together and join or merge. **5** *v.* To satisfy or fulfill, as requirements or a need: He was able to *meet* the needs of his students.

mi·grate [mī′grāt] *v.* **1** To move from one region or climate to another at the change of season: Birds *migrate* in autumn and spring. **2** To move from one place to settle in another.

mill [mil] *n.* A machine or device for grinding or crushing corn, coffee, etc.

mim·ic [mim′ik] *n.* A person or animal that copies closely the speech or actions of someone or something else.

min·er·al [min′ər·əl] *n.* A natural substance that is not a plant or animal and has a fairly definite physical and chemical make-up. Certain minerals, such as iron and copper, are necessary to animal and human health.

min·i·a·ture [min′(ē·)ə·chər] **1** *adj.* Very small; tiny. **2** *n.* Something made or represented on a small scale.

Mi·nos [mī′nəs] In Greek myths, the King of Crete.

Min·o·taur [min′ə·tôr] In Greek myths, a monster with a man's body and a bull's head. It was kept in the Labyrinth at Crete until killed by Theseus.

mi·nute [mī·n(y)o͞ot′] *adj.* Tiny.

mi·rage [mi·räzh′] *n.* A trick or deceiving appearance played upon the sense of sight, such as the appearance of water on a hot, dry pavement that is not really wet.

mis·sion [mish′ən] *n.* The task, business, or duty that a person or a group of people is sent forth to do.

mois·ten [mois′ən] *v.* **mois·tened** To make or become wet or damp.

mol·ten [mōl′tən] *adj.* Made liquid by great heat.

mon·arch [mon′ərk] *n.* **1** A large orange-and-black North American butterfly. **2** A ruler, as a king, queen, etc.

Moor [mo͞or] *n.* One of a Moslem people of northwestern Africa who conquered Spain in the eighth century. In literature, the *Moor* usually refers to Shakespeare's character Othello.

moor·ings [mo͞or′ingz] *n., pl.* **1** The cable, anchor, or rope by which a ship or boat is kept in one place. **2** A place where a thing is *moored,* or fastened with ropes, cables, etc.

mo·sa·ic [mō·zā′ik] *n.* A picture or design made from bits of colored stone, glass, etc.

mount [mount] *v.* **mount·ed** **1** To climb a slope or stairs. **2** To increase in amount or degree; grow greater.

mum·mi·fied [mum′ə·fīd] *adj.* Made into a mummy. A *mummy* is a dead body wrapped in cloth and prevented from rotting by certain chemical preparations. — **mum·mi·fy,** *v.*

mur·al [myo͝or′əl] *n.* A painting done on a wall.

myth [mith] *n.* A traditional story, usually about gods, heroes, etc., often offering an explanation of something in nature or of past events.

N

na·tive [nā′tiv] **1** *adj.* Being born, grown, or living naturally in a certain area. **2** *adj.* Belonging to a person by birth or place of birth: one's *native* language. **3** *n.* One of the original inhabitants of a place.

nat·u·ral·ist [nach′ər·əl·ist] *n.* A person who is trained in the study of nature as related to the Earth and living things.

nav·i·ga·tion [nav′ə·gā′shən] *n.* The art or practice of controlling the course and position of a ship or aircraft.

net [net] **1** *v.* To earn or produce after subtracting expenses such as taxes, etc. **2** *n.* A cloth of thread, cord, rope, or the like, knotted or woven together in an open pattern.

nim·ble [nim′bəl] *adj.* Quick and light in movement. — **nim·bly,** *adv.*

ni·tro·gen [nī′trə·jən] *n.* An odorless, colorless gas that makes up nearly four-fifths of the Earth's atmosphere. It is a necessary element to all living things.

no·ble [nō′bəl] **1** *adj.* Of having a high rank or title. **2** *adj.* Impressive or handsome. **3** *n.* A person of high rank or title.

---

add, āce, câre, pälm;   end, ēqual;   it, īce;   odd, ōpen, ôrder;   to͝ok, po͞ol;   up, bûrn;
ə = a in *above,* e in *sicken,* i in *possible,* o in *melon,* u in *circus;*   yo͞o = u in *fuse;*   oil;   pout;
check;   ring;   thin;   this;   zh in *vision.*

O
---

o·a·sis [ō·ā′sis] *n.* An area in a desert where vegetation or crops can be produced because of a water supply. — **o·a·ses** [ō·ā′sēz], *pl.*

ob·e·lisk [ob′ə·lisk] *n.* A square shaft of stone that tapers to a top shaped like a pyramid.

ob·jec·tive·ly [əb·jek′tiv·lē] *adv.* In a manner that is free from personal feelings or opinions; detached.

o·blige [ə·blīj′] *v.* **o·bliged** To bind or force (to do something), as by a sense of duty.

oc·ca·sion·al [ə·kā′zhən·əl] *adj.* Occurring or happening now and then: an *occasional* visit.

o·kra [ō′krə] *n.* The sticky pods of a small shrub, used in soups and as a vegetable.

op·er·a [op′ə·rə *or* op′rə] *n.* A play set to music in which all or most of the lines are sung rather than spoken. The singers in an opera are usually accompanied by an orchestra.

or·ches·tra pit [ôr′kəs·trə pit] *n.* The place just in front of the stage, usually lower than the stage, where the musicians sit.

or·gan·ism [ôr′gən·iz′əm] *n.* An animal or plant considered as a whole; any living thing.

or·i·gin [ôr′ə·jin] *n.* **1** The source of one's line of descent. **2** The beginning of the existence of anything: the *origin* of football.

or·ig·i·nal [ə·rij′ə·nəl] **1** *n.* The first creation or model from which a copy is made. **2** *n.* The first form of anything. **3** *adj.* Of or belonging to the beginning of something; earliest; first.

out·crop·ping [out′krop′ing] *n.* The appearance above the ground of a mineral that is usually found underground.

out·skirts [out′skûrts′] *n.* The outer edges or area far from the center, as of a city.

o·val [ō′vəl] *adj.* Having the shape of an egg.

o·ver·whelm [ō′vər·(h)welm′] *v.* **o·ver·whelmed 1** To overcome completely; crush, as with force or feeling. **2** To bury or submerge completely, as with a wave.

o·ver·win·ter [ō′vər·win′tər] *v.* To spend the winter.

P
---

pack·et [pak′it] *n.* A small package.

parch [pärch] *v.* **parch·ing 1** To make or become dry with heat; shrivel. **2** To make or become thirsty.

par·quet [pär·kā′] *n.* Flooring made of short pieces of wood arranged in a pattern.

par·snip [pär′snip] *n.* An herb with a large, carrotlike root that can be eaten.

par·tial [pär′shəl] *adj.* Involving or made up of only a part.

par·tic·i·pate [pär·tis′ə·pāt] *v.* **par·tic·i·pat·ing** To take part or have a share with others.

par·ti·cle [pär′ti·kəl] *n.* A very small amount, part, or piece; speck.

pa·vane [pə·vän′] *n.* A slow, formal dance performed by couples.

ped·es·tal [ped′is·təl] *n.* The base that supports a statue, vase, etc.

pen·in·su·la [pə·nin′s(y)ə·lə] *n.* A piece of land nearly surrounded by water, often connected to the mainland by a narrow bridge of land.

per·il·ous [per′əl·əs] *adj.* Full of risk; dangerous.

per·ish [per′ish] *v.* To be completely destroyed; die.

per·ma·nent [pûr′mə·nənt] *adj.* Continuing or meant to continue without change; lasting forever.

per·plexed [pər·plekst′] *adj.* Puzzled; bewildered.

per·son·nel [pûr′sə·nəl′] *n.* The persons employed in a business, engaged in military service, etc.

pe·so [pā′sō] *n.* The basic unit of money in several Spanish-speaking countries, such as Mexico and Chile.

phar·aoh [fâr′ō *or* fā′rō] *n.* Any one of the kings of ancient Egypt.

Ph.D. Abbreviation for "doctor of philosophy," the highest degree awarded by a college or university.

Phoe·nix [fē′niks] In Egyptian mythology, a beautiful bird said to live for hundreds of years before burning itself to ashes, only to rise again, young once more.

pierce [pirs] *v.* To pass into or through, as something sharp does.

pla·za [plä′zə *or* plaz′ə] *n.* An open square or marketplace in a town or city.

plume [plo͞om] *n.* A feather or featherlike form, especially if long and decorative.

po·di·um [pō′dē·əm] *n.* A platform on which the conductor of an orchestra stands. — **po·di·ums** or **po·di·a** [pō′dē·ə], *pl.*

poise [poiz] *v.* **poised 1** *n.* Ease of manner. **2** *n.* Balance. **3** *v.* To balance or hold in balance.

po·lar [pō′lər] *adj.* Having to do with the North Pole or South Pole.

pol·der [pōl′dər] *n.* A land area that was once under water.

pon·der·ous·ly [pon′dər·əs·lē] *adv.* In a heavy or boring way.

por·tent [pôr′tent] *n.* A warning or sign of what is to come; omen.

pounce [pouns] **1** *v.* To swoop down or spring, as in seizing prey. — **pounced 2** *n.* The act of pouncing; a sudden swoop or spring.

prac·ti·cal [prak′ti·kəl] *adj.* That can be put to use; useful: *practical* clothes for hiking.

pre·ci·sion [pri·sizh′ən] *n.* The condition or quality of being accurate or exact.

pre·dict [pri·dikt′] *v.* To state beforehand; foretell.

pre·his·to·ry [prē·his′tə·rē] *n.* The period or time before the first written record of past events.

pres·ence [prez′əns] *n.* The fact or condition of being present or existing.

pre·serve [pri·zûrv′] *v.* **pre·served 1** To keep from spoiling or rotting. **2** To keep from danger or harm; watch over.

prim·i·tive [prim′ə·tiv] *adj.* **1** Coming from or belonging to the earliest times. **2** Very simple.

---

add, āce, câre, pälm;   end, ēqual;   it, īce;   odd, ōpen, ôrder;   to͝ok, po͞ol;   up, bûrn;
ə = a in *above*, e in *sicken*, i in *possible*, o in *melon*, u in *circus;*   yo͞o = u in *fuse;*   oil;   pout;
check;   ring;   thin;   this;   zh in *vision.*

prin·ci·ple [prin'sə·pəl] *n.* **1** A law or way of action by which something works: the *principle* of gravity. **2** A general truth on which other truths are based: a *principle* of democracy.

proc·ess [pros'əs] **1** *v.* To prepare or treat by a special method: to *process* sugar. — **proc·ess·ing** **2** *n.* A method for producing something.

pro·ces·sion·al [prə·sesh'ən·əl] *adj.* Having to do with a *procession,* a formal, dignified line of people, cars, etc., moving from one place to another.

pro·claim [prō·klām'] *v.* **pro·claimed** To make known; announce publicly.

prof·it [prof'it] *n.* The amount of money made in business after all expenses have been subtracted.

pro·pel·ler [prə·pel'ər] *n.* A device for pulling or pushing an aircraft or vessel through air or water by means of rotating blades.

pros·per [pros'pər] *v.* **pros·pered, pros·per·ing** To be successful; thrive.

pro·te·in [prō'tē·in *or* prō'tēn] *n.* A compound, containing nitrogen, that is a necessary part of most animals' diets.

prov·erb [prov'ərb] *n.* An old and often repeated saying of advice or wisdom.

pub·li·ci·ty [pub·lis'ə·tē] *n.* Any information intended to bring a person or thing to the attention of the public.

pueb·lo [pweb'lō] *n.* **1** An adobe or stone building or group of buildings of the Native Americans of the southwestern United States. **2** (*written* **Pueblo**) A member of one of the tribes that live in such buildings.

pum·mel *or* **pom·mel** [pum'əl *or* pom'əl] *v.* To beat with the fists.

pur·pose [pûr'pəs] *n.* **1** The reason for which a thing exists; use. **2** What a person intends or wants to do; plan; aim.

pur·suit [pər·s(y)o͞ot'] *n.* The act of chasing or following.

Q
---

qual·i·fy [kwol'ə·fī] *v.* **1** To limit, add to, or soften: to *qualify* a statement. **2** To be or cause to be suitable or fit, as for a job.

qual·i·fy·ing [kwol'ə·fī·ing] *adj.* Causing to be suitable or fit, as for a job, office, privilege.

quar·an·tine [kwôr'ən·tēn] *n.* The keeping of persons or things that have been infected by contagious diseases away from others.

quar·ry [kwôr'ē] *v.* **quar·ried** To cut out stone from the earth.

quick·sil·ver [kwik'sil'vər] *n.* The metal mercury in its liquid form.

quick-wit·ted [kwik·wit'id] *adj.* Bright; smart; clever.

R
---

ran·che·ro [rän·chär'ō] *n.* A man who owns a ranch or works on one.

ra·vine [rə·vēn'] *n.* A narrow, steep canyon.

re·al·is·tic [rē'əl·is'tik] *adj.* **1** Showing things in a lifelike way. **2** Having to do with what is real and practical.

re·al·ize [rē'əl·īz] *v.* **re·al·ized** **1** To turn into an actual fact. **2** To understand or appreciate fully.

re·cess [ri·ses' *or* rē'ses] *n.* A hidden, inner place.

re·claim [ri·klām'] *v.* To bring land, as a swamp or desert, into condition to support farming, living, and so on.

ref·er·ence [ref'ər·əns *or* ref'rəns] *n.* **1** A statement, passage, or book to which attention is called. **2** The act of calling attention: She made no *reference* to the quarrel.

re·fin·er·y [ri·fī'nər·ē] *n.* A place where raw material, such as sugar, is made pure.

re·gal-look·ing [rē'gəl lŏŏk·ing] *adj.* Appearing regal or royal.

re·gret·ful·ly [ri·gret'fəl·ē] *adv.* Sorrowfully; unhappily.

reign [rān] **1** *n.* The period during which a king or queen, etc., rules. **2** *v.* To rule; govern, as a king.

rel·a·tive·ly [rel′ə·tiv·lē] *adv.* As compared with something else, or with a standard: a *relatively* small town.

re·lay [ri·lā′ *or* rē′lā] *v.* To send onward: *relay* a message.

re·morse [ri·môrs′] *n.* Great regret or anguish for something one has done.

rep·li·ca [rep′lə·kə] *n.* A duplicate or copy of something.

rep·re·sent [rep′ri·zent′] *v.* To be the symbol or expression of; stand for: The dove *represents* peace.

rep·re·sen·ta·tive [rep′ri·zen′tə·tiv] *n.* **1** A person chosen to represent, or speak for, others. **2** A typical example.

rep·tile [rep′til *or* rep′tīl] *n.* Any of a class of cold-blooded animals that crawl on their bellies or creep on very short legs. Snakes, crocodiles, lizards, and turtles are reptiles.

rep·u·ta·tion [rep′yə·tā′shən] *n.* **1** Fame. **2** The general opinion in which a person or thing is held by others.

re·sem·ble [ri·zem′bəl] *v.* **re·sem·bled** To look like.

res·er·voir [rez′ər·vwär *or* rez′ər·vwôr] *n.* A basin, either natural or made by people, for collecting and storing a large supply of water.

res·o·lu·tion [rez′ə·lōō′shən] *n.* **1** Firmness; determination. **2** Something decided upon.

re·source [ri·sôrs′ *or* rē′sôrs] *n.* (*often pl.*) A supply of something that can be used or drawn on: natural *resources.*

re·source·ful [ri·sôrs′fəl] *adj.* Skillful in finding ways of doing things or removing difficulties.

re·store [ri·stôr′] *v.* **re·stored** To bring back to an original condition: We will *restore* the paintings.

re·sume [ri·zōōm′] *v.* **re·sumed** To begin again after stopping.

re·treat [ri·trēt′] **1** *n.* The act of going back or withdrawing. **2** *v.* To go back or backward; withdraw.

re·u·nite [rē·yōō·nīt′] *v.* To bring together again.

re·veal [ri·vēl′] *v.* **re·vealed 1** To make known: *reveal* a secret. **2** To make visible; show: When the curtain opens, it will *reveal* a small room.

re·view [ri·vyōō′] **1** *n.* An article or essay discussing a book, movie, play, etc. **2** *v.* To go over and examine again. **3** *v.* To think back on. **4** *v.* To look over carefully or inspect.

re·volve [ri·volv′] *v.* **re·volv·ing** To turn, as around an object; move in a circle around a center.

rheu·mat·ic [rōō·mat′ik] *adj.* Having to do with or caused by rheumatism.

rheu·ma·tism [rōō′mə·tiz′əm] *n.* A painful swelling and stiffness in and around the back and in the joints of the knees, the hands, etc.

right an·gle [rīt ang′gəl] *n.* An angle formed by two lines perpendicular to each other.

rig·id [rij′id] *adj.* Stiff and firm; not bending: a *rigid* frame.

ro·dent [rōd′(ə)nt] *n.* Any of a group of gnawing mammals that have very sharp teeth that keep growing as they are worn down by gnawing. Mice and squirrels are rodents.

---

add, āce, câre, pälm;   end, ēqual;   it, īce;   odd, ōpen, ôrder;   tŏŏk, pōōl;   up, bûrn;
ə = a in *above,* e in *sicken,* i in *possible,* o in *melon,* u in *circus;*   yōō = u in *fuse;*   oil;   pout;
check;   ring;   thin;   this;   zh in *vision.*

roost [ro͞ost] **1** *n.* A place where a bird makes its nest and rests at night. **2** *v.* To come to rest; settle.

ro·tate [rō′tāt] *v.* **ro·tat·ing** To spin or cause to turn on an axis.

rud·der·fish [rud′ər·fish] *n.* Any of certain fish that follow or accompany a boat or ship. Also known as a pilot fish.

ru·ins [ro͞o′inz] *n.* The remains of something that has decayed or been destroyed: the *ruins* of old cities.

S

---

sac·ri·fice [sak′rə·fīs] **1** *v.* To give up one's life for something or someone else. **2** *v.* To give up anything important. **3** *n.* The thing offered or given up.

sam·pan [sam′pan′] *n.* A small, flat-bottomed boat used in China and Japan.

sar·coph·a·gus [sär·kof′ə·gəs] *n.* A decorated stone coffin, usually placed in open view or in a large tomb.

sau·ri·an [sôr′ē·ən] *n.* Any of a group of reptiles with scaly bodies and usually four limbs. This group is now restricted mainly to the lizards.

scale [skāl] *n.* **1** A series of lines and marks placed at regular points on an instrument for measuring distances or amounts. **2** A balance or other device for weighing things. **3** One of the hard, bony plates forming a covering on certain animals. **4** Comparative size, extent, or degree.

Scan·di·na·vi·a [skan′də·nā′vē·ə] *n.* The name for the present-day countries of Norway, Sweden, Denmark, Iceland, and Finland.

scav·en·ger [skav′in·jər] *n.* **1** One who searches through refuse, garbage, etc., for things to use, eat, or sell. **2** An animal, such as a buzzard, that feeds on dead things.

scent [sent] *n.* Odor or smell, especially if pleasant.

score [skôr] **1** *n.* A copy of a piece of music giving all the parts written for different instruments or voices. **2** *n.* The number of points won in a game. **3** *n.* A record of points won. **4** *n.* A grade or mark made on a test. **5** *v.* To make (points, runs, etc.), as in a game. **6** *v.* To rate or grade: to *score* test papers.

scor·pi·on fish [skôr′pē·ən fish] *n.* A fish with a poisonous sting. Also known as a common toadfish.

scout [skout] **1** *n.* Someone sent to find out about a rival, to find a person worth hiring, etc., as a sports *scout.* **2** *n.* A soldier, ship, or plane sent to get information about an enemy. **3** *v.* To observe or explore in order to obtain information. **4** *v.* To search, hunt, or explore.

scru·ti·nize [skro͞o′tə·nīz] *v.* **scru·ti·nized** To look at closely; examine very carefully.

scu·ba [sko͞o′bə] *n.* Equipment worn by divers for breathing underwater. *Scuba* stands for Self-Contained Underwater Breathing Apparatus.

scul·ler·y [skul′ər·ē] *n.* A room off a kitchen where vegetables are cleaned, pots and pans are washed, etc.

scut·tle [skut′(ə)l] *v.* **scut·tled** To sink (a ship) on purpose by making openings in it.

sea·far·ing [sē′fâr′ing] *adj.* Traveling by sea or making a living from the sea.

se·crete [si·krēt′] *v.* **1** To produce and give off: Glands *secrete* different fluids. **2** To keep from sight or knowledge; hide.

sem·i·cir·cle [sem′ē·sûr′kəl] *n.* A half circle.

se·rene [si·rēn′] *adj.* **1** Peaceful; calm. **2** Clear; fair: a *serene* sky.

sew·age [so͞o′ij] *n.* The waste matter that is carried off in sewers.

shai·tan [shī·tän′] *n. Arabic* An evil spirit.

shrine [shrīn] *n.* A place, box, or object that is sacred and usually holds sacred objects.

shut·ter [shut′ər] *n.* **1** The part of a camera that opens to let light through the lens and then closes rapidly. **2** A panel for covering a window.

sig·nif·i·cant [sig·nif′ə·kənt] *adj.* Important.

sil·la·bub *or* **syl·la·bub** [sil′ə·bub] *n.* A drink or dessert made of sweetened milk or cream mixed with cider or wine.

Sin·ga·pore [sing′(g)ə·pôr] *n.* A small country in southeastern Asia, off the Malay Peninsula.

sketch [skech] **1** *n.* A rough, hasty, or unfinished drawing or description, giving a general impression without full details: an artist's *sketch* for a painting. **2** *v.* To draw, outline or describe in an unfinished or incomplete way.

skip·per [skip′ər] *n.* The captain of a ship, especially a small vessel.

skit·ter [skit′ər] *v.* To skip or move about quickly.

slate [slāt] *n.* **1** A flat object that is written on with chalk or a special pencil. **2** A hard rock that splits easily into thin layers.

sloth [slōth, slôth, *or* sloth] *n.* **1** A slow-moving animal of South America that hangs upside down from branches by its claws and sleeps or dozes most of the day. **2** Laziness.

snuff·box [snuf′boks′] *n.* A small, decorative box for holding snuff. *Snuff* is a fine powder that makes a person sneeze.

so·ci·ol·o·gy [sō′sē·ol′ə·jē *or* sō′shē·ol′ə·jē] *n.* The study of people living in groups or communities, past and present.

som·ber [som′bər] *adj.* Serious, gloomy, or dark.

source [sôrs] *n.* **1** A person or thing that supplies information. **2** The beginning of a stream or river, as a lake or spring.

spasm [spaz′əm] *n.* A sudden tensing or contraction of a muscle or muscles.

spe·cies [spē′shēz or spē′sēz] *n., sing.* and *pl.* A group of living things that are alike and whose members can produce offspring.

spe·cif·ic [spi·sif′ik] *adj.* Particular; definite.

spec·i·men [spes′ə·mən] *n.* One person or thing of a group, or a small amount taken as a sample of the whole.

spine [spīn] *n.* **1** The spinal column; backbone. **2** The main support of something, as the back of a book binding. **3** A hard, pointed growth on a plant or animal. — **spin·y,** *adj.*

spire [spīr] *n.* The pointed top or roof of a tower, steeple, etc.

spout [spout] *v.* **spout·ed** To flow or pour out in large quantities and with force, as a liquid under pressure.

staff [staf] *n.* **1** A group of people who work together under a manager or chief: the *staff* of a hotel. **2** A stick or pole carried as an aid to walking, as a weapon, or as an emblem of authority. **3** Something that supports or maintains: Bread is the *staff* of life. **4** The five lines on which music is written.

stage pres·ence [stāj′ prez′əns] *n.* The qualities of poise and ability that help a performer become closer to the audience.

stam·i·na [stam′ə·nə] *n.* Strength; endurance.

sta·tus [stā′təs *or* stat′əs] *n.* **1** Position or rank: person of high social *status.* **2** State; condition: the *status* of a country during wartime.

stead·fast [sted′fast′] *adj.* Not moving or changing; firm and trustworthy. — **stead·fast·ly,** *adv.*

steppe [step] *n.* A vast, dry, treeless plain, especially one found in Soviet Europe and Asia.

stew·ard [st(y)o͞o′ərd] *n.* A person who manages the business or other affairs of another.

---

add, āce, câre, pälm;   end, ēqual;   it, īce;   odd, ōpen, ôrder;   to͝ok, po͞ol;   up, bûrn;
ə = a in *above,* e in *sicken,* i in *possible,* o in *melon,* u in *circus;*   yo͞o = u in *fuse;*   oil;   pout;
check;   ring;   thin;   this;   zh in *vision.*

strik·ing [strī′king] *adj.* Appearing strongly to the eye or the imagination; impressive: the *striking* colors of the trees in autumn.

stur·di·er [stûr′dē·ər] *adj.* More vigorous; stronger; firmer.

sub·due [sub·d(y)o͞o′] *v.* To overcome; gain control over or conquer.

sub·or·der [sub′ôr′dər] *n.* A small grouping of living things.

sub·ter·ra·ne·an [sub′tə·rā′nē·ən] *adj.* Under the ground.

sub·ur·ban [sə·bûr′bən] *adj.* Of or having to do with a town, village, district, etc., that is close to a large city.

suf·fice [sə·fīs′] *v.* To be enough; be sufficient.

su·pe·ri·or [sə·pir′ē·ər] **1** *adj.* Much better than the usual; extremely good; excellent. **2** *adj.* Higher in rank: a *superior* officer. **3** *adj.* Greater in size, power, ability. **4** *n.* A person of greater authority, ability, etc., than another: She is my *superior* at golf.

sup·ple [sup′əl] *adj.* Having the ability to bend or move easily.

sup·ple·ness [sup′əl·nes] *n.* The ability to bend or move easily.

sur·pass [sər·pas′] *v.* **sur·passed** To go beyond something else; to be greater, larger, etc., than something else.

sur·viv·al [sər·vī′vəl] *n.* The act of remaining alive.

sus·pen·sion bridge [sə·spen′shən brij] *n.* A bridge in which the roadway is hung from cables and fastened at the ends.

sym·bol·ize [sim′bəl·īz] *v.* **sym·bol·ized** To stand for; represent: A drawing of a huge tractor can *symbolize* strength.

symp·tom [sim(p)′təm] *n.* A sign of the existence of something, especially of a disease.

T

take ad·van·tage of [tāk′ ad·van′tij uv] *v.* **took ad·van·tage of** To use for one's own benefit or gain.

taunt [tônt] *v.* To insult or make fun of, with sneers and nasty remarks.

taut [tôt] *adj.* Tight; tense.

tech·nol·o·gy [tek·nol′ə·jē] *n.* The application of scientific and industrial skills to practical uses.

te·di·ous [tē′dē·əs] *adj.* Boring; tiresome.

tee·ter [tē′tər] *v.* To rock from side to side; seesaw.

tel·e·vise [tel′ə·vīz] *v.* **tel·e·vised** To transmit or receive by television.

tem·ple [tem′pəl] *n.* **1** A house of worship. **2** The flat space on each side of the forehead. **3** A building, usually of great beauty or size, that is devoted to some special purpose: a *temple* of the arts.

ter·ra·ces [ter′ə·sez] *n.* A series of wide, flat steps on a hill.

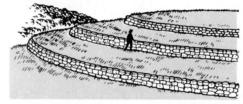

ter·rain [tə·rān′] *n.* An area of land or the earth, especially as considered with respect to its natural or topographical features or fitness for some use: The rocky *terrain* of the country made farming difficult.

The·seus [thē′so͞os *or* thē′sē·əs] In Greek mythology, the hero who killed the Mino-taur.

thrive [thrīv] *v.* To grow well: The plant will *thrive* in sunlight.

throng [throng] *v.* **thronged** To gather in a crowd.

tongs [tôngz] *n., pl.* An implement for grasping or lifting objects, usually consisting of a pair of hinged arms.

tra·di·tion·al [trə·dish′ən·əl] *adj.* Of, handed down by, or following tradition—customs, beliefs, etc., passed down from one genera-tion to the next.

tre·men·dous [tri·men′dəs] *adj.* **1** Unusually large; huge. **2** Unusually great; wonder-ful. **3** Dreadful; overwhelming: a *tremen-dous* disaster.

tren·ches [tren′chəz] *n., pl.* **1** Long, narrow openings in the earth. **2** Canyonlike places where the ocean is deepest.

trend [trend] *n.* A general course or direction: the new *trends* in art.

tri·bute [trib′yo͞ot] *n.* A speech, compliment, or gift given to show admiration, gratitude, or respect.

try [trī] *v.* **1** To determine the guilt or innocence of by trial. **2** To make an attempt.

tu·mult [t(y)o͞o′mult] *n.* Noise or uproar, such as that made by a loud, disorderly crowd.

tu·nic [t(y)o͞o′nik] *n.* In ancient Greece and Rome, a knee-length garment with or without sleeves, worn by men and women.

Tut·ankh·a·mun [to͞o·tang·käm′ən] Egyptian king born around 1355 B.C.

typ·i·cal [tip′i·kəl] *adj.* Having features common to a whole group; characteristic.

U

un·der·stud·y [un′dər·stud′ē] *n.* An actor who can take the place of another actor in a role, when necessary.

u·nique [yo͞o·nēk′] *adj.* **1** Unusual, rare, or notable: a *unique* opportunity. **2** Being the only one of its type: a *unique* gem.

u·ni·ty [yo͞o′nə·tē] *n.* The state of being or acting as one.

un·ruf·fled [un·ruf′əld] *adj.* Not upset or disturbed.

V

vague [vāg] *adj.* Not definite or clear: a *vague* idea; a *vague* outline.

vain [vān] *adj.* Useless. **—in vain,** *adv.* With no success.

va·ri·e·ty [və·rī′ə·tē] *n.* **1** An absence of sameness; change: We enjoy *variety* in our work. **2** A class of things; sort: a *variety* of rose. — **va·ri·e·ties,** *pl.*

var·si·ty [vär′sə·tē] *n.* The top, or best, team that plays for a school or college in a sport or contest.

vast [vast] *adj.* Huge; enormous.

vast·ness [vast′nis] *n.* Very great size, especially in terms of open space: the *vastness* of the ocean.

vault [vôlt] **1** *n.* A piece of gymnastic equipment, also called a "horse," over which athletes jump or on which they move. **2** *n.* A strongly protected place for keeping valuable things, as in a bank. **3** *v.* To leap or leap over with the help of a pole or the hands.

veg·e·ta·tion [vej′ə·tā′shən] *n.* Plant life: tropical *vegetation.*

ver·dant [vûr′dənt] *adj.* Green with plants.

ver·mil·ion [vər·mil′yən] *adj.* Bright orange-red.

ver·ti·cal [vûr′ti·kəl] *adj.* Straight up and down. The antonym for *vertical* is *horizontal.*

ves·sel [ves′(ə)l] *n.* A hollow container, as a bowl, pitcher, etc.

vex [veks] *v.* **vexed** To irritate; annoy.

vir·tu·al·ly [vûr′cho͞o·əl·ē] *adv.* Almost completely.

W

wad·dle [wod′(ə)l] *v.* **wad·dled** To sway from side to side in walking.

wain·scot [wān′skət *or* wān′skot] *n.* A covering for the walls inside a room, usually of wooden panels.

wan·ly [won′lē] *adv.* In a tired, faint, or weak way.

---

add, āce, câre, pälm;   end, ēqual;   it, īce;   odd, ōpen, ôrder;   to͝ok, po͞ol;   up, bûrn;
ə = a in *above,* e in *sicken,* i in *possible,* o in *melon,* u in *circus;*   yo͞o = u in *fuse;*   oil;   pout;
check;   ring;   thin;   this;   zh in *vision.*

wares [wârz] *n., pl.* Items for sale; goods.

wea·sel [wē′zəl] *n.* A small, slender animal with brownish fur that preys on smaller animals and birds.

wedge [wej] *n.* **1** Anything shaped like a V. **2** A narrowing piece of wood, metal, etc., that is shaped like a V. A wedge can be forced into a narrow opening to split something apart.

wraith [rāth] *n.* A ghost or ghostlike image or specter.

Y

yoke [yōk] *n.* A curved wooden frame with attachments used to join together two animals, as oxen.

Z

zo·ol·o·gist [zō·ol′ə·jist] *n.* A person who studies animals—their development, structure, classification, etc.

Index of Titles and Authors

H
I 9
J 0